By the Light of the Crescent Moon

◆◆◆

AILSA KEPPIE

◆◆◆

By the Light of the Crescent Moon

First published in 2021 by

Halifax, NS, Canada
www.ocpublishing.ca

Cover design
gracelaemmlerdesign.ca

ISBN - 978-1-989833-09-4 (Paperback Edition)
ISBN - 978-1-989833-10-0 (eBook Edition)

"Development is a lifelong series of necessary losses and subsequent gains. ... We become a mourning and adapting self, finding at every stage opportunities for creative transformation."

Judith Viorst, *Necessary Losses: The Loves, Illusions, Dependencies, and Impossible Expectations that All of Us Have to Give Up in Order to Grow*

Prologue

AS I REFLECT BACK ON MY LIFE, I realize the truth of the idea that life is a series of necessary losses and gains. Transformation gleams out from the darkness of my experience like a crescent moon in the night sky. It has taken time to understand that what seemed like an obstacle has often turned into a gift, a loss into a gain.

My life could best be summed up as an epic quest to experience love. To be loved, to love, to know what love is. Perhaps, as with any epic story, my quest began when I realized my own longing. Can anyone really love another person unconditionally? Maybe we can only feel the lack of love and wonder what wholeness would feel like. And so, I began the exploration of myself with the opposite question: Have you ever been hated?

I don't mean just disliked but really, deeply hated just for being there. I believe my mother hated me on a deep, subconscious level. It wasn't because of who I was or anything I'd done, it was merely the fact that I was a daughter, her first-born, and I was a mirror for her hatred of herself. Or more specifically, her inner child. Perhaps many women have grown up with mothers who hated them for being female. Perhaps we have passed on this hatred for generations. After all, our society has trampled women and the feminine for centuries; we must have embodied at least some of this hatred from the patriarchy.

The awareness that my own mother hated me haunted my early life without me even knowing it fully. Mostly, she appeared to be a loving and responsible mother, but a certain look would escape from her eyes now and then, and my body knew I was hated on some level. It was like the flash of a weapon being fired at close quarters. I reeled from the surprise and shock of that look.

As a child, I spent most of my free time in my room, on my own, as soon as I was old enough to have that choice. I loved to read, imagine, and go to places in my head that offered an escape from the bickering of my parents and the loneliness I felt in my family. I remember wanting my mother to hold me. Wanting to be understood, heard, loved. What child wouldn't want that? I could feel her presence, but it seemed to be behind a barrier. Kept from me somehow. I couldn't understand why I felt so alone and forgotten. Does everyone feel lonely in their family? I wondered this sometimes. My brother and I occasionally played together, but more often we each kept to ourselves. As I grew up and witnessed other people's relationships with their families, I found it hard to connect with their experiences. It was easier to float away, in my own mind, to a place where I controlled things and life was perfect.

My father likewise was incapable of closeness or intimacy, and I empathized with my mother as I saw her struggle to be seen by him. I also felt the emptiness of not being seen. My father had been sent to boarding school at the age of six, and to be fair, I can now understand his own need for protection. Of course, as a child, none of this matters. I only knew I felt more at home in my fantasies than I did in real life.

I suspect this could lead someone to replace real intimacy and connection with the fantasy of an idealized relationship. I believe this is what happened to me.

You might wonder where the title of this memoir comes from. I think I always knew there was a light in my story somewhere. The crescent moon symbolizes to me a time of rebirth, a fresh start, a re-emerging of the light, while also holding the mystery of not really being the source of that light. This is, in my imagination, what Islam did for me in my life. Every time I look at the small sliver of moon perched on top of a mosque now, it reminds me of the way I felt about myself then—not fully formed, but with a promise of fullness in the future.

This promise was neither that of the sunrise that promises a new day, bright and flourishing, nor even of the brightness of a full moon. This promise was subtler, the promise of the inner self—my inner self—that was waiting in the shadows. The child that was waiting to be called forth to play, to create, and to live in connection with my heart.

I think now that somehow, I needed everything to happen just as I am about to tell you, so that I could reach inward to that abandoned inner child and pull her out.

The crescent moon inevitably waxes to fullness, just as the night turns to day, and here, dear reader, I will take you on such a journey. This journey to the underworld and the darkness is not taken by the faint of heart, and I want you to know that I was not without my strengths and my allies. Do not fear—even if all seems lost, the light will prevail.

The crescent moon appears after the darkness, to show us the way. Let us begin.

Chapter
One

I LOOKED AT MY REFLECTION IN the mirror.
It was still early in the day, and the crescent moon
hung low in a clear sky. The cooler fall weather had
arrived, and it was the perfect time for this experiment.
I peered at myself. I was the same and yet not the same.

I had felt this split since forever. In fact, I couldn't
remember a time when I had felt whole. There had
always been a split between the me that was inside and
the me that I showed to the world. Looking in the mirror
always felt like I was looking at a stranger.

I had grown up on a small farm in rural Nova
Scotia. I was taught that mirrors were for vain people.
My mother and father had strong views on things like
"looks." If you put effort into your appearance, you were

somehow not getting what was really important. My father, for instance, never wore deodorant or worried when the hair on the back of his neck wasn't shaved. My mother was taller than him and spent much energy trying to be smaller than her five feet nine inches. Flaunting your unique beauty was not something we valued in our family.

I tucked a stray strand of hair under the large square of material I had wrapped around my head. I had picked out a beautiful cream with blue flowers. Somehow, even though the point of wearing the scarf was to cover our feminine beauty, our hair, I still wanted to cover it with something beautiful. I had always loved colour. It had scandalized my mother when I came down for breakfast one day when I was eight or nine years old, dressed in as many colours as I could find. My grandmother had always dressed in greens and browns, so Mom didn't exactly have a role model there. I chuckled remembering my mother's face.

Was it wrong to want to appear beautiful? Modest but pretty—it must be possible, right?

I felt doubt creep in. As I was growing up my parents had not actively put me down, but in those insidious ways that families are so good at, I had taken in the message that flaunting your beauty was wrong. I remember my mom saying, "Don't wear that makeup, you will look like a prostitute." So, I hid myself behind the persona of the good girl.

Mom had bought me boys' jeans when I was twelve,

saying that they would fit my body better as I didn't have
a waistline yet. I cringe thinking about it even now. I
had wanted to die rather than wear those jeans to school
when all the other girls had skinny jeans that showed
their curves. If only I'd had the right jeans, someone
would have asked me to the grade seven dance or even
just wanted to hang out with me after school. I pretended
I didn't care. I had other things to do. I stayed in my
room a lot. Taught myself to knit from a book. It didn't
matter. If I prayed hard enough, surely God would listen.

I spent hours imagining my knight in shining armour
rescuing me from my isolation and sweeping me off to
some faraway castle. In my vision I danced gracefully
in beautiful dresses and was eternally adored. I didn't
worry about how unrealistic this picture was. I assumed
the magic would happen at some point.

The bridge between fact and fantasy seemed
insurmountable for years, and I went through high
school still feeling that I wasn't sure how it all worked.
It never occurred to me until much later that my
fantasy life was what had kept me safe all those years.
Safe from the pain of isolation, emotional neglect, and
lack of connection.

I finally rebelled at fifteen. I believed leaving home
was the only option for finding my own way. I vowed to
get out of my local high school and away from home.
I spent hours researching, looking for a boarding school
that fit my talents; by this time, I had outgrown my local
music ensembles and opportunities. I finally found

Interlochen Arts Academy in the US. I asked my dad to accompany me on the piano as I recorded a few pieces for solo French horn. A few weeks later I was offered a scholarship for music at the prestigious American fine arts school.

Three years there passed in a whirlwind of growth and practice, culminating in the huge decision of whether to apply to top music schools for continued study. I marvelled at my friends' ability to sit for hours a day in the small practice rooms in the basement of our dorms. I didn't think I had that commitment. In one moment, while I was looking out the window and wishing I could go for a walk instead of practicing, I gave up the dream of becoming a professional musician. I didn't realize then that I was still running away from myself.

I thought maybe I would find more answers to life's questions in the field of science, so I applied to University of St. Andrews in Scotland to study physiology and was accepted. But my fears of unfulfillment and intimacy followed me. It had been harder than I thought to break out of the "good girl" mould, and I ended up staying stuck in my parents' idea of style and my family's way of being.

"Can't you wear anything nicer than jeans and T-shirts?" a friend asked with exasperation.

Her comment about my clothes cut deep. The hurt I felt finally led me to crack open my "good girl" persona and rebel against the messages I'd received growing up.

I had joined the trampoline club at the university
and begun to make a circle of friends. My first party,
I hung out on the edge of the crowd, feeling like I didn't
belong. Everyone was drinking and I didn't want to be
singled out, so I got myself a glass and poured water into
it, pretending it was alcohol. I made myself as invisible
as possible, in my head judging all the other people
for having fun. Deep down I was scared. Scared to lose
control, scared that all the bad things my mom had told
me about wild parties would happen to me.

With trepidation but increasing courage, I went
to a couple more parties and was surprised to find that
even though people got silly drunk, nothing horrible
happened to them. I let myself have a couple of drinks,
and in a desperate attempt to fit in, I kept going to the
club's social events. Aided by the effects of beer, I cast
off years of repression, although the guilt seemed to stick
to me like burrs. It wasn't long before I was invited to a
party in the next town. I abandoned caution and decided
to go. A first-year medical student named Tom also
attended the party, and we ended up reading a book
together on how to massage your partner. We were both
interested and ended up spending most of the night
working our way through the book, along with most
of our body parts. I found touch a much easier way
to connect than talking, and by the next day, we were
officially dating.

I remember my first kiss. Nineteen was old for a first
kiss, but looking back, I don't think I'd allowed anyone

near me before that. We had walked back to Tom's residence and were standing in that awkward way you do when you know you have to say goodnight, but you don't have a routine with it yet. He leaned down and softly put his lips to mine. It wasn't a long or particularly intense kiss, but I remember the way the fire in my belly surged up, and I floated home.

In subsequent years I experimented with wearing more stylish and feminine clothing, sometimes even erring on the provocative side. My favourite shorts had huge black buckles up the sides, and I frequently cycled around Bristol, where I had moved to do a foundation year of dance training, with a short dress and no bra, attracting many wolf whistles along the way.

As I looked in the mirror, it seemed only yesterday I was sewing sequins on a bra for the circus show I had performed in, and here I was, months later, covering my hair with a scarf.

I had decided that if I was going to dress as a Muslim, I would do it right. Maybe I was trying to redeem myself. Said had made subtle comments about my short dresses and colourful attire. I had bought longer skirts and looser tops since we'd been together. I wanted him to be happy with me, and by following Islamic guidelines, I made him smile. Doing things right was something that was applauded, recognized. People liked you if you did things right. If there was one thing the education system drummed into us, it was that doing things right gave you value. It had always seemed like a

struggle to be accepted in my peer group, but I was very
good at being good! As I positioned my headscarf, some
inner part of me recognized the irony that I was now
outwardly hiding more of myself, but I shut down that
voice in my head.

I pulled the scarf tighter under my chin and pinned
it on the side. There was definitely an art to wearing
a scarf. My first couple of attempts were clumsy, and
I ended up looking like I was wearing a pillowcase on
my head. I could feel the pin digging into me already,
and I felt a little claustrophobic. The corner that
wrapped over the top wanted to stick out, and I had
already used three straight pins in an effort to tame it
into submission.

I looked at myself again and sighed. I guessed
I looked alright. Would people be able to tell it was the
first time I'd worn the hijab in public? I pulled on my
new green coat and buttoned it up. It fell down to
my feet, which I had covered in black socks and shoes.
I felt much older than my twenty-five years. Perhaps the
clothes really do make you feel different. The only parts
of me that were visible were my hands and my face. Just
as it said in the Quran. I had picked up a copy of the
Quran recently in an Islamic bookstore and was doing
my best to read some every day.

I couldn't put my finger on exactly what had spoken
to me in the Islamic bookstore the day Said had taken
me in a few weeks ago. The beautiful male voice
reciting the lines of the Muslim holy text over the

speakers had brought tears to my eyes. It was a deep feeling of recognition, of coming home. I loved the symbol of the crescent moon perched atop the domed roof of some exotic looking mosque. It gave the impression of a new beginning. Like there was more to come.

I recognized the feeling of longing from my childhood. The haunting melodic chanting was calling to something that wasn't quite visible or even knowable. I knew this longing intimately. The chanting and the crescent moon and ultimately the quest for spiritual connection spoke to me.

I wasn't sure I felt quite the same love for the piece of cloth covering my head and the long coat covering my body, but for now I was committed to fitting in as much as I could. I still believed this was the quickest way to feeling happy. Looking the part—in this case, wearing the hijab—was the fast ticket to acceptance.

I smiled with satisfaction.

I was only going out for a walk, a test run, so to speak. I thought I'd slowly get used to wearing the hijab, work up to wearing it all the time when I was in public or had to be around non-related males. I had done my research, read the book on women's modesty in Islam. I was determined to be an inspiring example of a devout Muslim. I wanted to please Allah, and maybe I wanted to please my new fiancé too.

I had heard about Said before meeting him. His charm preceded him. In fact, the jealousy began when

another girl training at circus school got to do some
extra training with the acrobats from the Chinese State
Circus. She had been allowed to train in both acrobatic
and aerials, whereas I had been told to focus on aerials.
Ostensibly this was because of my "potential" in trapeze,
but in this instance that potential seemed to be a
drawback. She got to train at the professional circus
venue, and while she was there, Said hired her for the
summer to work in a show in England. It wasn't fair.
I knew I was better than her.

I shivered slightly at the thought that in the end,
I had won. Said had come to our end-of-year show and
had liked me and my trapeze partner, Tony, as well.
The day after finishing school, the three of us had gone
to work in the show, my first professional circus job after
finishing a year of dance training and another year of
circus and physical theatre.

Tony and I had embarked on the job with high
expectations. We were full of dreams of shows and lights
and action, so our arrival in Great Yarmouth was a bit
of a letdown. The boardwalk looked rundown, and
only a few scattered people strolled along the beachfront
with ice cream cones and stuffed toys. We had driven
up to the address they'd given us only to find the old
hippodrome building all locked up and no one in sight.
We had been told this was the place we would be
training and performing in the summer show. We waited
there for ages, looking at each other doubtfully. Were
we wrong? Had we been duped? Was there even a
show at all?

Just then, an unlikely threesome approached. An older man with an old coat that was a couple of sizes too big for him, a young waif of a girl with a tight bun pulling back her thin, blonde hair, and a handsome, Italian-looking man who exuded confidence and charisma. Tony and I stared, transfixed, as they drew nearer. We finally stood up hastily as we realized they were indeed coming toward us.

"You must be the new ones," the older man said, and indicated we should follow him. He turned to the other man and said, "Let's go to the café and chat about the show first."

"Okay." The handsome one turned to us and grinned. "I'm Said and this is Basil, the director." I waited expectantly for the blonde girl's name, but Said ignored her and swept on.

"Welcome to the show!" he said, very much like a ringmaster.

I smiled back shyly, noticing the muscles of his upper body through his fitted T-shirt. This was the famous Said I had heard about. I was a little awestruck as we entered a nondescript seaside café and sat down, pulling a couple of tables together to make room for the others who had appeared to join us.

"Coffees all around." Basil waved his hand and commanded the waitress. "Let's get down to business."

I found myself sitting next to Said and was feeling uncomfortably hot as I became aware of his body next to mine. I tried to keep my gaze forward and not turn to look at him, but it was hard to ignore his raw magnetism. The waitress had apparently noticed too, as she served him first, taking an extra-long time to set his cup down in front of him. Said gifted her his winning smile, causing a rosy blush to rise up her neck.

I kept my head down and tried to listen to the talk about the costumes, the set, and all the myriad things that still had to get done before the show opened in a couple of weeks. Said kept his arm next to mine on the table and drank his coffee in a way that made me imagine how his catlike movements would feel if we were having sex. I blushed at the thought and kept my head down even more.

After the meeting, Said asked if I had settled into the hotel already. I nodded, still finding my words hard to come by.

"Oh, okay then. I have to go there to move into my room. I was just wondering if you were going that way."

"Sure, I can come with you." The words tumbled out. "I still need to do a few things too."

"Great!" Said smiled straight at me. "It will be nice to have some help for once."

"Of course." I let my breath escape. I hadn't been aware of offering to help him move in, but I'd do anything to be around him for a little longer. I was smitten.

"Come on, the beach is beautiful, we can walk that way." He told Basil that he would be back in a bit and guided me expertly down to the boardwalk. "Don't mind Basil, he is all talk and no bite." Said walked beside me until we got to the sand and then ran forward a few steps and flipped expertly in a side somersault. "That's wild tumbling," he explained. "Moroccan acrobats are famous for that move."

"Oh," I said, amazed and a little shy—we were now being stared at by many of the others on the beach. "That was really good."

"I'll show you how to do that if you want. We can do some training between shows."

"Um, yes! That would be awesome!" I managed a few more words. "I'd like to learn to tumble, we didn't learn too much of that in circus school."

"Oh pfft, yeah, circus school doesn't know how to teach anything," Said scoffed. "I'll teach you properly."

I felt even smaller than I had at the café and wondered if I really was up to the task of performing in the show here. It didn't feel as if I was prepared at all. Said was only six years my senior, but he acted as if he knew so much more about life.

"Don't worry, you'll get the hang of it all," Said added, as if he could read my mind.

I was surprised that this handsome man had paid me any attention at all. The only boys that had ever seemed to really notice me were the class geeks in school. The type with cold, clammy hands, white skin from staying inside all the time, and no muscles at all. Said was the opposite of all that, with a quick smile and a body to die for.

Surprisingly it had only taken a couple of weeks

for him to put the moves on me. The other girls were insanely jealous. Said was the guy every girl wanted. Competition for Said's attention continued the whole summer. I know he loved the fact that everyone wanted him. He had reminded me of this fact every day.

"You are lucky I picked you. Look at all the other women that want me."

I had been so flattered he had picked me that I put up with his constant need for attention from the other girls as well. I worked the hardest, I trained the hardest, and in the end, I was the one who moved in with him. There was something satisfying in the proof that hard work does pay off, that prayers can be answered. I smiled smugly at the memories. I would make this relationship work, however hard it seemed. I could feel the hard determination rise up in me, almost to my throat, next to where the damn pin was still sticking uncomfortably into my neck.

I swallowed and stepped out of his flat. I say "his" because I had only recently moved in with Said, and I didn't quite feel it was my space yet. There were other women's clothes still stuffed at the back of his closet, and photos of past girlfriends stood in frames on the shelves in the living room. I had spent a few evenings alone there, listening to his phone ring and, when it went to voice mail, hearing female voices asking, where was Said and why hadn't he called? My heart always flopped wildly as I pondered the idea of picking up the receiver and telling them to back off, I was living with him now.

He had said we were getting married.

There was only a small doubt about this that made something deep in my gut clench in anxiety. We had joked about getting married while waiting backstage at the circus show. One of my costumes was a white dress; I was supposed to be a Russian princess while I assisted the juggler with his act. Said played the Black Knight, and he fit his costume to perfection. He looked so handsome in his black velvet shirt, which was open enough to reveal his chest. He looked like a cross between a pirate captain and a gypsy. It made all the girls swoon.

Someone walked past and casually mentioned that it looked like we were waiting to walk down the aisle. My heart leaped as I gazed adoringly at Said. I remembered my childhood fantasies of a knight in shining armour sweeping me up on his horse and galloping off. I knew Said had done trick riding in another show; it was so easy to imagine him in the role of my hero. I mean, here we were standing together in costumes that seemed to fit my fairy-tale image. Maybe it was meant to be.

"We could get married, you know," I said, only half teasing.

"Sure," he said, shrugging nonchalantly.

I forced him to speak to my parents on the phone that night to break the news of our engagement. As we walked to the phone booth he didn't seem as enthusiastic as I had hoped, but I forged ahead. He was distant as I chattered on happily, making plans for our life together. He stood at the phone booth, and when I handed him the phone, he took it and talked to my parents. That was all I needed to bring my fantasy to life. It didn't matter so much that he seemed a little too quiet. *Never mind*, I told myself, *I can make this work. I can will him to fit the role I have created for him.*

A few days later, flowers arrived at the circus venue, congratulating us on our engagement. My glowing face crumpled when Said tried to hide them, saying to everyone that it was a misunderstanding. I shook my head in confusion. But now I was here, living in his flat. Things seemed to have worked out.

A niggling doubt always stopped me from answering the phone at his place. I didn't want to jinx it, mess things up. Something invisible held me back. I wasn't sure. So, I kept quiet and tried to ignore the phone messages.

I concentrated on learning about my new religion. I loved the Arabic words, the beautiful recitation, the piety and passion that Muslims seemed to have for their religion and for Allah. All my life I had felt like I was looking for something, some connection or meaning. Glimpses of a deeper beauty and peace had come to me now and then, fuelling my desire for intimacy with God.

Islam called to my soul, and Said called to my child self, the one who had imagined the handsome prince courting me gallantly. He was Muslim, tall, dark, and handsome, with that exotic look that drives white Western women wild. He had shared some of his love for his religion with me, and I could see the desire in his eyes. His words soothed me as he talked of settling down, raising a family, practicing his religion more. He painted a picture for me, and I put myself in the middle of it. The fact that his imagined picture and the reality of the present moment didn't quite jive seemed but a small hiccup to me. I understood his dream, and I knew I could make that happen. Whether this was for me or for him, I didn't yet question.

I pushed all this to the back of my mind and set my steps toward the park at the end of the street. It was a damp, grey afternoon in Manchester, normal for this time of year. December could be a dreary month. I was used to seeing lights and greenery decorating the houses at home in Canada before Christmas, but here it was not so common. This part of the city had many immigrants, and Pakistani shops were more abundant than the quaint British butchers, bakers, and grocers I had become acquainted with in Scotland.

I wouldn't be celebrating Christmas this year. Strange. I didn't feel too bereft at that thought. I hadn't been home for Christmas with my family in a few years now. Christmas on your own was a much more subdued affair.

I thought maybe I'd call Mom when I got home. I was feeling somewhat sad. I hadn't seen my parents or my brother since they had come to see the year-end show at the circus school, and so many things had changed in my life. It was hard to know how to explain everything to them. Would they be happy about my new plan to get married and become a Muslim? This might be the most challenging news I had ever presented to them. Maybe I could fit in a visit home before the holidays? Break the news to them in person?

I felt better as I thought about this. It would be nice to go home and be with my family for a bit. I couldn't help feeling a little lost as I waited for Said to find work in Manchester. I had pushed my family away for a long time, but lately my feelings toward them were changing, and I missed home.

I wasn't working now or doing anything really. It had been a couple of months since we had finished our contract for Ford, doing circus shows at the Birmingham Car Exhibition. It had been wonderful to be working with professional acrobats and dancers. To have a makeup artist and costume fittings. I had begun to feel beautiful and inspired with ideas for new acts. But when Said invited me to come back to his apartment, my inspirations faded in the glow of his vague promises that we would build a life together.

I felt a slight pang of regret as I remembered performing in the circus. It had been fun and good money for a twenty-five-year-old. I had saved a few thousand pounds in only a few months and had felt like I might actually be making it as an adult. Said had suggested we send money to Morocco to build a house there. His family could look after it for us, and we would have a wonderful place for holidays, even to live there eventually. It sounded like a grand plan to me. I had not really thought of having my own house anywhere, let alone an exotic place like Morocco.

But if I kept with this path I was on now, my days of being onstage were over, maybe the money also. I had hoped to get more out of all my dance, voice, and physical theatre training. Now my days of being seen at all were basically over. A deep sigh escaped my lips, but as I breathed in the damp December air, I remembered my desire to become a true Muslim. It shouldn't matter if I made money or not or ever made the big time. Surely pleasing God was more important than doing what I wanted.

Only a year before, my life goal had been to see my name in lights. Broadway perhaps, the West End. A circus school friend and I had begun to plan our own circus show, a rendition of Peter Pan with circus acts, performed on a tall ship as the stage. Ideas and inspirations had flowed easily and bounteously. It had been almost too amazing to contemplate.

But then that inner voice began its ruminations. What if? What if you never make it, what if you end up on the street, begging for handouts? What if you go from one audition to the next, only to be told you aren't what they're looking for? Is it worth all that pain and rejection? The old patterns of doing what others expected surfaced with a vengeance. Being good was easy, living into my own greatness was not. Now the little voice in my head told me I would be rewarded for my persistence and piety, if not in this life, then in the hereafter. I let my breath out with a sigh. I had given myself permission to hide, and for now that felt better than the fear of my unknown greatness.

I have known The Voice for as long as I can remember. I believe it started off as a comfort. The Voice comforted me when I felt lonely or afraid or was tired of hearing my parents argue in the other room. The Voice was my companion, he could play my handsome prince, my long-lost friend, my erotic lover. He could always be counted on to be there. So, I am not sure when his persona began to change. Somewhere along the line, The Voice became not only protector, but persecutor. The comfort he provided became infused with thoughts like, "You don't belong out there, stay here and be safe with me." "No one wants to be with you anyway, why risk getting hurt?" "Other people won't live up to your expectations, I will do whatever you want."

The Voice shows up whenever it seems like I am enjoying things a little too much. The Voice knows exactly how to squelch my budding enthusiasm for any new creative project. It has a nasal quality that makes it sound like it's sneering all the time, making sarcastic fun of my ideas. Sometimes it seems that it is protecting me and keeping me safe, but at other times I want to punch it for being in the way of me really being free.

It's a male voice. I picture it as a tall, thin, reedy

man with a sharp nose and dark eyes that look at me with disdain. The Voice is mean, and I am too afraid to disregard it. I look to The Voice for protection—protection from some internal dread or fear. Like one of Bluebeard's wives, I do what I'm told to avoid punishment.

I sometimes wondered what I would find if I confronted The Voice. Skeletons? Evil? Annihilation? Yes, I think that's it, complete annihilation. I would no longer exist. At least that is what The Voice would have me believe.

I felt the snugness of my scarf and coat; I was safe inside myself. I walked a bit self-consciously to the end of the street and checked for traffic as I crossed over to the park. It was usually quiet at this time of day, so I had taken to going out for a walk almost daily. Said left for his job at the pizza place around three o'clock, and the twelve hours he was out stretched long and tedious as I sat alone in his one-bedroom flat, in a city where I knew no one.

Still, I told myself, it was nice to have so much time to do what I wanted. I had always prided myself on my ability to be creative and self-motivated. I stayed up to see Said after work, so we both slept in until almost noon every day, although I was usually a morning person. I would practice my few words of Moroccan as I lay in bed next to him.

"What would you like for breakfast?" I said in the odd sounding Arabic syllables.

I knew the words for toast, eggs, coffee with milk.
That usually covered it. I would slide out of bed and
shower quickly and prepare our breakfast. I enjoyed
setting the tray on our round coffee table, pouring the
coffee into mugs, and dipping my toast into the same
plate of eggs as he did. It was convivial, sharing food
this intimately. It was the Moroccan way, Said had said.
I licked the yolk from my fingers and gazed lovingly at
my handsome fiancé.

I shook my head as I walked and almost laughed out
loud. My life now was so different from only a year ago.
So different from anything I'd ever imagined. My dreams
and goals seemed to have faded now. Every day that
passed in this new city, with Said, felt more and more
removed from my old life.

This was not the first time I had changed course
and given up on a dream. I remembered my thought
process as I practiced for my senior French horn recital
at the arts school in the US. Would I ever make it as a
musician? I wanted to pour my soul into the notes, touch
people, make them feel joy, sorrow, angst, despair, ecstasy,
but something still remained locked away. I couldn't
open the flow of my own heart—at least not as much
as I wanted to. I also realized that much of the music
and emotions I wanted to express were beyond my direct
experience, and I couldn't access that place inside me
where I could create and feel everything I wanted. My
fantasies remained firmly locked up. I could see them
but I couldn't bring them into my earthly reality.

I glanced up from the path and saw a couple of young boys coming toward me, pushing their bikes. I looked down quickly. Dressing like a Muslim really did make me feel more modest, less outgoing, and not so inclined to chat to strangers on the path in the park. They were laughing and pointing at me, and I grew suddenly wary.

As they drew up next to me, one of the boys reached out and grabbed my scarf from the back and yanked it down. They both squealed with laughter and hopped on their bikes to pedal away, calling back, "Do you have hair?"

"Go back to your own country!"

"We don't want you people here!"

I blushed with indignation. I wanted to call back to them that I *was* from here. That I was white just like them. And, of course I had hair! But I kept walking and didn't turn around. Tears pricked in the corners of my eyes. I tried to fix my painstakingly arranged scarf, now all askew. I wanted to go back to the flat and lock the doors and stay inside. I tried to breathe normally. Should I finish my walk? No one else was around, and there was no one to see my embarrassment. I felt drained and exhausted, depleted from the outside and the inside.

I was about halfway around the small park and decided to muster my dignity and continue around to the gate where I had started. No other hoodlums were lurking that I could see. In fact, the only other people at the park were a mom and her young child over by the swings.

The voice in my head chimed in. *The trials of this life will be rewarded in the hereafter, as it says in the Quran.*

I had begun to read a version of the holy book with an English translation next to the Arabic calligraphy. The man at the bookstore had said the Quran was the actual word of Allah, "written down exactly the way it was revealed to the Prophet Muhammad," he'd said solemnly.

I found the meaning of the verses difficult to understand, but I prayed every day that I would become pious enough that the understanding would come to me. Said knew only a little of the explanations behind the written text and was not much help as I struggled to learn my new religion. He seemed happy that I was trying though, and I blushed when he complimented me as I excitedly shared some small tidbit of information. Obtaining knowledge was revered in Islam, as stated in this hadith, or saying of the Prophet Muhammad: "*Bismillahi Rahmani Raheem* (in the name of Allah), it is obligatory to have knowledge, so that we may act on that knowledge, call others to that knowledge, and have patience." I smugly shelved each sentence in my newly expanding memory.

I read about the etiquettes of learning in Islam. I had always been a good student, and I was determined to bring my best skills to my new-found faith.

From Ibn Kayyim al Josea I learned the six etiquettes of learning:

- Ask questions in good manner.

- Remain silent and listen attentively.
- Comprehend well.
- Memorize the knowledge.
- Teach it.
- Act upon it and keep to its limit.

I read that "one of the greatest sins is not gaining knowledge." Well, I would not fall into sin so quickly. I would learn as much as I could and be an exemplary student. The fact that this new obsession kind of made up for being lonely and isolated skirted in the periphery of my mind, but I paid it no heed.

Most evenings when Said had his friends over to visit, there was nothing else for me to do but study. I would make them tea and put a plate of cookies on a tray and leave it outside the living room door, knocking twice to let him know it was there and he could get it. It was not proper for me to sit with them, not now that I was a Muslim woman.

I often fought the feeling of being excluded. I wanted to join in the conversation, sit with Said, and get to know his friends. This pattern had started back in the circus. I had moved into his room, hoping to have more time with him. Every evening, we would come back and shower, and he would go down to sit with "the boys," saying he'd be back soon and I should just relax.

"You wouldn't understand anyway," he'd say by way of explanation. "We are speaking Arabic."

This was true, I knew, and I didn't really want to sit through hours of not understanding what they were talking about. It was better for me to sit apart and read, The Voice intoned insistently. I would be doing something that increased my faith, not just gossiping or wasting time chatting. Besides, Said always seemed so pleased with me afterwards.

"You are such a blessing," he would croon, hugging me tightly. "I love that you are trying to be such a good Muslim woman."

I embraced the study of Islam with vigour. I collected more books on Islam, much to Said's approval. To pass the time, as I sat in the bedroom I read books translated into English on all the topics and rules of Islam. Later, I would put questions to Said, and he would glow with pride at my desire to learn. He praised my studious habits and claimed that I would be one of the highest women in Paradise because I had come to the true path. When I asked a more difficult question, he often said it was better for me to find the answer myself, as it proved my desire to please Allah. He said he didn't want me to feel he was instructing me on how to act or what to say.

A different voice in my head sometimes whispered that he probably didn't know the answers himself and was cleverly disguising this by making it seem like he was helping me. But I would shoo this kind of thing from my thoughts. I was being unkind to doubt his intentions.

I had secretly been teaching myself to pray. I read the passages from the Quran in English for now, since I couldn't yet understand or say the Arabic. I felt shy to share this with Said until I could do it properly. I wanted him to be impressed.

Said had started praying more, I noticed. I told him about a dream I'd had where I heard the *adhan* so clearly it woke me up. The adhan is the voice that calls from the mosque when it is time for one of the daily prayers. When I told him, he got tears in his eyes and put his hands on my shoulders and said, "We should get up to pray Faj'r in the morning. You can wake me up and help me to do this, you are such a good woman." I had blushed and resolved to do even more and be better. His praise was like water for my soul, I craved more. Even the early time of the first prayer, about four o'clock in the morning, did not deter me.

I had worked with Said's friends only months before in the circus show. I had worn a sequined bra and harem pants as Said and I performed the bungee act together. The other girls in the show had all been jealous when I got to perform with Said. They walked onstage with me, in red velvet robes, while Said sat and smoked a hookah pipe. We were meant to be a drug induced vision of his imagination. The three of us walked seductively onstage and dropped our capes, lying down erotically on them.

Said made a point of looking lasciviously at the other girls and ignoring me, knowing it drove me wild with jealousy. I told myself it didn't matter, I was doing the act, and I was the one who walked home with him after the two shows we performed every day. The bungee belt was lowered over me, and I reached up to snap it onto the harness I wore around my chronically bruised hips. I winced whenever I put on the belt, but then the adrenalin took over.

I loved the feeling of flying through the air, dropping almost to the ground, pulling up strongly on the elastic to perform multiple somersaults before reaching up to catch the trapeze. Timing was everything, and Said and I synched our legs as we swung back and forth on the two trapezes, facing each other. He nodded, and I waited for the backswing, letting go of the ropes and falling backward as I was swung toward him. I reached my hands out—this was my favourite part. He reached out strongly and grabbed my wrists. It was a sensational feeling, to be "owned" like that. I smiled up at him, loving that moment when I was the only person in his focus. It was part of the act, we were meant to be lowered down as long-lost lovers. He played the part well—too well. I was besotted. We touched the ground and the moment was over. He turned to the cheering crowd, taking in their adulation.

My moment was over. I swept off one side of the stage, he went out the other. I couldn't wait for the next show, just to feel that thrill again, of being wanted.

My past relationships flipped through my head like index cards as I made my way upstairs to our dressing room. A very small number of cards really. I had been rejected or thrown away in the end by all of them. For some reason I couldn't quite comprehend, none of my past boyfriends had appreciated the qualities in me that I knew I had. Perhaps I hadn't known how to share my inner self. I had so many feelings! But the desire to be accepted and liked overshadowed everything. I withdrew even more, finding some kind of peace in a connection with God. Inside my head, God and I could have whatever kind of relationship I chose. There was a safety in that, which I depended on.

I hadn't really noticed, but over the years since I'd left home, the God in my head had become more and more critical. Demanding sacrifices of me that were harder and more challenging as time went on. I began to feel a sort of compulsion to prove myself worthy and to make sacrifices, which provided a way to dull the pain of disconnection from my inner desires. It was better not to feel at all than to feel the pain of not being fulfilled. I didn't know it then, but I had relegated myself to living a martyr's life.

My obsession with learning about Islam only somewhat alleviated the deep loneliness lurking in the depths of my heart. I sometimes missed my old life, the circus, performing, my friends, creating performance art. It seemed like I had jumped into another timeline; it was my life but in a different universe. A faint voice in my head questioned whether continual self-punishment was really the way to salvation. What's so wrong with feeling good sometimes?

The time came when I was ready to take the *Shahada*, the oath that would make me a Muslim: "I bear witness that there is only one God but God, and that Muhammad is the messenger of God." I was pledging to give myself over to the demands of this one God. The Voice in my head was cheering me on: *This is your chance to mean something to someone, to God.*

Said told me I was absolved of all my past sins. I was renewed, my past did not matter anymore. All my mistakes were forgiven. I wasn't sure I believed him, but I wanted to. I knew he hated that I had slept with other men before him and even experimented with a female friend too.

Said told me that I had erased all of his past sins too because he had shared Islam with me and I would take him to Paradise by my conversion. It was his influence that had helped me to see the right path, and so he shared in the reward. I wondered vaguely what he thought of his own past. Did he feel shame for all the women he had been with and not married? Did he have to think about all that every time he said the Shahada in his prayers?

As I continued my first walk outdoors in the hijab, my mind wandered unbidden to memories of me and my friend in the showers at circus school. We had been exploring our ability to be comfortable with our sexuality onstage, and I had found myself fantasizing about being with a woman. I had yet to determine whether this was a part of my unexplored sexuality or just a passing phase. The opportunity arose sooner than I imagined.

She was sitting on the benches in the locker room, and I had just finished in the shower. The room was open and I had to walk past her to get to my clothes. I found myself being drawn to her lips. What would it be like to kiss her, another woman? I stopped in front of her and slid onto her lap. When I kissed her full on the mouth we both forgot everything else, including the fact that I was still dripping wet. I was surprised to find that my body responded as readily to a woman as it did to a man. A tingling deep inside my belly spread a warmth down between my legs. Her hands were on my back and she pulled me to her as we kissed. One of my hands grazed her breast, and instinctively I started massaging it gently, and then with more urgency. I kissed down her neck, both my hands on her chest now. She moaned and her legs parted as I slipped down to explore her with my tongue. It was exciting to feel my way around. I knew what to do, as I could feel what my own body would want.

I quickly shut out those thoughts, they made me feel uncomfortable. My body reacted in ways I knew would make God angry, and Said too. *You should be happy you are coming to the right path and absolving your sins*, The Voice insisted angrily. I shook myself out of my reverie and walked more quickly, willing my body to obey.

The truth was, I was afraid. I was afraid of my own

desires, afraid of my passion, and afraid that I would lose control if I ever let that part of me lead the show.

Maybe you are just a slut. The Voice was louder, reverberating. My stomach tightened. I hadn't meant things to go there again in my mind. I didn't know what to do with my erotic energy. The memory arose of its own accord. During my time in circus school, I had befriended an American guy visiting the UK for a year abroad. He and his roommate had introduced me to the alternative party scene, and I had guiltily participated in some explorations with the two of them that I had never revealed to anyone. I found it hard to withstand the barrage of images and sensations that flooded my brain.

Running naked down the hallway between their rooms, it had seemed impossibly fun to be desired sexually by two men at the same time. They had both been aroused by me, and the intoxicating power of this was still lurking in the shadows of my body's memory. Even now, my vulva swelled, unbidden, at the thoughts.

Walking faster and tightening my legs together to numb the sensation, I questioned myself. How did I let myself be used like that? Was I being used? I felt ashamed, as if I had done something wrong, while at the same time I felt angry at myself for my shame. It wasn't like I'd done something hundreds of other people didn't do at some point.

I drew my hijab tighter across my chest, trying to suppress the memories. *You were a whore*, my inner voice said. *You have no modesty at all.*

I rounded the last corner of the park and headed back across the road. I had had enough of wearing the hijab for one day, and I couldn't wait to get home and take everything off again. I had almost reached the steps to the flat when I saw the way was blocked by a woman in bright pink clothes. She looked Pakistani or Indian, and she had a large bag with her. It looked like she was visiting someone in the building. I waited for her to move, but she stayed, blocking my path to the door.

"Can I help you?" I asked.

"Do you know if Said is home?" she asked, in a tone that was too familiar for my liking.

"No, he isn't here now," I snapped, "but I am his fiancée, can I help you with something?"

She started, and her eyes dropped.

"Well, um, I, um, I bought this duvet cover set for him," she mumbled, but then she squared her shoulders and looked me in the eye, sizing me up. "May I come in and put it on? My name is Rani, by the way. I have known Said for a long time."

She pushed her way in as I unlocked the door. I didn't want to be rude to a long-time friend of Said's, if that's truly what she was. I had never heard him mention her. She seemed to know her way around the apartment and quickly stripped the covers off the bed and began putting on the new linen she had brought with her. How did she know where everything was in here, I wondered, especially in the bedroom? Who was she really? Had Said purposely kept her a secret?

I stood helplessly in the hall, wondering how I could get her to leave. She finished her transformation of the bed and fished a card out of her purse, which she tucked against the pillow. She gazed around and seemed to satisfy herself that Said was indeed out.

"Tell Said I came by," she instructed brazenly. "My name is Rani," she said again. She looked me up and down. "Make sure you tell him I was here."

Then she turned, walked out the door, and flounced down the street. I watched her walk to the corner and then, in a daze, turned and shut the door behind me.

I sat down on the sofa in the small living room. I looked around, feeling adrift, not at home. These were not my things, this was not my apartment. Even the pictures on the shelf were of some Turkish girl Said had dated for a while, not me. What was I doing here? I got up and wandered into the bedroom. I got a chair and climbed up to look in the top of the wardrobe space. I pulled out a couple bags of clothes, and a pair of ballet shoes that looked incredibly tiny fell out of one of them. I picked them up. Some other woman's stuff. I pushed everything back in the bag and shoved it back on the top shelf. I didn't want to look at it, didn't want to know whose it was. Maybe sometime I'd just put it all in the trash and hope Said didn't notice. My chest felt tight, and I was feeling physically ill. I put the chair away and pulled at the duvet cover distractedly. I wasn't sure that I wanted to sleep in the bed she had made up. Damn all the women Said had been with before!

I wanted Said to clean the ghosts of girlfriends past out of his apartment. I wanted him to put my picture in the frame in the living room. I wanted him to show me I mattered.

I had left all my old clothes at my last apartment. My short dresses and jewellery. My book of erotica, a dildo a friend had bought for me. Much of my old way of life had already disappeared. It added to my feeling of having lost my anchor, who I was. I first noticed this when I was still in circus school. We had been challenged to experiment and try so many new characters, discover new parts of ourselves, that it had become hard to tell who I was anymore. I rose to the challenge of being innovative with an almost explosive energy. I was, after all, an Aquarius. We are made for innovation and quirkiness! However, I had begun to feel more and more as if I was just being different, with no connection to who I really was inside.

A panicky feeling settled in my stomach when I thought about it. Said—and with him, Islam—had come along at the right time, with a plan, a set of rules on how to live my life. I could dedicate myself to a spiritual path and to a life partner and family at the same time! It seemed perfect. Instead of a seemingly endless, lonely path of discovery, I could take on the God-given rules and way of life of a practicing Muslim woman. End of story. Peace, happiness, Paradise. Sighing, I wondered why I was not holding onto these things for more than fleeting moments.

I looked around for some way to vent my feelings.
I wanted to smash something into tiny pieces. Nothing
here was mine, and I couldn't bring myself to harm
Said's things; I still needed his love. Even more angry
at this thought, I pulled out my old diaries, pages I had
written about my life before Islam. I ripped out the pages
and tore them up. Pictures of me in school tumbled out,
and I crumpled them up, stuffing them deep in the
garbage can so I couldn't come back later and fish them
out. I wanted it all gone, I wanted myself gone. I didn't
want to feel so angry, so afraid and helpless. I breathed
out, looking at the shreds of my life. A coldness
descended on me then, and the feelings were gone.
I picked up the mess and threw it all away. Numbness
shrouded all my senses.

I couldn't stop my mind from wondering how many
girls he had brought here, to his small apartment. Had
he promised them things too? I knew he had almost
married a girl from Cuba, a gymnast whom he had
worked with in the circus. Would I be different? I didn't
want to listen to the doubts in my head. I hoped we
would soon get married. We had talked about it. I was
learning about Islam, and I had said I was happy to
stay home and have children. I would support Said to
practice his religion. He wanted to get a different job,
one that allowed him to stay in one place, grow his
beard, pray at the mosque on Fridays, wear the clothing
of a practicing Muslim. The men had prescribed
clothing too: baggy pants with the hem above the ankle

and a long shirt. I wouldn't be alone. He painted such a clear picture of marital bliss and spiritual contentment, I couldn't say no.

I resolutely turned my mind away from the woman at the door, the pictures on the shelf, the clothes in the wardrobe, and I filled the kitchen sink with soapy water. I would clean up, there were oil spatters on the wall behind the stove, all the way up to the ceiling. I rolled up my sleeves and attacked the grime, hopeful that doing something purposeful would supplant my errant thoughts. I thought of the line from *The Sound of Music*: "When someone closes a door, somewhere God opens a window."

I turned my eyes up to the window and smiled with grim determination. I would focus on pleasing Allah. He would take care of me. My life would mean something. It had to.

Chapter
Two

THE NEXT MORNING, I AWOKE with a nagging feeling of unease that pierced right through my chest and made it hard to breathe. I turned over to look at Said lying next to me. His arm was thrown up over his face as he slept, and I noticed the bulging bicep muscles that had grown in the past few weeks. I joked that he could just walk into a gym and put on muscle. But this morning, my body did not respond in the usual way to his masculinity.

The words came out before I thought about it. "Yesterday someone came to the door looking for you," I said, wanting him to drag the words out of me. "It was a Pakistani woman."

"Oh?" he groaned sleepily. He put his arm down,

not quite opening his eyes.

"Yes, she came to the door with a duvet set for your bed." The words started tumbling out now. "Didn't you notice the new bedding?" My voice shook slightly. "Her name was Rani."

My heart beat harder in my chest, and it felt like all the breath was being squeezed out of my body.

"Oh yes," he mumbled vaguely, "Rani, she was at college with me. Don't worry about her, she was just crazy about me."

"Yes, I could see that," I snapped, frowning slightly. "The question is, how did you feel about her?"

I regretted asking this as soon as the words left my mouth. I didn't want to know about his other girlfriends. I wanted him to say he had forgotten about all of them after meeting me. I tried to silence the protective side of The Voice deep inside that doubted he would ever say anything to me that could take away the fear. The fear that he didn't really feel about me the same as I did about him.

Said pulled me closer to him. "I didn't care that much about her, she was just a silly girl. I love you." He started to kiss my neck and I giggled, pressing closer to him. I knew I could arouse him with my body, and the power of this knowledge gave me the courage to ask.

"So, do you think we should go to the mosque and get our marriage certificate soon?" I gazed up at his eyes, trying to read his answer before he spoke.

"Sure, let me speak to the boys, we can maybe go

on Thursday."

"Really?" I squeaked.

"Are you happy with me?" His eyes searched mine. "Do you love me?"

"Yes, you are everything to me." I lowered my gaze and melted into his arms. "So, Thursday?"

He nodded and kissed my head. I forgot everything else but his arms around me.

The next two days stretched interminably long. I paced from the living room to the bedroom and back so many times I lost count. I couldn't wait to be married to Said. Secure. Vague thoughts of loneliness fluttered in the back of my mind. I had no friends or family to come with me to the mosque. It wasn't that they wouldn't have come, exactly. I hadn't asked them.

I struggled to understand my own tangled emotions. My parents had always been very supportive of my wild and crazy decisions, but I hadn't included them in much of my life since I had left home. It wasn't that my family was so bad; at least, there was nothing I could put my finger on. I had just known I needed to get away in order to find some breathing room. As I waited now for my "happy ever after" ending, I could feel the familiar emptiness in my heart. Spending hours in my room as a young girl, finding ways to occupy myself, I could avoid listening to the endless bickering of my parents downstairs. The fantasies I could spin by myself seemed so much more fulfilling that I made them my reality. Perhaps it was not so different now.

I brushed the thoughts away again. Said would come through, he was my prince, my knight in shining armour. Being married to him would change everything.

I usually made decisions and told my family about them later. I didn't want to go through the third degree of explaining myself every time. I often didn't know why I decided to do something until I did it. It just felt right. Feelings and hunches were not considered valid reasons for life choices in my family. Maybe, in this case, I was worried they would talk me out of it.

I hadn't yet mentioned to Said my idea of going home for a visit. The time had never seemed right.

I busied myself with cleaning and my daily walk. Things would work out. I had Allah now. Family and friends were not important.

Thursday came at last. I got up early to shower and put on the Moroccan striped jellaba Said's mother had sent me. I was vaguely aware that I was wearing nothing of my own, nothing that held memories of who I had been before. I shook my head and looked at myself in the mirror. I looked like a stranger, but not in a bad way. My face shone with what everyone now told me was *noor*, divine light. That was worth a little wardrobe shift! I fixed coffee and toast and then woke Said.

"It's Thursday!" I said excitedly.

"Hmm?" he said sleepily.

"Thursday! We are going to the mosque today to do the *nikah*, the marriage." I looked at him suspiciously. "You remember, right?" I felt the tightness in my chest

again. I hadn't bothered him about the marriage much
this week, because I didn't want him to change his mind.
Had he forgotten altogether? I had been so good about
letting him organize things. I'd asked very little about
the actual ceremony, comforting myself with the thought
that at least he was going through with it. Now I
wondered if he really had set anything up.

"Oh, yes, right," he mumbled. "Yeah, Mourad and
Mounir are coming with us. You have your passport?"

The breath escaped my lips as it hit me that this
was really happening. "Yes!" I answered excitedly.
"How do I look?"

He rolled over and opened his eyes properly.
"Beautiful, *habiba*, my beautiful."

I blushed. "Breakfast is ready."

"Okay, let me just have a shower."

I waited impatiently for him to finish getting dressed,
and we made small talk as we ate breakfast. I had so
many questions but no idea how to ask any of them.
I munched some toast shyly and hurried to clean up
the dishes.

As we were driving to the mosque, Said told me
about the dowry.

"So, in Islam, I am supposed to give you and your
family a gift or money. It's yours to keep. It's more a
token gift now rather than an elaborate bride price that
they used to do." He laughed. "Sometimes they would
give camels or goats."

I smiled. "Well, I don't need camels or goats. I just

need you."

Said took my hand. "That's why I'm marrying you. Anyway, if the imam asks me, I'll just put down twenty-five pounds, okay?"

"Sure, that is fine," I answered quickly, just relieved to know he was actually going to marry me, officially. That small voice noted that twenty-five pounds didn't sound like much, but surely, he loved me as much as he said he did. Material things didn't matter. I wasn't one of those women who needed a huge wedding, gifts, a dress. I knew there were more important things. I had never really imagined myself having a big wedding anyway, even when all my friends in school were drooling over pictures of brides and sunsets. Laughing inside, I remembered my childhood daydream of riding off with a prince, on his horse. I guess this was kind of similar. I was marrying the Black Knight from the circus show. Of course, we were no longer performing together. Said had yet to find his feet with a new role in life. As much as I was not sure who I was becoming, I wasn't sure who he was becoming either.

On the way home, I wondered in a somewhat dazed frame of mind how I had become a married woman with so little fuss. The imam had given Said and me a lecture on sharing the household chores. Well, mostly he had told Said to help me with the dishes if I asked him to. That was the only memorable part of the wedding, that talk about dishes. I just felt kind of numb. I decided to talk to Said about going home to see my family. He was

in a good mood about the wedding, and I thought
it would be a good idea to take advantage of that.

"What would you think about me going home for
a week or so?" My voice quivered as I realized this meant
more to me than I was previously aware. Even though
I pretended I didn't need them, I really did. I wanted
to be held by people who cared about me as I stepped
into this new era of my life. I needed something to be
acknowledged and held sacred.

"Sure!" Said answered with a huge smile. "It is a
great idea to go and see your family."

I wasn't sure he was understanding me properly,
as I had meant to say I would go on my own, but
before I knew it, Said had jumped on the idea of
a trip to Canada.

"You want to come with me?" I was a bit confused.
I hadn't expected this turn in the conversation.

"Of course I do!" He beamed. "I want to see your
parents again and show them how I am going to treat
their daughter."

"Oh." I tried to pull my thoughts together. He had
only offered me twenty-five pounds as a dowry, and now
he wanted to come with me to Canada? "Do you think
we can afford to go?"

"Of course," he said again, a tone of anger
creeping into his voice. "We can use our savings from
the circus work."

"Oh," I said again, feeling like I was missing
something important. Hadn't we agreed to save money

for a house in Morocco? "Well, if you think it's a good idea…"

"Family is the most important thing." This started a rant about the virtues of respecting family in Islam. I found myself in a daze, barely hearing him. I couldn't understand his views sometimes. He seemed to turn on a dime from one ideal to another. It made me feel like I was going crazy.

I held on to the seat belt, clutching it tightly. Was this how you were supposed to feel after getting married?

The Voice replied smugly, *The Quran has rules and suggestions for everything, all aspects of life. We will follow that and be blissfully happy*. I guess I had to learn to trust.

Said turned abruptly at the next lights, and we came to a part of the city I didn't know.

"Where are we going?"

"We have to get you a ring," he said, matter-of-factly. "I can't take you to your mother without a ring."

"Oh." I was still having trouble keeping up with his thoughts.

"Here, we can get one here." Said turned into a back alley and parked the car. "Come on, I have a friend who has a shop here."

I climbed out of the car, still in my Moroccan jellaba. I felt conspicuous and uneasy. Ever since the episode in the park, I didn't really like going out in public, especially to a place I didn't know. Said ushered me into a small, dark shop.

"*Assalamu alaikum*, brother." He held out his hand

to the man behind the counter. "How are you? How is your family?"

"Very well, brother Said," the shopkeeper answered warmly, putting a hand on Said's shoulder as he shook hands. He was dressed in the long shirt and short pants the Muslim men wore. His beard was long and well-kept.

"We need a ring for my wife." Said turned to face me, aligning himself with the owner of the shop. This was one of his gifts, an ability to make everyone like him. I blushed as he said those words, "my wife," and turned to look at the rings eagerly.

The shopkeeper said, "Of course. You must have a look at my finest rings."

"You can make a deal for me, brother?" Said winked. "I am a poor man, newly married."

My face coloured with shame then, and I turned away, embarrassed to be talked about like that.

"Come here and see which one you like." The man beckoned me close to the counter, and I peered into the case again, but with less enthusiasm. Most of the jewellery was way too gaudy for me. I noticed one ring that looked like my mother's wedding band.

"Oh, that one looks like my mom's." I spoke and pointed without thinking.

"Perfect," Said said, clearly relieved it was not extravagant. "We can get one like your mom's. How much is it?"

"Oh, that is only a zircon, not real diamond." The shopkeeper tried to turn Said's eye to the rings in the middle of the case with larger stones.

"That's perfect." Said smiled and clapped him on the back. "No sense in displeasing Allah by being arrogant," he continued. I smiled weakly. I was disappointed he didn't think I was worth more than the cheapest fake ring, but what could I say to that? I didn't want to be arrogant. I held out my hand and let Said put the ring on my finger. It felt cold.

That weekend, Said took me to visit his cousin Mourad and his wife, Bilkys. They lived not far away and had been married a year. Said boasted that Bilkys had really wanted him but that he had not been interested in her, and so she had settled for his cousin instead. My heart thumped. I guess that was a compliment? It didn't feel like a compliment, it made me feel anxious. At least he was living with me, and married to me now too, I reminded myself—I had the paper from the mosque to prove that, and the ring on my finger. I told the doubts in my head to shut up.

"I hope you and Bilkys will be friends," Said prodded as he parked the car.

The smell of rice and chicken and Indian spices drifted out as we walked up the steps, and my stomach rumbled. I had been hungry quite often recently. The twinges in my uterus, announcing the beginning of my monthly menses, had been more severe than usual, and I was a few days overdue. I tried not to let my irritability over my physical discomforts show as we were ushered inside by a dark Indian woman in a brightly coloured *shalwar khameez.*

"Bilkys, this is my wife, Aishah." My heart swelled as Said announced me as his wife. It didn't matter that he had changed my name to a Muslim one. Maybe it was because Said's friends found it easier to pronounce than Ailsa. Aishah was the most favoured wife of the Prophet Muhammad, he had told me. I should be honoured to share her name. Did it matter that I was giving up my own? I had changed so many things already in these few short months since we had been together, I almost couldn't remember my own self. I surrendered my name without much of a thought. I was his wife, that was enough. I could live with the name Aishah, if it kept him with me.

The house smelled faintly of mould, and I tried to quell the slight feeling of nausea that rose in my throat. Bilkys offered us tea and I accepted a cup gratefully as I sank onto a big floor cushion in the living room. Said and Mourad immediately began speaking in Moroccan. It sounded to me like they were arguing, but Bilkys assured me that was how they talked to each other. She seemed to enjoy the role of know-it-all, so I let her tell me all about the circus, about Said's mother, whom she had met a couple of years ago, about Morocco. Apparently, she and Mourad were travelling to Morocco soon to visit, as she was pregnant with their first child, a fact she announced proudly.

I looked dubiously at her stomach. I couldn't honestly say whether it was a baby or a few extra pounds, but I smiled and congratulated her anyway. I was beginning to suspect I might be pregnant too, but I didn't let the possibility really take hold in my mind. The evening crawled on, and I could feel my head nodding. The TV was on and Bilkys had lapsed into silence watching some drama. Said and Mourad had eaten and gone out to the mosque to pray. I began to wonder if anyone would mind if I curled up and had a nap. I stretched my legs out cautiously and Bilkys looked over.

"Are you tired? The guys might not be back for a while. You know what they are like when they get talking. Do you want a blanket?"

I nodded. "Yes, thanks." I did not know what the guys were like when they got talking, but I didn't want to let her know that, so I took the blanket and curled up on the cushion. I really wanted to go home to our apartment and go to bed. I prayed that Said would not be too long.

A few minutes later, or so it seemed, Bilkys shook me awake and asked if I wanted to pray. It was time for the last prayer of the day, Isha'a. I mumbled something and opened my eyes, hoping the men would be back and I could go home. She handed me a scarf and showed me where the bathroom was to make *Wudu*, the ritual cleansing for prayer. I stumbled up and followed her, noticing that we still seemed to be in the house alone. Sighing, I closed the door and went through the ritual that I had been practicing at home.

Three times rinse your nose and mouth.

Three times wash your face.

Three times wash your hands and arms.

Wipe your wet hands over your head and ears.

Three times wash your feet.

I smiled as I dried my hands and remembered that if you farted after all of that, you had to repeat your washing all over again, as farting broke your ablution. I didn't fart.

Some of the rules of Islam seemed ridiculously picky. Still, I wrapped the scarf around my head in the required way for a woman to stand before Allah in prayer and went back to the living room. Bilkys had laid out the prayer mats pointing southeast, the direction of Mecca, and was all ready to pray. I stood next to her and we placed the sides of our feet together. I could feel her arm against mine. We were supposed to be close so that Shaitan, the Islamic name for Satan, would not be able to come between us as we prayed. I was glad of her company although her seeming expertise in Said's likes and dislikes and general interest in him caused my inner dislike of her to bristle. She made me feel inferior and inexperienced. I put those feelings away as we prayed, though; I meant to give her the benefit of the doubt. I didn't really want to make enemies of Said's friends and family. I had no friends of my own here, and my family was all back in Canada.

We finished the prayer and tidied up the mats. I offered to help her with the dishes, but she said not to worry. I looked at the clock, it was getting late.

"When do you think Said and Mourad will be back?" I asked her.

"Well, the prayer time in the mosque was an hour ago, so they should be back soon."

Prayer times in Islam are very exact; there were schedules printed for each time zone and even by city. The times of the five daily prayers were set according to the sun. Fajr, the morning prayer, was prayed when the first thread of dawn showed on the horizon. In England, this often meant getting up really early, like four o'clock. The prayer was invalid if you were too late, after the sun had risen. You could always ask forgiveness and pray it anyway, but there was a guilty feeling of having failed somehow when this happened. Noon prayer, late afternoon prayer, sunset prayer, and night prayer followed similar rules. Ideally the men would pray in the mosque itself. It surprised me to learn that it was actually frowned upon for women to pray every day in the mosque. When I asked Said why, he explained that women weren't allowed in the mosque when they were bleeding, so if they made a habit of going to pray there and then they didn't go for a week, everyone would know they were on their menses. Of course, this was something that should be private, so it was just better for the women to not go to the mosque except on special holidays. His explanation kind of made sense to me, but it also felt like a slight to women, not to be allowed to perform this ritual of prayer in the same way as men. Still, I told myself, I had much to learn about this new religion.

I couldn't be expected to understand it all right away.

Growing up I had never been told outright that women were second-class citizens, but this was conveyed to me in many subtle ways. Women were meant to be well-rounded and versed in many things, but not for the sake of ever shining themselves, only to make sure their children were introduced to the arts, music, culture, and the sciences. At the age of twenty my mother had given up a full scholarship to do her PhD in order to get married instead, which, now that I was married at twenty-five, seemed ridiculously young. It was as if she also had needed the security of a husband in order to survive in the world. I believed what Said said and what the books told me: women needed a guide, someone to keep them from going astray.

Even for men, praying in the mosque five times a day could be difficult, especially if you were working in a *kuffar* country (a place of the unbelievers). Said tried his best to pray as many times as he could in the mosque, and if he was at work at the time of prayer, he would roll out a mat in the back of the pizza shop, or the gym, or even outside. Anywhere on the earth was a place of prayer, except for bathrooms. Bathrooms were one of the main locations of the *jinn*, an unseen race of beings not unlike humans but different. People were made from clay, while the jinn were made of fire. Angels were also part of Allah's creation and made from light. The jinn had free will just like humans, so some of them were Muslim and some of them weren't. The unbelieving jinn were referred to as *shayateen* and could whisper troubling words in your ear if you were not strong in your beliefs.

I sighed, sitting down a little stiffly on the couch next to Bilkys. Just then, the door opened and in walked the men. Said was smiling and laughing.

"Did you girls have a good time?" he asked jovially.

I smiled without replying, and he looked at me sharply.

"Stay and have some coffee!" Mourad invited. Said nodded and came to sit next to me on the sofa.

"What's the matter?" he said, too loudly to allow me to answer honestly.

"Nothing." I shook my head. My back ached and I didn't feel like drinking coffee. "I just don't feel that great."

He patted my knee and Mourad asked me how I liked Manchester, and I resigned myself to staying a bit longer.

After what seemed like another few hours, I nudged Said and asked quietly if we could go home.

"Okay," he said, "we can go soon. I'm just going to take a quick look at something on his computer. He wants to show me this program where you can read the Quran online. I'll only be a few minutes. Maybe you want to look at it too?"

The Arabic script was beautiful, and the Imam's voice on the recording made my heart open, as it always did. There was no mistaking the true beauty of the Quran recited well. My eyes were heavy though, and

I couldn't concentrate on listening for more than half a page.

I didn't know if I would ever get used to the long visits that seemed to be the normal thing in my husband's culture. I had grown up mostly in rural Nova Scotia. My mom had adhered to a strict childhood routine as we were growing up. Family mealtimes, quiet periods for play on our own, and planned social visits were my usual experience. This idea that you would drop in and possibly stay all day at someone's house was not in my vocabulary. I felt like I was running a marathon of social niceties, and I couldn't wait to get back to my own space after only a short time. Tonight was no exception, and I finally touched Said's arm and said I'd like to go home. He nodded and got up grudgingly, still talking to his cousin and not looking at me.

"I'm going to take Aishah home," he said in Mourad's direction. "I'll come back later."

I followed him dutifully to the front door, sighing in relief at the thought of getting home.

Said started in as soon as we got to the car. "You didn't really make an effort to be nice. It was rude to ask to leave like that."

Angry words rose up in my throat, but I clamped my jaw shut and kept silent. Finally, I said, "I'm sorry. Thanks for taking me to visit them."

He didn't say much, and when we got to our street, he stopped outside the door and stayed in the car.

"Aren't you coming in?"

"I'm going to go back and see Mourad for a bit longer and maybe visit some other brothers from the mosque. I'll be back later. You go ahead and go to bed if you're tired, baby."

I did suddenly feel drained. "I'll see you later then."

I could barely make it up the steps to the flat, but once I got in the door, the feeling of surrender in my body was almost comforting. Much of my childhood was spent in this same cocoon of safety, alone in my room. I'd imagine whatever I wanted in my head, and the imagining often became more real to me than anything else: my parents' bickering, the isolation I felt at school, the deadening effect of pretending to be someone I wasn't. Not that I really knew who I was then. And, to be honest, I was wondering if I was having a bit of an identity crisis now. Things had shifted so radically in my life, and I seemed to be taking on yet another role, to which I had no real connection. *You just have to make the best of this path now that you are on it,* The Voice whispered almost seductively.

I was beginning to settle into a routine, here in Manchester. I had taken to wearing the scarf and my long coat whenever I went out and had begun experimenting with cooking some more exotic dishes. There was a halal meat shop down the hill from our flat, and in my desire to please both my husband and Allah, I had taken to walking down there to get our chicken legs and sometimes beef as well. Said loved tandoori chicken, and I had found the spices, premixed, in the Pakistani

grocery shop next to the butcher. I revelled in the feeling
of playing house and having the time to spend cleaning,
cooking, and making our home feel comfortable.
The home was a sanctuary and the woman's domain.
I understood that women should remain in the home
unless it was a necessity to venture out. I felt safe at
home, and it was easier to stay in than to put on
my hijab just to wander about. The menial tasks of
the home felt grounding and kept my mind occupied.
I didn't want to think too deeply; I was afraid of what
I would find.

There were times I felt lonely for other friends,
though. Said was gone for long stretches of the day.
A friend of his had landed him the job at the pizza
takeaway, and he was spending time after work with
the guys. A few of the acrobats had taken apartments
in the vicinity, and he had made many new friends at
the local mosque as well. I complained to him one
evening that I felt isolated, without anyone to talk to.
I was jealous of his freedom to visit people whenever
he wanted. I had not made any close friends in the few
months we had worked together in the circus. Moving
in with Said had effectively shut down other relationships
there. I had called my closest friend from university and
told him that I could no longer continue our friendship
as I was a practicing Muslim now and could not speak
to men outside my own family. Most of my other friends
found we no longer had much in common and had
stopped reaching out to me. The radical shifts from

music to biology to circus were difficult enough for them to fathom, but moving from Canada, to the US, to Britain, had compounded the distance. The final straw was the move from being a Quaker—I had attended meetings from childhood into university years—to taking up Islam. It was just too hard to explain my journey, not really knowing the reasons myself, and I was afraid my friends would see the cracks in my perfectly built up demeanour. I wanted no questions asked.

I didn't want to name my feeling as sad, but a heaviness had settled over my heart. I fought this feeling of grief and abandonment by working even harder to be a good Muslim and perfecting my role as wife and partner. Turning away from the unpredictability of real relationships, I reached toward the relative safety of being one with Allah.

And now, we were going to see my family. Said had told me to book us tickets to go for a week, and I was happy to be seeing my parents soon. But there were so many changes happening, it was a little overwhelming. I wanted to put my head on my mom's lap and cry, like I used to do when arriving home for the holidays from boarding school.

I picked up some more books on different aspects of living a pious life. Whatever I read, I acted on as well as I could, wanting to emulate the great women of Islam at the time of the Prophet Muhammad. I had taken down the pictures of Said's old girlfriends and shoved them in a box. I replaced the spaces in the frames with Arabic calligraphy or scenes from nature. I knew that having a picture of a person kept the angels from entering the space, and I felt convinced there was a different energy now that we had no portraits up at all in the house. I was pleased to have a reason to put away the photos of his old girlfriends, all in the name of piety. Said had been appreciative of the new décor and never mentioned wanting the old photos. I was grateful to him for that small thing and forgave the fact that he hadn't removed the pictures himself. My mother had taught me to always try and see the best in people, even when I thought they didn't fully deserve that consideration.

Said offered to take me back to the Islamic bookstore. We hadn't been there since before the marriage ceremony, and I had been nagging him to take me somewhere; I was tired of being stuck at home. I could have gone out on my own, but for some strange reason I couldn't really put my finger on, I didn't want to go out much. I forced myself to walk every day for exercise, but the rest of the day I just amused myself in the apartment. So, going to the bookstore, which was on the other side of town, seemed like a big outing.

We walked into the small shop, and as before, there was a recording of the Quran recitation playing. Said turned to me, eyes shining, and said, "Listen to that! It's Saad Al Ghamidi, a famous reciter of the Quran."

It was beautiful and I nodded and smiled, happy

to see him in a good mood.

"Pick a book, baby," he continued. "I'll get you something as a present."

As I was browsing the shelves, I came across a book about the temptation and sin of music. My heart constricted as I opened the cover and read the first lines. Music? Was it really the temptation to evil? I couldn't quell my curiosity and asked Said to get me that book. It felt masochistic and yet holy at the same time. Such a big sacrifice surely was worth a huge reward.

I kept the book closed until we got home and I could be alone. For once I was glad Said was going out. I pulled out the book and began to read.

"The heart can only have one love, and it must be Allah," the book stated. "Music, by its very nature, encourages sins such as dancing and licentious behaviour, and takes the heart away from piety."

I cried, thinking of how much I loved the beautiful, heart-stirring music of the great classical composers, the sensuality of jazz, the cultural diversity of the many world music tapes I had carefully copied and collected over the years. I was swept back to high school, my senior recital. I had worked hard to put together a complete concert showcasing my various ensemble and solo repertoire. Music had been a means of touching people, stirring their souls. My French horn had been my constant companion for years. Music was a doorway to my inner self. Sometimes it helped me connect to my feelings, my longing, and sometimes it was somewhere

I could hide from the pain of being in the world. Either way, it kept me alive.

So, I cried as I read about how it was wrong to listen to anything but the recitation of the Quran. Did I really have so many bad habits and sins? I was torn. My music collection stared at me resentfully from the corner of the bedroom, still in boxes. I had not listened to any of my tapes since moving in with Said.

Who was I kidding? I had to commit to being Muslim one hundred percent, I couldn't hide behind not knowing anymore. In a fit of righteous action, I took my entire music collection and threw it in the dumpster outside our building. My heart thumped and my palms were sweaty, but in my head, I cried, "*Allahu akbar,* Allah is great," and I turned my mind away from the wrenching anguish in my heart. I would do anything for God. *You would do anything to be loved,* The Voice whispered.

In my copy of the Quran, it said: "And the first to embrace Islam of the *Muhajirun* (those who migrated from Makkah to Madinah) and the *Ansar* (the citizens of Madinah who helped the newcomers) and also those who followed them exactly in faith. Allah is well pleased with them as they are well pleased with him. He has prepared for them Gardens under which rivers flow (Paradise), to dwell therein forever. That is the supreme success."

I was a success. I had heard the call of Islam and had not shirked my duty. I would do everything in my power to be a good Muslim, even an exemplary Muslim.

I secretly hoped for some kind of validation, some recognition of my supreme sacrifices. People were ultimately disappointing in this regard, but in my head, Allah approved of me, smiling down and promising me a beautiful place in Jannah, the final abode of the righteous.

Looking back on my decision not to pursue my studies in music, I think it was another sacrifice I thought I had to make to the insatiable God of life. If I gave up another thing I loved, then I would be loved, be free, be able to live the life I was meant to live. Perhaps it was a protection against the pain of everything. If I framed it as a sacrifice, I could feel like a martyr. Martyrs were revered, even if only after they died.

I have come to realize that I was terrified and didn't know it. Afraid of what connection would feel like, afraid to reach out. The pain of the longing and the sacrifice were infinitely preferable to the pain of rejection, or even worse, indifference. Better to move on to something else than smash into my fear of my own greatness.

Standing next to the dumpster, my tapes in a heap inside, I took a moment to look up at the sky. The moon was bright and I looked at it for a while, soaking in its comforting presence.

We were leaving for Canada in a week for our visit. Would my parents approve of all these changes in me, in my life? Part of me craved their approval, and part of me wanted to push them as far away as possible. The internal conflict was almost unbearable. It was easier to shut down my confusing feelings rather than process them; it was too overwhelming.

I went back inside and picked up the sponge in the kitchen. I started scrubbing the counters vigorously. Tears rolled down my cheeks unheeded as I gripped the sponge even tighter.

Chapter
Three

THE DAY DAWNED BRIGHT AND clear for our flight to Halifax. The holy month of Ramadan was starting the next day, and I was nervous about my first experience of fasting. Not only was I taking my new husband home to meet my parents, but we were going to be abstaining from food and drink during the hours between sunrise and sunset. This was going to be a lot for my mom and dad to take in.

As the plane landed I nervously adjusted my headscarf over my long coat. I looked at Said, wanting support, and he smiled encouragingly. "You look beautiful, habiba. Your parents will love us."

I sighed and stood up as we came to a halt. "We will soon find out, anyway."

Whatever I was feeling was swept aside in a few minutes as I caught sight of my parents waiting beyond the arrival doors. My mother standing with pursed lips, a couple of inches taller than my dad, who looked preoccupied with something in the other direction. My heart leapt. I hadn't realized how much I had missed them.

Mom saw us and waved eagerly. I waved back, holding my hand in front of my body so I wasn't so conspicuous. Said caught the interaction and called loudly, "Hey, Mom! Hey, Dad!"

I cringed. Was he actually going to do a whole charming son-in-law thing? I didn't much like this showman side of him, it always made me feel left out somehow. He was centre stage again and loving it.

I hugged my parents, allowing myself just a small amount of collapse as I felt their arms around me. Then the moment was over, and I was introducing Said, who was beaming and hugging them warmly in a show of affection that seemed a bit over-the-top to me. My mom was lapping it up though and telling him how happy she was to meet him.

"I got her a ring like yours," Said said, and lifted my hand to show them the ring.

"How wonderful!" Mom exclaimed, while my dad nodded amicably. Did he have to make a big deal of that already? I covered up my annoyance by grabbing our suitcases and marching toward the door.

The drive to my parents' house brought back

memories of the many times I'd come home to visit over
the years. I sat in the back seat with my mom, while
Said chatted in the front with Dad. He struggled a little
to engage my father in conversation, and every once in
a while, he would turn to my mom and elicit her support
and encouragement. She was always aware of making
people feel comfortable and made a great sidekick to
Said's stories about the circus and his life in Morocco.
She oohed and aahed at all the right places.

I slumped back in the seat, somewhat annoyed
to be left out of the conversation but relieved to have
a few minutes for self-reflection. I wondered if I was
really ready to come home for a visit. It didn't feel
the way I imagined it would.

We crested the hill where the sweep of the Bay of
Fundy stretched out ahead of us with the majestic Cape
Blomidon rising as a red gash out of the water, and I felt
a wave of emotion. This view had always signalled that
we were nearly home. The familiar feelings swept through
me, along with a sense of unease as I realized how much
I had changed. Coming home with a husband and a new
religion was a tangled mess of pride and disbelief.

As we pulled into the driveway, I had a moment
of panic as I remembered a few years ago bringing
a boyfriend home for Christmas and not being allowed
to stay in the same room. Would my mom let me share
a bed with Said this time? Stepping into the kitchen
brought a rush of old memories, the wood stove in the
corner, the homey clutter covering every available

surface. I put my suitcase down and stood there taking it all in.

"I've put you in the corner room, your old bedroom," Mom said.

"Thanks, I'll take our bags up there." I sighed with relief. At least I wouldn't have to explain anything to Said about the sleeping arrangements.

We came down to plates of snacks and hot apple cider. The smell of the country I'd grown up with. "This looks amazing, thanks!" I popped a cookie into my mouth.

"Tomorrow we start Ramadan and fasting," Said stated, looking pointedly at me. "We will be fasting from food and drink from sunrise until sunset," he continued, looking at my parents.

"Oh yes," Mom said, smiling. "We are interested to hear more about your customs and culture."

"Ramadan is the holy month in Islam," Said began, dropping into his lecturing voice. "All the other months of the year, we work for ourselves and our family, but this one month is for Allah."

"How nice," said Mom. She had definitely fallen under Said's spell already. Everything he said was agreed to and encouraged with smiles and nodding. He could be engaging when he tried. I had already forgotten this about him, as he didn't seem to turn on the charm for me anymore.

That night I set the alarm for four o'clock the next morning. "We have to eat before the beginning of sunrise, right?" I looked over at Said for confirmation. This was my first Ramadan, and I was nervous about fasting for the whole day.

"Yes," Said nodded. "Dates and milk are what the Prophet Muhammad, peace be upon him, often ate."

"Okay, I think my mom usually has dates, and there is definitely milk, so that should be possible." I turned over in bed. "Goodnight, baby."

"Goodnight," Said whispered.

I woke with a start at the sound of the alarm, and I shook my head trying to remember where I was. The glowing red numbers read 4:00. Ugh. Too early to want to eat, but I remembered we were fasting today, so I rolled up to sit on the bed sleepily.

"Come on," I poked Said. "Let's go and eat before we pray Fajr."

Said was surprisingly quick to get up and pull on his long white candora. We crept quietly down to the kitchen, and I got out two glasses for milk. I found the dates in the cupboard, rolled up in a bag with the nuts and other baking supplies. I took out a handful and put them on a plate. Said and I munched quietly, not really talking much. We didn't want to wake up my parents, and four o'clock in the morning is not a time for talking.

"*Allahu akbar, allahu akbar,*" Said began, quietly chanting the adhan or call to prayer. I had grown to love hearing this over the last few months. It is a beautiful way to gather people for prayers, and I loved the ritual of it. As he finished the last line, I headed to the bathroom to make ablutions. It felt peaceful and even holy to be up this early and getting ready to pray and fast for the day. I felt very spiritual.

As Said washed, I set out the small prayer mats for us and found my big scarf to cover my head. I was sitting quietly when he came over and stood slightly in front of me to lead the prayer. The man always leads the prayer and stands in front of the woman. The submission was not just to God but to my husband also. I felt this as I prostrated myself behind him on the mat, my face close to his feet as he bent forward also. This dynamic was slowly emerging in our relationship too, but I liked the idea of being cared for and protected. I was to stay a foot behind and beneath him, and my job was to raise him up and bring him honour and reward by being a pious wife, and hopefully mother to our children. It was nice not to have the responsibility of everything on my own anymore. I didn't yet understand the dark places where this could lead.

The subtleties of the dynamic continued throughout the visit with my family. In many ways, I was happy to accept his guidance and leadership. I had always been very independent and even rebellious, and it seemed fitting to let myself be led now; I was tired of doing so much on my own. I sank easily into the role of supporter for Said and found this led to the least friction in our newly formed marriage.

Said completely charmed my parents in the week-long visit, assuring them of our love for each other and that our blissful union would lead to lifelong success. It all sounded like a fairy tale, my childhood dreams in real form. I felt complete.

The week passed quickly and we left Canada to fly back home. The sadness at leaving was somewhat mitigated by the fact that we were travelling, so we could break the fasting for that day and eat. Travelling was seen as a hardship in the Islamic texts, so eating was advisable for those days. The equivalent time could be made up after the month of Ramadan ended, along with any days of menstruation for women, as we were not allowed to fast during our cycle either.

I found out later that making up days of fasting after Ramadan was ten times harder than fasting during the month of Ramadan, when everyone was oriented to that. But for now, it was nice to be travelling with my husband, eating, and looking forward to our life in England as a married couple.

When we got back to Manchester, the sky was grey and overcast. The heaviness was unsettling. The days began to blur together, and I couldn't believe it was already early March. We had been married nearly four months already! One night, I awoke with a pain in my abdomen, like someone had pinched me on the inside. I rolled over and looked at the clock by the bed. The red numbers glowed 3:00. Ugh. I sighed and tried to get comfortable. Said was facing the other way and I curled myself around his back, hoping the comfort of his physical presence would help me drift back to sleep. My period was a week overdue, and I was feeling bloated and irritable. I wanted to squirm and cry and punch something all at the same time. Instead, I held my breath and tried to be still. I willed myself to lie there and not wake Said by reciting the words of the Quran I had been learning in Arabic: *Bismillahi rahmani Raheem* …all thanks be to Allah, the most merciful, the most kind. …I eventually drifted off to sleep again.

The next morning, I woke up late, feeling a bit nauseous. *I hope I'm not getting the flu or something,* I thought, annoyed.

"What are you making for breakfast today?" Said asked sleepily.

"Breakfast? Why do I have to always make breakfast? You know, when we first met in the circus, you used to make me breakfast in bed!" I snapped unreasonably. "I don't know what I'm making for breakfast," I continued, grumbling, as I walked through to the kitchen. Said had not spoken another word, which was just as well.

I put the coffee on to perk and got out the bread to make toast. The smell of the coffee almost made me throw up. *Huh, strange, I usually love my coffee in the morning.* My head felt light and I held on to the counter for a second as the room started to spin. Crap! The last thing I needed was to be sick right now.

The coffee gurgled and I poured two cups and put

the toast on a plate. I didn't have the stomach to make anything else. Said could make his own damn breakfast if he didn't like what I made! I slammed the cups onto the tray and carried it into the living room. I could hear him in the shower now, so I sat down heavily and began to cry. *God, this is stupid. What the hell is wrong with me?* I wondered. I was just blowing my nose and drying my eyes when Said came in with a towel around his waist. He flexed his pecs teasingly, and I rolled my eyes.

"What's wrong?" He stopped posing and noticed my tear-stained face.

"I don't know." My lip trembled and I took a deep breath, afraid I'd start blubbering all over again. "I just don't feel good today."

"Oh, well, you just take it easy today at home. I have to go out anyway," he said, in what I'm sure he thought was a comforting tone.

"Where are you going? You are always going out! Why can't you ever stay at home with me?" As I heard myself speaking, I wondered how anyone would want to stay at home with me.

Said looked hurt. "Why don't you go to see a friend?" he offered, in an effort to placate me.

"I don't have any friends!" I almost shouted. "I don't know anyone in Manchester, and I don't go out 'cause you don't take me anywhere, and I'm not supposed to go out a lot now that I'm a Muslim."

Said gazed into his coffee cup.

"Maybe I can take you to pray at the mosque

on Friday. You might meet some other sisters."

"Okay," I said, slightly mollified. "I still want to spend more time with you though. I miss you. You are out so much and I don't get to see you like before when we were working together."

"I know. But you understand it's better for my faith not to be in the circus anymore. I am working with other Arab brothers now. I go to the mosque on Fridays. It's better, it's what I want." Said stood up then and took his cup to the kitchen. "I have to go out and see some new Libyan brothers now. They just arrived in Manchester, and we are helping to get them settled. I'll be back later. Don't get stressed. Have a nap or something."

I looked down at the tray. "Okay."

I didn't really want to have a nap, and I didn't want to stay at home on my own all day. I could feel the anger making my jaw tight, but I didn't say anything. I wished I didn't feel sick.

A couple of weeks passed and my period still hadn't come. My breasts felt sore and I seemed to be extra irritable. A sneaking suspicion had begun to play on my mind that I might be pregnant, and now it was becoming a real possibility. I wanted to be happy about this. Well, maybe more than that, I wanted Said to be happy about this. Having children and raising a family is important to Muslims. A few years earlier I had sworn I would never have kids. I had been busy with creative projects,

singing, circus school, and friends. I wasn't completely
sure what had changed since then. I couldn't quite
connect to the me of even a few months ago. A fog
had settled around me, and I felt cocooned in a shroud.
It wasn't a completely terrible feeling; I loved feeling
protected and safe. The fears around what I would do
with my life or how I would make a living had faded into
the background. All that I was aware of was Said, and
our small apartment, and the life we had together.

I sighed. I wanted to love my new life, but there
were so many restrictions. I wasn't supposed to talk to
men, I couldn't listen to music, I had to cover myself
when I went out. I struggled with how to make the best
of my situation, or more to the point, how to make
myself better so it didn't feel so suffocating. More than
anything, I wanted to feel loved and accepted. I practiced
finding a way to make everything seem like a good thing.
"When God closes a door, somewhere he opens a
window." Wasn't that right? Was I a bad Muslim, an
ungrateful person because I wasn't happy?

I gazed out the window of our flat. A baby would
be a good thing. A saying from Hasan Al Basari that
I had read recently came to mind: "By Allah, in the last
twenty years, I have not said or done anything but I
thought, does Allah like this action?" Allah wanted us
to have children, to increase the population of Muslims
in the world. Being a mother was holy work. A baby
would give meaning to my cloistered life.

Said was at work until late again that night; he often

didn't finish his shift until two or three in the morning.
I decided to go to the pharmacy and get a pregnancy
test. I wanted to know for sure.

Fairly recently, I had begun to wear a more extreme
version of the burka and a veil when I went out. The
more time I spent alone, the more I retreated from social
contact. The mosque was one of the few places I visited.
A Pakistani woman I had met there had shown me how
to sew my own burka-style hijab, and I had poured my
creative energies into cutting and sewing a long black
gown that fell from my head all the way to my feet.
I think I missed being creative; I had always loved
making things. Now that I wasn't creating circus acts or
music, I channelled my energy into cooking and making
useful things for the apartment. Making my own hijab
seemed a fun way to have some input into how I looked.
I could pick the colour from the muted neutrals that were
deemed acceptable for women's Islamic outerwear. The
headband was secured by an elastic band underneath
the fabric, which held it in place over my scarf and veil.
I had purchased a pair of black gloves to go with my new
outfit, and I was pleased with the results. I loved how
it cleverly stayed put on my head and covered every inch
of my body shape, and Said seemed pleased with my
newfound piety.

I felt safely unseen when I went out in my burka,
which wasn't as often these days. It was too much trouble
to get everything on just to go for a walk. Besides, wasn't
the point of wearing the hijab not to display yourself

in public?

I got out my burka for my trip to the pharmacy. I wrapped my head first with a long scarf, then the veil fastened over that, and finally the burka slipped over everything. I took my gloves and my purse and locked the door behind me.

I groaned when I realized it was raining. Wet weather soaked the bottom of my burka and made it stick to my legs. There were a few drawbacks to the outfit. I debated going back inside and pulling on my rain pants underneath, but I couldn't be bothered. I resigned myself to getting wet feet and marched purposefully toward the main street. Said always said he could tell it was me walking from a long way away because of how I moved, even if I was in a group of women and we were all wearing nearly identical burkas.

I was wet and uncomfortable by the time I returned home. I decided to have a bath and then take the test. It was hours before Said would return home.

I stripped down to my underwear and started the water. I looked at myself in the mirror. My breasts definitely looked bigger. I had not needed to wear a bra all through dance and circus school. I cupped my breast in my hand. Said had commented when we first got together that he could hold my entire breast in his hand. I shivered remembering his touch on my bare skin. He had said he loved my body. It had been only a few months since I had stopped working in the circus, right before getting married, and I still looked good. What would it be like to be pregnant though?

I stepped into the tub and sighed blissfully as I sank into the water. I hadn't realized I felt so tired. I closed my eyes, moaning softly. Now that I was relaxing, I was aware of the increased sensation "down there." Hmm, weird that it should be so noticeable, so persistent. Calling me.

My hand moved down of its own accord. My fingers finding the soft folds and stroking, very gently. It seemed already to be aroused and soft, and my pressure increased as quickly as my breathing. I came with an intense, short breath that felt like lightning down my legs and into my belly. I turned over in the bath and pressed my palm against my pubic bone. I wanted Said to be there right now.

The warm water soothed the desire and I turned over again, feeling energized. I got out and dried myself then opened the pregnancy test packaging. I had bought the double one, just in case. I sat on the toilet and held it under me. One minute, the box said. Wait one minute and then check the small window. I waited.

Two lines meant yes, one line meant no. I stared at the box. Okay, that must be one minute. I took the stick and turned it over, holding my breath. There was the first line…and there, faint but visible, was the second one! I was pregnant! I checked the box again just to make sure I understood. Yes, the directions were clear, it was positive.

The rest of the day dragged on, and I found it

hard to concentrate on anything. My head seemed
to be floating around completely separate from my body.
I wasn't sure how I felt about the pregnancy, so I decided
finally that if Said was happy, I would be happy. It didn't
occur to me to wonder why I didn't think it was
important to have an opinion. I just glossed over that.

I had become adept as a child at distancing myself
from my body and my feelings—sometimes it was too
painful, sometimes too lonely, often it was just easier
than dealing with my feelings in the present moment.
The underlying terror of reaching out and encountering
a black void of nothingness kept me inside the safety
of my head. So even though there was potentially a
new human growing inside of me, I pulled away from
it. It didn't seem quite real. Perhaps Said's excitement
would make it real for me.

What seemed like an eternity went by until I heard
the door open. I went to greet Said. My smile froze
as I caught sight of his face, and I pulled back.

"What's wrong?" I inquired, worried.

"Nothing," he said, sounding defeated.

"Really?" I said. "You look pale."

"It's nothing," he mumbled, and I moved aside
to let him pass. He sat on the couch.

"Well, I have news for you," I hinted, trying to tease
him, as I sat playfully on his lap.

"Oh? What's that?"

"Well, what do you think about being a dad?" I
asked, my voice breaking despite my effort to control it.

He looked at me and tears shone in his eyes. "You're pregnant?"

"I took the test today. It was positive," I replied. "Are you happy?"

He buried his head in my chest and said it was the best thing that had ever happened to him. I released the breath I didn't know I was holding. My fingers played in the curls that trailed off near the nape of his neck.

"Now tell me what's wrong," I whispered.

He sighed and pulled away. "My friend is closing the takeaway, so I can't work there anymore. Also, Philip asked me to come back and work in the circus. Well, he actually asked if you and I wanted to do the feet-to-feet act this season." He stopped and looked at me. "I don't want to work in the circus anymore. I'm tired of it. I want to have a family and practice my religion more and settle down."

"Of course," I soothed, "you have to do what feels right." I fleetingly imagined what it would be like to perform with Said now. I still felt I would like to know what I was capable of as an aerial artist. But I had not trained for over four months now, and although I looked good, I was feeling out of shape. And now with the pregnancy...I sighed inwardly and smiled at Said.

"We are going to have a family, and you can find another job. We can make this work." I sounded confident, even to my own ears. It was surprising to hear myself. My mind was already racing with plans to help him find work and for us to find subsidized housing.

I had thought of taking a part-time job at the local college, but now that I was pregnant, it didn't seem like it made sense.

"You always make me feel better," he said and kissed me. "Come to bed."

"But you haven't eaten yet. I made dinner," I replied, hesitating.

"Come on," he pulled me up and began undressing me before we even got to the bedroom. "I need you."

Half an hour later, I dragged myself out of bed again to heat up the dinner. I didn't feel hungry at all now. I could have just gone to sleep. The clock said 3:00. Ugh!

"Do you want to eat now?" I asked again.

"Yes, I'm just going to watch a bit of TV before I come to bed. You can just put the food on a plate for me if you don't want to stay up."

"Okay." I put on his big terrycloth bathrobe and went to get his dinner. I looked at the chicken and rice. The nausea swept over me and I gagged then threw up in the sink. I rinsed my mouth then plated up a generous portion for Said and put it in the microwave. The smell began to make me feel queasy again, and I hurried back to the bedroom. I took a deep breath and decided I couldn't eat anything now. Said came in from the bathroom where he had taken a quick shower.

"You okay, baby?"

"Yeah." I climbed into bed again. "I don't think I want to eat now."

"Okay, you need your rest now." He tucked me in. "I'll be back soon."

I was asleep almost instantly.

Chapter
Four

SUMMER ARRIVED AND WITH IT a welcome break from the morning sickness. Early in June, Said sat drinking his coffee with me, and as I prepared to clean away the breakfast dishes, he put his hand out and stopped me.

"Hey, how about we go to Morocco for a visit?" His eyes lit up with excitement as he asked, and my heart melted.

"Now?" I was both excited and taken aback at the suddenness of his offer.

"Well, in a couple of weeks," he said. "My mom wants to meet you, she wants us to have a wedding ceremony there. What do you think?"

I looked dubiously at my growing belly and shook

my head. "Well, it might be good to go and visit, but I don't think I want to do a wedding now that I'm already pregnant. Do we have the money to go?"

"We can just go for a couple of weeks." Said was already set on it, I could tell. "I think we can manage it."

"I guess we are going then." I smiled at him. I was nervous about meeting his family, but it felt good to be taken to Tangier as his wife.

"Wonderful!" he exclaimed and stood up. "I'll look at getting the tickets today."

I hummed as I washed the dishes. It was definitely exciting to have a trip to look forward to. The weeks of feeling ill and staying home were beginning to wear on my nerves.

A couple of weeks later we landed in the small Tangier airport. The hot breeze blew across my face as we climbed down the steps from the airplane and onto the tarmac.

"There is my mom." Said pointed up at the wide window where a crowd had gathered to watch the plane land. He waved excitedly and pointed at me. I waved as well, trying to hold my scarf from blowing off my head. Said hadn't warned me how windy it could be here.

It was not much cooler in the terminal building. I was aware of the sweat trickling down my back.

"Come on, let's get the suitcases and go meet my mom." Said took my hand and guided me to the luggage carousel. Our suitcases were small compared to the huge boxes and bags that many of the Moroccans were picking up. The parcels were wrapped and squeezed into many colourful shapes, not like the luggage I was used to in Britain or North America. People jostled and shoved one another to get their belongings, and I found myself pushed to the back of the crowd as Said went forward to grab our bags.

Returning to where I was standing, he grinned. "How do you like Morocco?" He laughed. "Come on, baby, let's go introduce you to my mom."

I followed him, curious to meet the woman who figured so largely in his life. A large, round woman hurried over to us, beaming. She grabbed Said and kissed his cheeks, speaking a torrent of Arabic that I couldn't catch at all.

"Aishah!" She turned suddenly to me and pulled me into her ample embrace. I kissed her cheeks, trying not to mind the smell of sweat that enshrouded her. The heat was beginning to get to me too, and I wondered how long it would be before we could get washed and changed.

Talking non-stop, Said and his mother bustled me out of the airport and into a large, white taxi. I sighed and sank back into the seat, grateful I didn't have to join in.

I watched the palm trees go past as we drove. The land was flat and scrubby, the trees planted along the middle of the road didn't really provide any shade or shelter. It didn't have the lush, tropical feel of the Caribbean—it was hot, dusty, and dry, more of a desert

feel. The houses were either bare concrete and brick
or whitewashed, which gave the landscape a bright feel.
There were many people out walking, the women with
colourful robes, the men in more earthy tones.

We pulled up outside a two-storey house, with
a balcony on the second floor from which I could hear
Said's sister, Fatima.

"Duh, duh!" She had been born deaf and had never
been to school. She had made up many of her own signs
and could communicate fairly well with people close to
her. She pointed excitedly then thumped heavily down
the stairs to open the door for us. She erupted out of
the house and went straight to Said. She looked almost
exactly like a younger version of his mother. She reached
over to me, and I allowed myself to be enveloped again
with sweaty hugs and kisses.

Said paid the taxi driver and we carried our suitcases
into the main room on the ground floor. There was only
one small window, but because of this the room was
thankfully a bit cooler. I sank down onto the sofa and
looked around. The room was quite big, and to my eyes,
bare. The sofa extended along three quarters of the wall,
and two large coffee tables were placed in the middle,
covered with cloths and a vase of fake flowers, which
I would later learn was the requisite décor. A platter
of cookies also sat on the table, covered with plastic.
Fatima had already disappeared to make the traditional
mint tea, and I could hear her clanging away in the
kitchen upstairs.

The aroma of mint preceded her as she came back downstairs with the tea. The round tray was full of tiny tea glasses and the silver teapot in the centre. It was beautiful and exotic and I loved it. I was served first, and I felt the honour of being the guest. The tray of cookies was passed to me every time I had an empty plate until I had to smile and put up my hand. "Please, no more! Thank you."

The two weeks flew by with a trip to the beach and another to the marketplace. I spent a couple of hours a day on the roof, sunning myself in the Mediterranean heat. It felt wonderful on my growing belly, to lean back and feel the sun on my skin. So different from the wet and grey of Manchester. I enjoyed my time in Morocco, and the memory of the sun, the food, and the weather stayed in my mind as we said goodbye to Said's family.

The next few months passed in a slow, ponderous sameness. I had begun learning to read Arabic and recite the Quran with a few other women. We also had a sisters' study circle once a week. We met on Thursday evenings, the night before Jumua, the Muslim holy day. I loved the feeling of sisterhood and belonging. I had signed up to attend the local college to learn the art of floristry; I was collecting unemployment payments to supplement what Said earned and had to show I was attempting to find a job. The course was interesting, but wearing my veil all day while trying to arrange flowers was frustrating. I was tired much of the time, and my daily walks had dwindled to a couple of turns around the block and occasionally a pregnancy yoga video I had bought. My mind craved the kind of creative outlets and stimulating discussions I'd had in circus school. Somehow, learning Arabic and Islamic doctrines did not inspire the same passion. I berated myself for not appreciating the study of the religion as much as I used to love other topics. Was I bad? I should try harder to please Allah.

Your *deen*, or spiritual life, should be the most important thing in your life. I threw myself even more into learning about Islam and its history. My new Muslim friends encouraged me to memorize the sayings of the Prophet Muhammad, and we competed with each other to gain knowledge of our faith. My voice, which only a year earlier I had trained to sing musical theatre numbers, was now used only for recitation of the Holy Quran. I prided myself on learning to pronounce all twenty-six letters of the Arabic alphabet and the rules of reciting, called *Tajweed*.

"Assalamu alaikum, sister Aishah," the sisters always greeted me. "May Allah be with you." I studied the sayings of the Prophet. I had asked Said for a wedding gift, a complete set of Imam Bukhari's collection of the sayings of the Prophet Muhammad. There were a number of volumes, and they were divided into quotes on various topics that covered almost every aspect of daily life. I found the sameness of being at home tiresome; I craved new learning and ideas. I challenged myself to memorize the sayings, and with the sisters' encouragement, I even learned the lineage of scholars who had passed down each quote or *hadeeth*. Some were irrefutably correct, according to the modern sheikhs, while some quotes had doubtful narrators and so were not to be taken as truth. I wondered how they determined who were the trustworthy narrators and who weren't. I slowly infused my thoughts with the opinions of the scholars.

Allah had many names in the Quran, and we looked at the meaning behind them. Ninety-nine names was a lot. Some were easier to grasp, like "the most merciful." I could imagine God was merciful more easily than understanding "the avenger." I wished we could talk more about the underlying meanings of these names or qualities of Allah. I wanted to understand and know what God was and perhaps gain insight about myself and my life. I was told to ask questions, but when I did ask, the answer was often, "Practice the actions of prayer and remembrance, and everything will become clear in time," which was incredibly frustrating. It seemed that with all the talk about peace in Islam, there was also a forced surrender, which had the opposite effect. It raised an anger in me, a rebelliousness that I had to quell. The Voice became my own persecutor, and my creative self fell into the role of victim. I began to crush my own thoughts and opinions; no need for an external force.

I did my best to be silent, to pray, and to ask forgiveness for feeling frustrated. This was only sometimes successful. Having attended Quaker meetings as a child, the idea of silent prayer and direct communication with God was not foreign to me. In fact, I found many similarities between Quakerism and Islam. The reverence around simple daily tasks, the individual reverent focus during prayer times, and the idea of working on the self were all familiar. I was yet to realize that my self had all but disappeared.

I turned again and again to my books and to my new-found sisters in Islam. I could find peace and connection here as I had in my childhood. Sometimes the effort of doing all the work myself got to me. I knew I had to try harder. I was doing my best to fit in with my new friends. I even wore Pakistani tops and pants every day, leaving my pre-Islamic clothing in the closet untouched. Even my outer self was changing to fit the prescribed look, all in the name of being accepted, another word for "loved." Was this the love I was searching for?

We studied the pillars of Islam and helped each other to fulfill all of them to the best of our abilities.

"Sisters, we should try not to watch TV," one of the women said. "It is *haram* to look upon another person that is not covered up. You should not waste the precious time Allah has allotted you in this life watching sitcoms or dramas that are not furthering your understanding of God. Our time should be spent in prayer and *dhikr* whenever we are not actively fulfilling our roles as good wives and mothers. We should raise up the standing of our families in the eyes of God."

I noticed that a few of the sisters were not always
following the rules we had discussed. Not showing them
up in the group became another way to make myself
feel better. If others were making mistakes, I needn't
feel so guilty about my own.

Said was pleased. He read occasionally too, but
not with the same fervour that I did. He encouraged
me to visit the sisters and learn everything I could. I
could not help thinking that he enjoyed the fact that
I was whining less about spending time with him.
But I worked hard to dispel such thoughts. I buried my
resentments and sadness under the blanket of piety.
The sisters became my support. I quickly became known
as one of the most pious women in our community.
The brothers were pleased to have me visit their wives.
This was the highest compliment a woman could receive.

A letter arrived in the mail in early November,
a month before my due date. It was from the housing
department of the local council. We had applied for
a larger house, as I was expecting a baby. Getting a
council house would mean our rent would be paid, and
Said's lack of work wouldn't be such a trial. He had tried
attending college for computer skills and then later for
car mechanics, but both courses had failed to ignite any
passion for learning. In fact, he seemed to be falling into
a depression and often spent his mornings in front of
the TV, only getting off the couch in the evening to go
and visit the brothers at the mosque. I would work even
harder at making a nice breakfast and being cheerful

around him. As my stomach tightened with the pregnancy, it masked the tightness of worry that sat, unrelenting, deep in my core.

I slit open the letter and my face broke into a smile.

"Baby! Look!" I exclaimed, waving the letter as I waddled into the bedroom. "We got offered a house!"

"Oh?" Said mumbled sleepily. "That's nice." He rolled over and I moved around to the other side of the bed.

"Come on," I said, "let's go look at it! The appointment is in two days, and I want to see where it is."

Said groaned. "Can we go later?"

"Please, baby, come on. I want to move in before I have the baby, and I want to see where it is. My parents are coming to stay in three weeks!"

"Ugh, okay. Let me get up then. Can you make coffee?"

"Yes, thank you!" I kissed him as he turned over to get up. "Hurry up and have a shower."

I hummed as I made the coffee, even though technically Muslims shouldn't sing unless travelling or to quiet children. I made sure I didn't sing the words to the song that came unbidden into my head—Gershwin's "Summertime"—and I kept the humming barely above an audible level. The sultry melody moved something deep in my soul. My hips moved sensuously and for a moment I forgot everything but my body.

Snap out of it, The Voice urged. *You aren't supposed to enjoy music anymore.*

I put two pieces of bread in the toaster and got out the cheese and butter. I knew what would put Said in the mood to be considerate. The toast popped and I slathered it with butter and sliced pieces of cheddar to go on top. I arranged the toast on a plate and put it on the table next to his coffee. I really hoped the house would be nice. I was excited to move into a place that wasn't filled with the ghosts of Said's past. A home that was ours.

Half an hour later we were driving down the hill to an area of government housing. It was obvious from the grey concrete blocks and modular design that this was the place. Pathways wound their way between the modules, and we looked for the number that they had offered us in the letter. Number 273 was right on the main road. It said in the letter that it was a three-bedroom house. There were no curtains in the windows and it looked empty, so we peeked in.

We could only see the ground floor, but I gasped as I saw the cracked tiles and dirty walls. The kitchen looked like a construction site.

"It doesn't look ready to live in. How are we supposed to move into that?" I looked down at my belly, feeling the full weight of it. "I can't even do much to help at this point." I sighed.

"Don't worry, baby. We'll be okay," Said said. "I'm sure it will work out."

I leaned my head on his shoulder. I wanted to believe him.

Later that week we were given the keys to our new house, along with some rolls of wallpaper and cans of paint. Said and I packed our few belongings and made a few car trips up and down the road to move it all into our new place. The living room seemed huge compared to our one-bedroom flat, and having three bedrooms seemed positively spacious! I was exhausted from the move, and I plunked myself on the couch in the middle of the uncovered tiles in the main room. I was hungry as well, and the gaping holes in the kitchen where the appliances should go did not look promising.

"I have to go out soon," Said said as he set the last box down next to me. "Do you want me to bring you some pizza?"

"I guess so." My stomach growled. "Can you get me some fruit and yogurt or something now though?"

"Sure," he answered. "Do you have any money? I can run to the corner store."

I fished around in my purse and found a ten-pound note. "Here, take this. Maybe get some milk too. I think we have tea bags here somewhere."

He closed the door behind him, and I promptly burst into tears. How could we make this demolition site into a home before the baby? My parents were coming in a couple of weeks, just before my due date. I felt overwhelmed and moody. I lay down on the couch and pulled my coat over me as a blanket. Within minutes I was asleep.

When I awoke the next morning, my neck stiff from
sleeping on the couch, I was surprised to see Said already
awake and even more shocked to see him painting the
kitchen. I swallowed the nausea that rose in my throat
at the smell of the paint, and forced a smile. He was
making an effort.

"Hey, darling." I gave his bum a squeeze. "That
looks nice."

"I wanted to get some decorating done for you."
He smiled, looking almost boyish.

I felt lighter than I had for weeks. His smile lit up
my entire world. And more than that, he genuinely
seemed to enjoy the painting. I was so happy he had
found something to do that put him in a good mood.

His burst of energy lasted for the next few days.
I had space to think about the baby. My hospital bag
was packed, and it seemed an interminable wait now
for the pains to start.

A friend of Said's had offered him a couple of shifts
a week at a pizza takeaway. After he left for work one
evening about a week after the move, I was restless and
uncomfortable. My belly had stretched to such a large
size I couldn't fit into anything but Said's old track pants
and a T-shirt. My back ached but I didn't feel like sitting
down. Said had been painting off and on, and the house
was beginning to show signs of being liveable. Friends
were getting new carpeting so gave us their old stuff, and
they had thrown in a set of floor-to-ceiling curtains as
well. I had set up the kitchen, and our mattress was laid

out in the upstairs bedroom on a rug on the floor.

I sighed and waddled upstairs to look at the bathroom. It had been left a dark blue, and there were no tiles on the wall for the shower. We had some boxes of white tiles and adhesive, and I opened the box to have a look at them. Plain white, they would make the room seem lighter. I picked up the adhesive and read the instructions. Didn't sound too difficult.

By midnight that night, I had the back wall tiled and ready to grout. The pains in my back had intensified and were starting to feel more like labour pains. Said should be back from work soon. Maybe I'd mention going to the hospital to check on things. Come to think of it, he had been staying out late a lot recently. He had said he was going to the mosque to pray, but that would have been over hours ago. I laid down on the mattress, and the pains got worse. It was now one o'clock. Should I call him? I looked over at my hospital bag in the corner. There was no way I was going to sleep.

I sighed and rolled over. At 1:30 I called Said.

"What are you doing still awake?" he asked, surprised.

"I can't sleep, I think I might be having labour pains."

"The baby?" he yelled excitedly.

"I'm not sure," I said, trying not to panic. "Maybe we should go to the hospital and check it out."

"Okay, I'll be home soon."

"Where are you anyway?" I couldn't hide the irritation in my voice.

"I'm just sitting down with some brothers here from Libya. Don't worry, baby, I'll be home soon."

I hung up and felt my hand shaking. I bent over with the next pain. I hated when he talked to me like a child. I waited for the pain to subside and then took my bag downstairs to wait for him. I put on my scarf, veil, and burka. At least that covered up my scruffy pants and T-shirt. I smiled at myself for caring how I looked. None of it would matter anyway, once I was in the delivery room.

I was almost asleep in the chair when the car pulled into the driveway.

"Are you okay, baby?" he asked as he walked in.

"Yeah, but I think we should go to the hospital. The pains are coming regularly now, every few minutes."

"Okay, come on." And he took my bag. No apology for being out half the night, no explanation. I sighed inwardly. I wasn't in the mood to pick a fight.

We checked into the maternity ward, and as I was wheeled off to a room to be checked, I could hear Said giving instructions to the nurse.

"I don't want any men in the room with her," he was saying. I could hear the nurse's voice answering back but not her exact words. I strained to hear what was going on.

I felt apprehensive and wished he would come and hold my hand rather than worrying about who else was in the room. I knew that on some level it was his way of protecting me, keeping my modesty intact. I also knew

I should feel loved and cherished, "like a pearl hidden in the oyster shell," as the Quran said. I wished the pains would go away, that it would be over quickly. I tried to breathe, but I was beginning to realize that this was not going to be as easy as I thought.

Said sat with me for awhile. I could tell that he didn't like seeing me in pain. I tried to smile and talk with him in a normal way. I was tired and irritable though and just wanted this part to be over. They decided they needed to break my water and explained that I would notice the labour pains getting stronger. The pain was intense. I felt like I was on a runaway train. I wanted to get off. Turn around. Take it back. I had had enough already. Each minute on the clock ticked by so slowly. It was three o'clock and I just wanted to go to sleep. Said looked at the clock too.

"I think I am going to go and pray Fajr at the mosque," he said quietly. "I'll be back soon. The nurse said it would still be awhile. You'll be okay." His eyes looked pleadingly at me for permission to leave.

"Fine, whatever," I growled. "Don't be too long though."

I didn't really want him to go, but I didn't want him to stay either. I was getting frustrated and the pains were taking all my attention. I didn't have the energy to discuss it.

As soon as Said left, what had been intermittent pains became one long, never-ending pain. I moaned and tried to move in the bed. I couldn't breathe through it—it just didn't stop. Tears pricked the corners of my eyes. My head pounded. The moans got louder. I began to lose control. Panic was welling in my chest. *I can't do this. I can't. Do. This.* Tears were now pouring down my cheeks. I didn't think it was possible, but the pain was getting worse. Not in manageable waves, like the labour pains I had read about, but in one huge, mounting wall of pain.

I think I started screaming, I'm not sure, but the nurse came in and put a cloth on my head. She tried to soothe me and calm me down. I didn't want to be calmed. I wanted this to be over.

"Just make the pain stop!" I shouted.

"As soon as your husband is back, we can consider an epidural," she said.

"Where is he? I can't do this."

"He said he was coming back soon. You are doing great."

I could have choked her. I was most definitely not doing great. I was not doing well at all. I wanted to scream at her. She had her back to me and was talking about getting a form for me to sign to have the epidural. Where was Said?

What seemed like an eternity later, Said returned. He took one look at me sobbing and moaning, and he started crying too. The nurse got a signature and the okay from Said to do the epidural. She mentioned something about the possibility of being paralyzed. I barely registered this as I signed the form. I beseeched

Allah to make this work out okay. I couldn't handle any more pain. I asked forgiveness.

Said stood in front of me as the anaesthetist put the needle in my back. I gripped Said so tightly I think I left marks.

"There you go, it's all done," the anaesthetist said matter-of-factly.

I lay back down on the bed and slowly registered that the pain was gone. All I could feel was a strange numbness in my lower body. My eyes closed and I dozed off and on for a couple of hours. I didn't know if Said was with me or not, and I didn't care.

Through the haze, I heard them saying it was time to push. I tried. I just felt so tired. I didn't seem to be much good at this either. I heard them talking about getting the baby out quickly. I could almost feel the cold metal of the forceps reach in and grab the head. I felt disconnected from my lower body. I could feel the pressure, but it didn't seem to be my body. One last push and I felt the pressure subside. The baby slid out and suddenly there were people rushing. Said kept telling them to get out. He didn't want men in the room. The nurse, rather than argue, just grabbed the baby and ran out of the room.

Where were they taking my baby? Was it alright? I was spent. I couldn't even ask a coherent question. I heard a cry from the next room, and within minutes they brought our beautiful baby to me.

"We just needed to resuscitate her," the nurse

explained, smiling. "She's okay now though. You have a little girl!"

The nurse put the bundle in Said's arms, and his face softened with wonder. Tears were swimming in his eyes as he looked at me. "I'm so proud of you. I have a daughter."

He held the baby close to his face and whispered the adhan in her ear. I could hear the Arabic words as he recited, "Allahu akbar, Allahu akbar." God is great. This is the ritual for Muslim babies, for the first words they hear to be the Quran.

We named our daughter Omaima, which means "young mother" in Arabic. I had selected it from a book of Islamic baby names. Looking back now, I see the irony—it was I who was the young mother.

Having a baby was hard work! She cried at night, I was grumpy, my stitches got infected, and I couldn't sit down comfortably. After a week in the hospital trying to learn to breastfeed, it still wasn't working well. It seemed to me that Omaima stubbornly refused to latch properly and screamed louder than all the other babies on the ward. I was tired and stressed. I felt like a failure. I couldn't even feed my own baby. I wanted to go back to how things were before the baby. I wanted to laugh and sit on Said's lap and feel his arms around me. I wanted to get a good night's sleep and plan my day in a sane way. I wanted to feel in control and on top of things.

I felt none of that.

You should be grateful, The Voice intoned. *You are doing holy work, populating the earth with Muslims.* Said and I had talked about how many children we wanted, and the number seven came up as the ideal number. I couldn't imagine doing this six more times.

"How are things going at the house?" I asked Said when he came to visit. I was hoping my parents were helping to fix up the living room and our bedroom at least. They had fortuitously arrived just after Omaima was born.

"Fine."

I wanted details, but I didn't have the energy to question him further.

"My cousin offered me a job at the gym he is opening," he announced, sounding excited. "I can train people there and help out at the desk."

"That's great!" I smiled encouragingly, glad to hear he would be doing something productive for the family. In the days following Omaima's birth, Said had had difficulty coping. I wanted him to be happy. But he still didn't look happy.

The nurse finally suggested I go home and see how breastfeeding went there. I still felt like I could barely walk, and going to the toilet was an excruciating ordeal. I didn't feel ready to take my baby home. My mother took charge and, for once, I was happy to let her—I needed her help. I sighed and sat back as she bundled the baby in her snowsuit and buckled her in the car seat, a gift from my aunt.

My mother loves setting up spaces, arranging furniture, creating the perfect balance of beauty and functionality. She is good at it too, I could see the improvement the moment I stepped in the door. I pushed down the resentment and guilt at having her redesign my space. She had managed to make our living room functional. We even had a seating area with a sofa and chair and coffee table. I lay down, already exhausted, and when my mom put Omaima next to me, I found she latched on all by herself! I looked down at her in amazement, not daring to breathe or move an inch, in case she stopped. She was sucking away contentedly. In that moment, I dared to hope that I could do this.

The first days at home flew by. The day of my parents' departure, I could feel the panic rising in my chest again. My mother had made me snacks, held the baby in the morning so I could nap, and done the dishes. What would I do now that she was leaving? I had not managed to cook a meal or clean the house since I'd come back from the hospital. The baby seemed to take all of my time, and then some.

Said, on the other hand, seemed happy once my parents were gone.

"It's just us again," he said, smiling. "I don't feel comfortable with other people in our house." *He likes to be in control*, The Voice whispered. My parents got in the way of his influence, and he had backed off while they were with us. He couldn't show his mood swings or let down his mask of happy pride at being a new father. Perhaps my panic stemmed partly from knowing I would have no one to buffer his neediness once we were alone again.

"I hope I can manage everything," I said doubtfully.

Said showed no sign of having heard me, diving straight into his own agenda.

"Well, I need to go and see Phillip, I'll take Omaima with me. They will all want to see her!"

Phillip was the circus owner, and Said had known some of the circus people for years. I could see his pride as he talked about showing off his baby. I wondered briefly why he didn't seem to want to include me in his plans. Was I no longer worth showing off? Now that I had birthed a child and my conversion to Islam was old news, did I represent nothing of value to him? I swallowed the lump that arose with these thoughts and lashed out instead.

"Well, she needs to be breastfed often. How long will you be?" I wanted a break but I was worried.

"I won't be long. Get her ready, and I'll take her today," he said and got up, thereby indicating the conversation was finished.

"I have to feed her first," I said, feeling a little panicky. "And are you sure you can change her diaper and everything?"

"Oh, I'll get someone there to help me if I need it." He wasn't calming my nerves at all.

I picked up Omaima and jiggled her awake. Her tiny mouth latched on and started sucking. At least she was feeding well now. I held her protectively. I didn't really want to be away from her so soon.

"Have a rest, baby." Said looked down lovingly. "You look tired."

Tears welled. Was it really care I was seeing in his eyes? No matter. I let myself feel the relief of even a few hours alone to rest.

"Okay," I gave him a watery smile. "I'll get her ready to go."

I waved, still teary, as he drove off with Omaima strapped into her car seat. A huge pang of loneliness enveloped me and I stumbled to the couch to have a good cry. A couple of hours later, I woke up. I had nodded off. I leaped up and checked the time. It was later than I thought. Said should be back soon, the baby would need me. As if in answer, my breasts suddenly felt hard and full. I decided I should call him.

"Hello?"

I could hear voices in the background. "Said? Where are you? How's Omaima? Is she okay? Is she hungry? Will you be home soon?"

"I'm just here with Auntie Mary, Phillip's mother," Said replied laughing. "Everyone loves Omaima."

"But she must be hungry. Is she okay? You should be coming home." I couldn't help sounding concerned and a little bit cross.

"Yes, I'm coming soon, don't worry. Omaima is fine, she hasn't cried at all."

"Well, the drive home is an hour and a half!

You should be on your way back," I snapped.

"Okay, okay, don't get all snappy with me. We are fine, and I'll be home soon." His voice had an angry tone, and I knew it was a warning.

"Okay, I am sorry, I didn't mean to snap. I'm just worried about her."

"Don't worry, I'm her father. I can look after Omaima too!"

"Yeah, I know. It's just…" I wasn't really sure why I felt so worried. "Come back as soon as you can, okay?"

"Okay, don't worry." His words had no effect at all. I was nervous and irritable, even after my nap. I went into the kitchen and gazed around absently. I filled the sink with water and began to clean up. At least that would keep my hands busy, and maybe keep me calm. My breasts ached, overfull with milk.

A couple of hours later, I had done all the little chores I had the energy for. Said still wasn't home. I put the kettle on and had to clasp my hands to keep from wringing them. Where was he? Of all the inconsiderate, annoying, irresponsible things! The baby needed me! Why was he not here with Omaima?

I glanced at the phone. Should I call him again? I didn't want to risk angering him further—he might not come back for a while, just out of spite. I shook my head, startled at my own thoughts. So many times he had stayed out late. Was there an honest explanation every time, or did he really mean to hurt me? I took a deep breath. It would be okay, he wasn't so stupid as to keep the baby from feeding for too long. My breasts ached and I contemplated using the breast pump. I didn't want to pump though, I wanted my baby!

Just then, I heard the car in the driveway. Five hours! He had been gone for five hours! I dashed to the door and almost ripped the car seat from him on the way in.

"Why were you gone so long?" I threw over my shoulder as I unbuckled the still sleeping Omaima.

"Don't be like that," he growled. "She was fine. Look, she's still asleep. Everyone loved her and she had a great time."

There was no point in fighting. My baby was more important now. I hardly dared feel the seething anger in my chest, and the thought of confrontation terrified me. I could not even put my feelings into words. Terror, panic, rage were all mixed up and left me feeling there was no way out but to dissociate altogether and deal with the matter at hand.

I peeled the snowsuit off her little body and took her to the couch. She had woken up a little and began rooting for my nipple eagerly. With a sigh of relief for both of us, I put her to my overfull breast. I had to squeeze my nipple into her mouth to get her to latch; milk squirted onto her cheek. My body relaxed, her rhythmic suckling soothed me. There was something almost sexual about breastfeeding. It gave me that same blissful feeling of euphoria. Lately it had almost replaced my need for physical intimacy with Said. I didn't really miss sex much. I gazed adoringly at my daughter.

Nothing else mattered in the whole world when she was in my arms. A baby was so easy to love.

I could see that Said was disappointed I hadn't even bothered to kiss him in greeting. I felt slightly guilty, but couldn't he understand how worried I'd been? My anger stirred again and I held Omaima tightly. He looked at us on the sofa and turned, sighing. I felt the sense of dissociation wearing off, but it was replaced by the pain of a desperate longing. Where was the love I thought I had been promised? The love I had worked so hard for, even giving up my self in the process?

"I'm going to the mosque."

"But you only just got back!" I called after him as he went into the hall, desperation making my voice rise, making me sound on the edge of hysteria.

"You need time with the baby. I'll be back later." He put his shoes on again.

"Don't you want to eat or anything?" The panic rising above the anger now. I didn't want to be alone again so soon. I didn't want to be alone at all. Abandoned, my worst fear.

"Don't worry about me," he muttered, "I'll get something with the brothers."

"All right." My heart sank. I didn't have much to offer him anyway. I hadn't yet returned to cooking proper meals. Maybe it was better that he went out. I wasn't a very good wife at all. Turning the anger inwards on myself helped with the pain I felt in the moment. My body deflated almost instantly, just leaving an overwhelming tiredness.

My sadness didn't go away completely over the next few months, although at times I almost forgot it was there. I lived in a blur of diapers and breastfeeding. Said had agreed to let me go out two mornings a week to learn Arabic and Quran recitation with a few other women. He kept the baby next to him in bed while I was out. At least they both seemed to like napping in the morning. Said had been a bit distant lately. He said he found it hard to share my attention with the baby. I wanted him to understand how things had changed for me. Looking after the baby was all encompassing. How could he expect me to have time for him in the same way as before?

Sometimes I felt guilty for neglecting him and tried to make it up to him. I made tea for him and let him watch TV while I cleaned up, even though part of me was angry that he didn't help. He had a job now, he had a right to relax. Sometimes, though, when I had been up for hours with the baby, I snapped at him.

"Can't you help me?" I shouted irritably.

He looked at me with that odd look he sometimes had, like he was distancing himself. "I don't want you to come to rely on me. What if I have to go away to work? You have to be able to do things on your own."

My mind reeled. *"What if I have to do things on my own"? What the fuck?* Was he planning to go away? Was he leaving me? I didn't realize it then, but at that moment my sense of safety in our marriage disintegrated.

I cried in frustration. I had no rebuttal for that. I couldn't fight back. Sometimes I just wanted him to help, like right now. *Get a hold of yourself,* The Voice said sternly in my head. *He's right, you should be able to do things on your own.*

I hated that voice.

Chapter
Five

I DON'T REMEMBER EXACTLY HOW IT happened, but somewhere in the first few months after Omaima's birth, Said began sleeping in the spare room. He came home late from work and said he didn't want to disturb me. I was up early with the baby every day and had to admit I didn't pay much attention to him at all. I had been feeling sick to my stomach the last few days and finally complained to him about it.

"I need a break. I don't feel good," I said, an edge of whining in my voice. I hoped he would take me seriously. I felt like he should have known I needed some time on my own, without the constant demands of the baby. Didn't he get it?

"All right, I'll take Omaima to stay with Bilkys

for the day," he said, then sighed in a resigned way. His cousin's wife had had her baby a few months before me, and we had become friends of a sort since that first visit over a year ago. I didn't have many friends, and we now lived close enough that I could walk to her house. A few times, when I really needed to get out of the house, I had loaded Omaima up in the pushchair and walked the kilometre or so over to Bilkys's place. It was a pleasant walk when it wasn't raining. I enjoyed looking at the row houses with the small, neat front gardens. It never ceased to amaze me how small things were here in England compared to the wide, open fields where I had grown up. It was a relief just to be in different surroundings for an hour or two.

"Okay." I rolled over in bed and closed my eyes. Why was I so tired? I didn't even care where he went with the baby, I just wanted to be alone. I wished that Said would watch her, take more of an interest in his daughter. He still didn't seem to really know what to do with her. He said he felt that such a young baby was better off with her mother. I guess I could understand that. I reasoned that he would take her out and be a dad when she was a bit older.

I felt like I was going to be sick. Maybe I was sick. I tried to think whether any of the sisters I studied Quran with had the flu. I couldn't think of anyone who might have made me sick. I just felt like hell. I stayed in bed all day. I didn't have to think about the baby, and I deserved one day of doing nothing.

I pulled the covers over my head and wished I could be somewhere else. Somewhere far away, with a beach and waves lapping at the shore. I drifted off, still dreaming.

The next day I went for my Arabic lesson. I took the baby with me. I am not sure when I started taking her with me instead of leaving her at home with Said. He had begun complaining if I was gone too long or if the baby cried, and it had just become easier to take her. I was getting to be a pro at breastfeeding now though, and I could do it under my scarf while sitting on the floor with my notes in front of me and not miss a beat of the recitation. I still felt slightly sick, and after the lesson as I was chatting to another convert to Islam, an Englishwoman named Lorna, she looked at me and asked if I had done a pregnancy test.

"A what?" I asked, shocked and not sure I'd heard her properly.

"A pregnancy test." She smiled. "You might be pregnant. That's why you are feeling sick."

"How could I be pregnant? I haven't even gotten my period after the baby," I argued. "I am still breastfeeding!"

"Well, maybe take one just in case." She laughed. "It happens."

I shook my head in disbelief. It couldn't be another baby. Omaima was only six months old. A knot of fear tightened in my stomach. I went home via the pharmacy and picked up a test. I had to be sure. Thankfully the baby was asleep when I got home, and I had no trouble peeing these days. It seemed I needed to go all the time. I decided to get it over with and did the test. I made a cup of tea and left Omaima asleep in her car seat. My heart skipped a beat as I went back to get the stick. I turned it over slowly.

My eyes took in the two pink lines. Was that positive? I checked the box. Two pink lines. Yup, positive. I sat down on the edge of the bath. I didn't know what to feel. How would I make it through this again so soon after the last one? Would Said be happy? He had been happy the first time, but I had my doubts about whether he was still happy with the outcome of the first pregnancy. His importance in the family had dropped down a notch, and he was no longer getting as much attention from me. What would he say now? Would I lose even more of his attention if I had another baby?

I blurted out the news as soon as he came home.

"You are?" he looked kind of dazed. "Well that's great!" His face broke into a smile, and the knot in my stomach relaxed slightly.

"I can't wait to tell the brothers! They will be so happy for me!" He got up excitedly and went to get his shoes.

"You're going out again now? You only just got home."

Said kissed my cheek and patted my belly. "Have a rest, baby. I'll be back soon."

I'll be back soon became his mantra over the next few

months. It seemed that I was more of an asset to him now than a person. He needed me to complete his image as the successful Muslim man. He had grown a full beard and wore a long shirt that fell below his knees, with light cotton pants that had to be hemmed above the ankle. It had amused me how particular he and his friends were about the right pant length; if it was too long, you were not following the rules of Islam. He had also become stricter about the way I dressed and even requested that when the mailman came to the house I put my gloves on and reach around the door so I wouldn't be seen.

My world had shrunk so much in the last year. I used to love to travel, go to shows, walk around, and sit in cafés just to people-watch. As the birth of my second baby loomed nearer, I felt the isolation more acutely and was filled with trepidation. My parents couldn't come this time, and I worried about the first few weeks. How would I cope with two babies and no support? Omaima was only a year old and still breastfeeding off and on.

I broached the topic with Said. "We have to talk about what we'll do when the baby comes." Part of me was hoping he would see that he had to pitch in more at home, be around for his family. I didn't actually say this though, as I knew it would make him sulky and withdrawn if I complained too much.

"I could get my mother to come," he replied unexpectedly. "She would love to help with the baby, and Omaima too for that matter."

My face fell. That wasn't the response I wanted.

I didn't really know his mother, and I couldn't speak enough Moroccan to talk to her yet. His suggestion was such a surprise, I didn't know what to say. I wondered how he always managed to create a scenario where he didn't have to be responsible himself. Still, maybe it was a good idea to have someone. Better than nothing, I rationalized.

What the absolute fuck? The Voice protested. *You deserve more support and attention. You are having his children!*

Quiet, I told The Voice. *I need him to love me. Don't blow this.*

"Okay, I guess." I heard the words come out of my mouth as if someone else was speaking. "You'll have to get a visa for her to come." This slight attempt at gaining control of a situation that was spinning rapidly away from me felt small and impotent. Of course, he would get her a visa, and I would have to deal with not only him, but his mother as well.

"I'll talk to her today and ask her." He got out his phone. "I'm sure she will be happy to come and help. My sister can look after my dad while my mom is here with us."

I didn't relish the idea of sharing my house with his mother. Would she want to change things? Would she approve of me as a wife and mother? I wasn't sure at all that I would live up to her idea of a daughter-in-law. On our visit to Morocco I always had the feeling she was sizing me up and wishing I was a little more "Moroccan." I didn't have the same desire to have

the new trend in curtains or fashion as Moroccan
women seemed to have. I let my baby cry herself to sleep
sometimes. I didn't know how to make the flat, round
loaves of bread they ate; mine always turned out
different. It's not that we disliked each other, it wasn't
that strong, but we had such different outlooks. She and
I were from different worlds. The heaviness in my heart
matched the feeling in my body. I felt like a huge stone
was weighing me down. I felt too tired to attempt to
explain my feelings to Said. I just gave a strained smile
and stayed quiet.

He dialled Morocco.

"Allo? Mama?" Said broke into a torrent of Arabic
I didn't understand. They talked for a long time, and
I tuned out after a few minutes.

He finally hung up. "It's all settled! She's coming."

"Oh, okay." I felt flat. The boiling resentment, anger,
and disappointment of a few minutes ago had vanished,
and I felt nothing. I was getting more and more used
to this detached void of feeling. I wasn't sure if it was
the tiredness of being pregnant again or something more
sinister.

Safiyya, my mother-in-law, was ecstatic to be asked
to come. By the following week we had arranged her
visa and bought her ticket. Said thought the break from
working on her feet all day would be good for her. No
doubt it would, I knew she worked very hard. Perhaps
it was the destiny of all women to work hard.

I wasn't really looking forward to her coming.

I had finally become comfortable with my routine with Omaima. She was sleeping better now, although I sometimes had to leave her to cry herself to sleep at bedtime. I liked having my evenings to myself, but that wouldn't last long—the next baby was due in a couple of weeks. Said seemed happy though. I knew he really missed his mother, and he was worried about her. At least that was what I imagined he was feeling. His mom had always doted on him and did everything specially for him, cooking his favourite dishes, staying up to make sure he didn't need anything when he came home from the café with his friends. I had felt even more inadequate when we visited Morocco. Was I supposed to dote on him like that too? No wonder she had high blood pressure and was probably pre-diabetic—she spent every waking moment doing things for other people. Seeing a doctor in Morocco cost money, and they hadn't had much extra to spend on health care. Maybe we could take her while she was here. I couldn't help but feel some sympathy for her.

The day of her arrival was soon upon us.

"I'm going to pick up my mother from London tomorrow," Said reminded me.

I looked up at him. "Okay." I smiled understandingly. "I'll get a chicken and make dinner for when you bring her back." I knew that was what he wanted. "I'll pick up some mint and some olives too. Make her feel at home."

Said smiled and I felt an echo of the warmth his smile used to evoke in me.

"Thanks, baby, that sounds good. I'm just going to the mosque for prayers and to see the brothers. I'll be back later." He kissed my forehead and patted my belly as he went out.

I'll be back later. There it was again. My throat constricted with unshed tears, and the small spark of feeling was roughly extinguished. I really wanted him to stay at home for once. I missed the old days, before we were married. We used to lie in bed for hours making each other laugh. He would make me breakfast in bed. Things had changed, and I couldn't quite put my finger on how. I felt like I was living in a story, and I wasn't the author.

I got up and waddled to the kitchen. The baby had really moved down in the last couple of days. I couldn't wait for the birth to be over. Hopefully it would be easier than last time. I shuddered and picked up a cup on the counter and washed it out. The kettle was full and I flicked it on to boil. I'd make some tea and get an early night. Tomorrow promised to be a busy day of shopping and cooking and then welcoming his mom.

The next afternoon I was just putting the finishing touches on the roast chicken and salad I had made when the doorbell rang. Surely Said wasn't back yet? I went to answer it and was surprised to find Bilkys and another Moroccan friend at the door.

"Assalamu alaikum, Aishah," they gushed. "We brought some food over for Safiyya. We didn't think you'd be able to cook."

"*Wa alaikum salam*," I replied, forcing myself to smile. "Actually, I did just cook chicken. But thanks." I didn't want to seem rude, but really, I wasn't completely incompetent. I stepped aside to let them in. They went to the kitchen and began unloading their food as if they owned the place.

"Do you have a big plate?" the other lady asked. I think her name was Nadia. "I want to put this on the plate and arrange the salad with it."

"Um, sure." I pointed to the plates in the cupboard and slid my chicken over on the counter. It didn't look half as good as their meal. I tried to wrap it up and put it away while they were busy, so they wouldn't notice. I felt like I might cry any minute, so I kept my head down. Yet again, I felt like I wasn't good enough. I couldn't even cook a meal for my mother-in-law without help. I knew the pregnancy hormones weren't helping my emotional balance at the moment, but I couldn't help it.

"There," Bilkys said as she put some delicious looking handmade sweets on top of a pretty napkin-covered plate. "I think that will do." She turned and gave me a sickly-sweet smile. "You really should be resting in your state, you know."

"Yes," I mumbled, like a chastised child. "I was just going to sit down with some tea."

"Oh! There they are!" Nadia squealed, as the car turned into the driveway. She rushed to the door and flung it open. "Safiyya! Said!"

The bulky frame of Said's mother clambered out
of the car, a bit awkward in her bright, Moroccan
jellaba. The scarf covering her hair was larger than
normal and a lovely cream colour that matched the trim
of her jellaba, a long, straight robe that served to cover
her clothes underneath. Nadia and Bilkys rushed out and
hugged and kissed Said and his mother multiple times.
I hung back, not really sure where I fit in. Said was
standing in the middle of the driveway surveying
the scene with pride, as if he was a king and this was
his domain. He didn't look at me or notice that I was
hanging back at the door.

My mother-in-law came over finally. "Aishah, how
are you?" She spoke only Moroccan, but I understood
a few things.

"I'm fine," I answered in my halting Arabic. I kissed
her on both cheeks and stepped aside to let her come in.

"Where is my little Omaima?" Safiyya looked
around eagerly for her only grandchild.

Omaima was just then crying out. All the noise had
woken her up.

"Oh my!" Said's mother said. "You mustn't let her
cry. Where is she? I'll get her." She looked around
worriedly, trying to locate the direction of the cries.

Great, I thought, *just great.* Now I was a neglectful
mother as well as an inadequate cook. I led the way
upstairs, trying to hide my frustration.

Omaima was standing up in her crib, wailing at the
top of her lungs.

"Sh, sweetheart," I pleaded quietly as I lifted her out. She stopped and stared. Safiyya had followed me into her room.

"Habiba," Safiyya crooned, "come to me. You are beautiful. Look at you."

I let the now wriggling Omaima down and she toddled over to her grandmother. Safiyya beamed and picked her up proudly. She turned and started downstairs with the now quiet Omaima in her arms.

Perfect, I thought, *just perfect*. I wasn't needed in the kitchen, and now I wasn't needed as a mother. The heaviness in my belly sank even lower. The weight of everything I was feeling almost brought me to my knees.

I followed meekly. At the bottom of the stairs I tried to catch Said's eye. "I need to change her diaper," I mouthed silently. Said nodded and said something to his mother. She turned to me and let me take Omaima to change her diaper.

No problem there, I was still okay to clean shit apparently. I got a little more forceful than usual with the clasp of the diaper, and Omaima squealed in protest. I finished and hesitated. I wanted to stay upstairs. I could hear Nadia and Bilkys talking simultaneously in Moroccan downstairs. I did not feel like being sociable for hours in a language I barely understood. Omaima wriggled out of my grip, and sighing I took her hand as she headed toward the stairs. A pang of guilt ripped through my chest. This was Omaima's grandmother, but I could barely swallow the resentment that arose like bile in my throat.

I stayed upstairs for as long as I could with Omaima, taking my time on the stairs. Besides, I was two weeks shy of my due date, and everything just seemed like too much effort. I was dragged out of my reverie by the sound of Said calling me.

"Are you coming down?" he asked, a little impatiently.

"Yes, coming." I sighed again and picked Omaima up. This would be quicker, and I wasn't in a patient mood.

"Come on, baby, my mom wants to see you and Omaima," Said said under his breath.

I pasted a smile on my face and walked back into my living room.

At least I didn't have to be the hostess. Bilkys had already made tea and was serving the biscuits and fruit. Said looked at her appreciatively, and I felt tears prick my eyes again. I was angry and hurt. I had worked hard all morning to clean and cook, and all for nothing.

Bilkys passed me a glass of Moroccan mint tea and pushed the plate of biscuits closer to me. I knew she was only acting this way in front of Safiyya. She wanted to be seen as the sweet, efficient Moroccan wife, even though she was married to Said's cousin and not him. I contemplated reminding her of this fact but decided I had better keep my rebellious side in check. Love seemed in short supply these days, and I didn't want to jeopardize the trickle that was still flowing my

way. I would fight for my right to be loved by my
own husband.

Jealousy rose in me again. I never forgot Said telling
me how Bilkys used to visit Blackpool when he and
his cousin were there with the circus and how she had
wanted to be with him but had settled for his cousin.
He had repeatedly told me how lucky I was to have him
when so many other girls had failed. It was as if I should
feel guilty for the times I didn't appreciate him.

I took the tea and tried to look interested in the
conversation. I hoped Bilkys and Nadia would leave
soon. I wanted to get his mother settled and relax. After
what seemed like ages, I gave Said "the look," and he
walked his cousin's wife and friend to the door, promising
to bring his mother over to visit them later on. The one
benefit to having guests was the fact that Said never
wanted to look bad in front of other people, so it gave
me a small grain of power.

When he came back into the room, his mother
looked over at me and asked Said to tell me something.

"What is it?" I asked.

"She was saying that when you have the new baby,
she could take Omaima back to Morocco and raise her
there. You'd have a new baby to care for, and she would
love to help."

"What?" I didn't want my children to be taken from
me. "No! I don't want her to raise my children."

"She is just trying to help. Don't worry about it,
it's just the way she thinks." I could tell he was already

feeling trapped between me and his mother. Well, he had better choose carefully between us. My anger barely concealed behind my smile, I got up and began clearing the dishes. Safiyya got up to help.

"Sit," I said, motioning with my hand for her to stay and talk with Said.

Said rose and followed me to the kitchen instead, putting his hands on my pregnant waist. He whispered in my ear in a menacing tone, "Don't be ungrateful, that is a generous offer for her to make. Many grandmothers in Morocco help raise the children."

I cringed. "Tell her thank you very much, but I am keeping my children with me. She can help tomorrow when she has rested up from her journey." I nodded to him, attempting to keep my face composed and friendly. I didn't want her help, I didn't want anyone's help. I just wanted to be alone.

Said took his hands off me abruptly and returned to his mother.

I noticed Omaima had stayed put in Safiyya's lap. Fine, I would do the dishes. I didn't care if everyone else wanted to visit. I couldn't understand them anyway. Whatever.

As it turned out, Safiyya helped with the cooking quite a bit. Said was enjoying having her here and invited all his friends over for tea or dinner, knowing she would provide the food without complaining.

She caught us fighting one morning about the cost of chicken.

"We can't afford to keep doing this. I don't want to have to walk to the butcher's every day for more meat either. You are going to have to cut back on hosting your friends here." His mother saw the look on my face and began scolding Said, without really knowing what we were fighting about. She knew that I was unhappy, and she told him to make me happy.

I couldn't help smiling inside. At least she was on my side in this. He should make me happy, or try anyway. Weren't you supposed to make each other happy in a marriage?

The next morning my water broke. I felt the wet gush of liquid as I rolled over in bed. Luckily, I had followed the advice in my pregnancy book and put plastic sheets on the bed a few weeks ago. I got up apprehensively. Weren't the pains supposed to start after the water broke? Would I go through labour more quickly this time? I sat on the edge of the bed and grabbed a towel to put between my legs as I hobbled to the toilet. I didn't feel any pains yet, but looking at the liquid dripping down my legs I knew I should go to the hospital.

"Said," I whispered, "we need to go to the hospital."

"Hmm?" he mumbled sleepily. "What's wrong?"

"My water broke," I answered. "We should go. Maybe wake your mom up and tell her to keep Omaima here for now."

"Okay." Said struggled to open his eyes. He had only got home a couple of hours ago from the mosque and whatever he and the brothers got up to after prayers. *His fault for staying out half the night*, I thought spitefully. Now he could pay for it by getting up and taking me to hospital.

"Mama," he patted his mother's shoulder, "we are going to the hospital now. Stay here and take care of Omaima for now, and I'll come back and get you when the baby's come." I understood the gist of his words, although he spoke to his mother in Arabic.

"Yeah, yeah." She sat up quickly. "Go, look after her, I'll be fine with Omaima." It was only three o'clock, but she looked ready to wake Omaima up right then and make sure she was okay. I didn't reflect too long on what she would or wouldn't do, as the ache in my belly was getting worse. I clutched my bump and made my way down the stairs.

After fifteen months of caring for Omaima, mostly on my own, I felt somewhat more assured as I returned home later that day with baby Safia. Her birth had been much easier than the first one, and I hadn't even needed stitches this time. Breastfeeding was old hat now too, and I settled in on the couch as soon as I got home.

Omaima, not wanting to be left out, climbed up as well and wanted to feed on my other breast, even though she had mostly stopped breastfeeding a few weeks ago. Part of me was glad she still wanted to be with me. I thought again of Said's mother taking Omaima back to Morocco and hugged her protectively. I didn't want anyone to take my babies.

Now that I had had Safia, I began to resent my
mother-in-law always telling me how to do things.
I didn't feel like trying to communicate with her, and
I didn't have much in common with her experience.
When Said was home, it was okay. He could translate
for us, and he was adept at making people feel good
when he wanted to. And, of course, his mom adored
him, which was what he really craved. My adoration
and attention had been channelled elsewhere for months
now, and I no longer had the patience or time to pander
to him the way I had when we were first married. I felt
guilty for this. I was supposed to be a wife first and a
mother second. But I couldn't find that place in myself
much anymore. I felt cocooned in a reality where only
my babies and I existed. It was sometimes lonely. I didn't
know how to share this place with him. I resented the
fact that he could come and go so easily and I was stuck
at home. On the other hand, I just wanted to enjoy being
with my babies on my own. Adding a second baby more
than doubled the work, but it was work I was used
to now. I didn't have the mental or emotional energy
to deal with Said as well. Survival was my only plan.

Somewhere inside, a voice protested that there was
more to life than survival. That marriage and raising
a family could be wonderful and sweet, a shared journey
with your loved ones. Was that just a pipe dream?
Another voice answered in a snide manner, *You don't
deserve to have all that. Life is only about suffering.* The first
voice was always silenced by the stronger, critical

one, for now anyway. Maybe one day things would
be different.

After a couple of weeks, Said's father began to
complain that his wife wasn't around to look after him
and that Fatima, Said's handicapped sister, just wasn't
the same, so Safiyya got ready to return to Morocco.
My father-in-law's complaints struck me as a familiar
refrain; didn't Said do the same thing?

We all piled in the car to take Safiyya to the airport.
Surprisingly I was sad to see her go. She had kept Said
happy and well fed; she loved to cook. She was generally
a happy soul and loved nothing more than to hold her
grandchildren in her arms. Sitting for hours with them
was not a burden for her, and I marvelled at her seeming
ability to sacrifice her own desires so selflessly for others.
Part of me wondered why I could not do this so willingly.
Was I flawed somehow? Spoiled perhaps? I just couldn't
measure up to this seemingly impossible standard. It
never crossed my mind that for her, being a grandparent
was the only thing on her mind, aside from Said, who
it seemed was always her first love. It struck me that
he never lacked for love as I did. His mother was besotted
with him. The love of a mother for her son could be a
fierce thing, something I could never hope to compete
with no matter how wonderful a wife and mother I was.

I was relieved to have my house to myself again.
I no longer had to plaster a smile on my face all the time,
I could show my frustration if I wanted to.

I tried to keep up some of what Safiyya had done

around the house. I made tea for the brothers that Said invited over. They sat upstairs in the spare bedroom that we had made into the TV room. Sometimes I asked him to help more with the kids and the chores; I resented it when I saw him sleeping late, watching TV, or relaxing. He would explain again that he didn't want me to become dependent on him, he wanted me to be able to manage if he ever had to go away for work. I still had no logical response to this. It sounded like it made sense, and yet intuitively I felt this was not right. He wasn't away right now, and I did need help sometimes.

"Are you going away?" I asked, a little worried.

"Well…I haven't completely decided yet, but Phillip has asked me to go to Dubai and work with the circus for three months this summer. I'd like to go."

"Oh." I really had nothing to say to that either. "Well, I guess if it's a job…" Something was off with his logic, but in my baby-addled state, I couldn't put my finger on it. Going back to work with the circus—wasn't that what he had wanted to get away from? The wheels of my mind squealed with the effort of my thought process. He had told me he wanted a family, wanted to be with me, wanted us to practice Islam. Now he was suddenly going away to have fun, be in a show, all the things we had enjoyed together when we first met. How was that fair? I'd be stuck here with two kids while he went back to the life we had first shared together, except now, he'd be enjoying it without me. I shook my head, confused, but kept quiet.

"Yeah, I haven't been getting much work around here. You know that, baby. I can make some more money," he reasoned.

It was obvious he wanted to go. He wanted me to agree with him. How could I force him to stay here, where he didn't feel fulfilled? I knew he missed the circus and the show business life. I missed it too.

"I don't know," I said. "How long would you be gone?"

"Just three months."

"When would you leave?" With that question it was basically a done deal.

"In two weeks." It sounded like he had already accepted the job, and I could feel my insides tighten. A sense of betrayal rocked my body. Why hadn't he said anything?

"Oh," I said again, aware that I sounded like a broken record. I was shocked. Three months on my own with the kids—an eternity.

Safia woke up then and started whimpering. I went to get her from the basket. She was tiny and perfect, and I couldn't help smiling at her as she opened her eyes and began rooting for my breast. I did love my babies, but still, something felt off.

"Will you send me money?" I asked.

"Yes, of course. I'll be back soon, baby." He planted a kiss on my forehead and turned back to the TV. "Go and see to the kids, we can talk later."

Downstairs I sat on the couch, Safia tucked under

one arm and Omaima lying with her head on my lap
playing with my other breast. A few tears trickled down
my cheeks, the only concrete evidence of my inner
turmoil. I could no longer recall exactly what had upset
me so much about the whole conversation. I felt cheated
somehow, like I'd been promised something for all my
sacrifice, and instead, I was getting nothing.

I thought about the window, the one that God always
opened when he shut a door. Why did it always feel like
doors were slamming in my face? I gazed out the living
room window. I'd be okay. I prayed silently to Allah
for courage, patience. One of my Muslim sisters had
joked about resting being something you did in the grave,
not in this life. It did seem to be true. God must know
what he was doing though. We were never tested beyond
what we could endure, were we? I sat and breathed,
tears still trickling down my face. Sacrifice and patience,
these were qualities we were rewarded for, right?

Right?

Chapter
Six

THAT SUMMER PASSED IN A blur of baby chores. I walked to the park, changed diapers, fed everyone, did laundry, shopped for groceries. A friend and I made a deal to call each other every night after dinner to chat about our day. She had kids too and a husband who wouldn't even let her go out of the house. It helped to tell someone your frustrations, those little things that happened in your day, small disasters and triumphs. A couple of times, I packed Omaima and Safia into the pushchair and went to her house for Pakistani curry and handmade roti or flatbread. She was a great cook. I loved the different flavours of the food. She was adept at eating on the floor with the children all gathered around the same big platter.

It felt good to share a meal. It felt like a family. When it was time to go, we hugged and a look passed between us. We knew the pain and struggles behind each other's eyes. We didn't need to say anything.

It might seem odd that Said and I didn't talk that much on the phone while he was away. This was before cellphones took off and even before it became commonplace to talk via the Internet. He called once or twice a week, we shared a few words. I told him the kids were growing, and he told me about his work. I think I didn't want to share too much because I would feel the loneliness more that way. If I kept a smile in my voice, and the "everything is fine" mentality, I could get through the days.

Said had primed me to do everything on my own, and I began to find ways of succeeding at this. It was summertime, and after breakfast I would open the door from the living room to the garden and take the laundry out to hang on the line. Omaima would come on her toddler tricycle, and Safia would be tied securely onto my back with a long cloth. This was a trick I had learned from Said's mother, and I was grateful for it, as having my hands free and the baby firmly attached let me get a few things done.

Before long, I couldn't imagine having Said around. My life with the kids was full and all encompassing. He faded further away.

Three months had passed quite quickly, it seemed to me, when one morning the doorbell rang. I put down the basket of laundry I'd been taking upstairs and went to answer it. Said stood on the step, grinning. His head was shaved bald, and his beard had grown. I hardly recognized him.

"Hi, baby!" He laughed. "I'm home."

"How come you didn't tell me you were coming today?" I asked, bewildered. "I would have gotten ready."

He laughed and grabbed me to him. "I missed you so much," he mumbled, then kissed me.

I tried to relax my body into his and be happy that he was home. I just felt disgruntled that he hadn't warned me.

"I missed you too," I said, though I wasn't sure I had really. I had settled into a routine that was doable, I had friends that understood and shared my daily battles. What had I really missed about Said? His dick? I almost laughed out loud and turned to hide the smirk on my face. My friend and I had talked about our husbands and what was required to keep them satisfied. I had laughed when she admitted she gave him a blow job before sending him to the corner store for milk, just in case he was tempted by seeing other women. It was true, sex had been relegated to a marital chore more than a fun pastime for most of the sisters. I liked to think my marriage was different, but as I struggled to enjoy my husband's present groping embrace, a shadow of doubt flickered through my mind.

He looked around as he came inside. "Where are my babies?"

"Omaima is upstairs sleeping and Safia is here in the living room." I moved forward to lead the way. Picking Safia up, I turned her to face her father. She was three months old and able to hold her head up and smile now. Said took her from me and bounced her up and down in front of his face.

"My little Safia, you've grown," he cooed. She took one look at his big beard and heard his masculine voice and promptly burst into tears. "Oh, don't cry, baby," he said smiling at her. "Baba's home!"

She screamed even louder, and Said handed her back to me, looking a little hurt. "She wants her mom."

"I think she doesn't recognize you," I said. "It's been a long time."

"Hmm. Well, where's my Omaima?"

"She's asleep," I said again. "She goes to bed at six thirty."

"Well, let me go and see her." Said bounded up the stairs, and I sighed. It always took a long time to get Omaima to sleep, and now I would have to do it all over again. I went into the kitchen and put the kettle on. *I guess it's nice to have him home*, I said to myself. Guilt flashed through my mind as I realized I had to talk myself into being pleased.

I made us some tea and took it to the living room. Safia was still fussing and I got the pillow I used for breastfeeding and made myself comfortable. Omaima must have been fast asleep because Said came down then and joined me.

"Are you happy I'm home?" he asked, a slight wistfulness in his eyes. He had always been fairly sensitive to my energy, especially when it wasn't turned toward him.

"Of course," I replied, a little too quickly. He had been away for three months. For my own survival, I'd had to find other ways to cope than to rely on him, just like he had told me to.

"I started wearing the niqab and burka," I said shyly. This was a more fundamentalist version of the hijab. The black veil fitted under a full head-to-toe covering, and black gloves and socks completed the outfit. Sister Umm Abdullah showed me how to make the whole outfit and had informed me that this was how the women dressed in Saudi Arabia. Following this dress code meant we were even more pious, as the holy city of Mecca, the birthplace of Islam, was in Saudi Arabia. I was proud of my creativity and I had liked sewing my own covering. "I made a dark blue one and a black one." Many of the sisters at the study circle wore outfits like this, and when I went to the Friday prayers at the mosque it was a bit intimidating to be surrounded by women in black. I wanted to fit in, but it gave me the feeling of being indistinguishable from any other woman, which was the whole point I guess.

"Oh! I'm so proud of you, baby." Said had tears in his eyes. "You are the best thing that ever happened to me. You know, even I will be rewarded in heaven for having such a pious and good wife."

Funny, I thought, *you being rewarded in heaven was not what I was thinking about at the time.* In any case, I smiled. "Do you want to see them?"

"Sure," he said, nodding.

I put Safia in the bouncy chair and got the scarf that went underneath, then fastened the veil around my head, pulled the burka over everything, and finally put the elastic around the back to hold it all in place. I flipped up the top part of the veil so that my eyes could be seen through the slit.

"What do you think?" I asked, turning around.

"I think you look beautiful. You are full of noor, spiritual light."

His compliment warmed my heart a little, and I was glad to feel a bit closer to him again.

"Can we go to the Islamic conference in Birmingham? It's next week, and some of the sisters are going. There will be a sheikh and lots of talks. Umm Abdullah has asked me to help her at her stall for Islamic clothing."

"Sure," Said said. "I'm glad you have made some good friends while I was away."

"Yes, I've been studying a lot," I said proudly. "I am even giving a talk on charity in Islam for the sisters circle next week."

"I'm so proud of you. You bring many blessings for me." Said kissed my hand.

A few days later, Said came in and told me his cousin Mourad was going to Morocco for a month and had

asked him to work in his gym for him again while he
was away.

"Will you get paid?" I asked. By now I knew that
many times these "favours" were expected to be carried
out with no obvious return. Moroccan culture demanded
that familial ties be honoured without expectations. I still
found this difficult to swallow, especially when Said's own
wife and kids often were kept waiting for hours or had
to go short so his friends could eat. I could feel myself
tense up, afraid of the answer.

"Well, I'll be able to work out, and Bilkys said
she would make me lunch every day," he explained
somewhat sheepishly.

"Hmm." I turned away and busied myself with
fixing the sofa cushions. What could I say? He wouldn't
change his mind, and he had already given his cousin
his word.

Every day for the next few days, I was regaled with
gushing praise of the amazing lunches Bilkys had made
and brought over to the gym, personally. From what
I gathered, she also sat and chatted to Said while he
ate and kept him company so he wouldn't feel so bored
sitting at the gym all day.

"Would you like me to pack you a lunch today?"
I asked. The way he went on about how considerate
and thoughtful she was had made me a little jealous.

"Oh, that's okay, baby. I know you are busy
with the kids." He smiled and pecked me quickly on
the cheek. "I might be a bit late tonight. I am going

to the mosque to meet some new Libyan brothers.
Don't wait up for me."

"When will you be back?" I asked, feeling heavy.

"Probably not until after Fajr prayer," Said
answered.

I sighed inwardly. The early morning prayer
was around four o'clock at this time of year, and
he sometimes just stayed up to pray if he was up late
working or visiting. It made sense but it usually meant
I was getting up for breakfast by the time he was coming
home to bed. I missed him holding me while I slept.
It seemed like we hadn't slept together like that for years,
since before the kids.

"I miss you," I said suddenly, turning to him. I
missed the feel of his body against my back, his insistent
touch when he wanted to be intimate, even just the
warmth of someone close by.

"Aw, I miss you too, baby." He pulled me into his
chest in that way that used to make me feel safe and
loved but I realized now just kind of fuelled my
disgruntled fury. Confused at my own reaction, I bent
my head, so he didn't see my face.

My day passed, as it usually did, with a long series
of tasks relating to the kids. I had developed a fairly good
system of coping with two babies only fifteen months
apart. After breakfast, I usually got them ready to go out
and took them to the local park, the same one I had
walked in for my first outing with my hijab, except
now my destination was the swing set and not the
walking path.

Diapers, clothes, shoes, coats, double pushchair, snacks, and finally my black burka and veil, and I was ready for the morning outing. Omaima sometimes walked part of the way on her own. I encouraged this as it made the uphill part easier without her weight in the pushchair.

Our house was farther away from the park than Said's old flat had been. I liked having more space, and we had come a long way toward furnishing the entire house. One of the three upstairs bedrooms functioned as a sitting room for Said and his friends, and our TV. I did not sit in there often.

Omaima had the second small room and Safia had her crib in the walk-in closet in the hall. This seemed like the easiest way to keep the girls from waking each other up when they weren't sleeping well. Said and I had the largest bedroom. Our mattress on the floor seemed to make sense as I didn't worry about the kids falling out if I brought one or the other back to bed with us in the early mornings.

I couldn't recall spending much time with Said in bed at all recently. Safia often woke up at four in the morning and was restless and fussy. Said was often only just going to bed at that time, and so I had adapted by taking the baby down to the living room and napping on the big floor cushions while Safia crawled around the room. I had child-proofed this area as much as I could, as most of my day was spent in there. The only furniture was a plastic climbing frame and slide, a gift from my parents, and a bookshelf that allowed me to put a few things out of reach. Big floor cushions worked well as seating, and a couple of storage bins for toys. Even Omaima hadn't figured out how to open doors yet, so I was fairly safe to stay with the girls without having to chase them everywhere. By the time Safia had tired herself out again and was ready for a morning nap, Omaima was waking up and ready for breakfast. Fooling myself into thinking I had slept well was a necessary survival skill. After being out late Said usually slept until noon, and so my morning routine had developed without him.

This morning was no different than usual. I had woken up early with the baby and come downstairs with her. I was vaguely aware of the fact that Said's side of the bed was still empty. A gnawing feeling of unease began to grow in my belly, but I brushed it aside. He had said he was going to be late getting home. I checked the clock: 5:30. I thought the Fajr prayer should have been over an hour ago. The bitterness that I had been feeling more often lately rose up in my throat. He never seemed to be home these days.

I sighed heavily and rolled over on the cushions as Safia crawled near me. I must just be tired with the kids. I couldn't seem to fall asleep again though; it promised to be a long day. Just then I heard the door click.

"Said?" I called out. "Is that you?"

I got up and went into the hall. He was taking off his shoes and coat with a resigned air, almost sheepish.

"Everything okay?" I asked, feeling that the least he could do after spending extra time out at the mosque was come back in a good mood.

"Yeah, I'm fine," he said in a voice that sounded anything but fine. "I'm just going to go to bed for a bit."

"I could make you tea if you want," I offered, trying to make him smile.

"I can't." He choked on the words, almost as if he was going to cry.

"What's wrong?" I asked again, really worried now.

"It's…it's…I can't tell you." He looked up at me then, with tears in his eyes. "I'm so sorry, Ailsa."

I reached out to hold him. "It's okay, I love you," I said, trying to comfort him.

"No! You don't understand…" He faltered. "I love you so much too." Then he turned quickly and went upstairs.

I felt my own tears coming, anger and frustration also. What could possibly be so bad that he couldn't tell me? I was his wife after all. Just then, Safia started to fuss, and I turned to pick her up.

"Sh, sweetheart, everything's okay." I rocked and soothed her, holding on to her little body as much to comfort myself as to quiet her. "Everything's going to be okay," I whispered.

A week later, I still had not gotten to the bottom of Said's sudden and unexplained depression. He hadn't said much to me at all and had not stayed in the house except to sleep and eat quickly. I was worried. The kids kept me occupied most of the day, but the evening stretched long and lonely as I turned everything over in my mind. It had all started after his cousin had gone to Morocco and he was helping out at the gym. His cousin's wife had been frustratingly anxious to make herself useful to him and had also called a few times to ask if Said could come over and check various things that she was having trouble with in her house. A small but persistent doubt began to form in my mind. I knew she had always had the hots for him. I tried to put the thought out of my head. Said was married now, with two children, and a practicing Muslim. She was married with a baby too, for that matter. It didn't make sense. Still, now that it had occurred to me, I couldn't get the idea out of my head. I resolved to ask him about it. That would put my mind at rest.

I gave the girls a bath and put them to bed. Safia was beginning to sleep on a schedule, and I was grateful to have a part of the evening to myself. I was impatient for Said to come home and decided to call him and ask when he might be back.

"Hello, baby?" I asked, when I heard his voice. "I was wondering if you might be back home soon. I want to talk to you."

"I'll be home soon," he replied quickly. He always said that. I wanted a more definite answer.

"When? I really need to talk to you," I pushed.

There was a hesitation on the other end of the phone, but he answered in a resigned voice, "I'm coming now."

"Okay. Please come soon. I just got the kids in bed."

"Okay, I'll be there soon." And he rang off.

I felt nervous and jittery. For some reason, I was dreading this conversation. Of course, I was just being silly, and he would tell me it was something else, I didn't need to worry. I fixed the sofa cushions in the upstairs TV room, straightened the carpet, put the clean laundry in our bedroom, and made some tea. I heard the car pull in to the driveway. At least he hadn't taken long to get home. I went to the door.

"Hey," I said, smiling flirtatiously, "it's about time! I could hardly contain myself," I teased.

He didn't respond, just smiled weakly, and I moved aside to let him in. Already this was not going well. My body closed in on itself and I felt the tightness in my belly.

"Do you want some tea? I just made a pot," I asked a little nervously.

"Sure, okay," he answered distractedly, pulling his phone out of his jacket and looking at it. I hadn't heard it ring, but he seemed intent on looking at his messages. "I have to go out soon though."

"Oh," I said, my face falling. "I thought we could spend the evening together."

"Well, pour me some tea then, and we can sit for a while." He smiled at me and I felt a bit mollified.

I brought the tea and the cups upstairs, with a plate of cookies. I was anxious to please him after not seeing him much that week.

We sat down and I handed him a cup of tea.

"So, what did you want to talk about?" he asked.

"Well…" I hesitated, not quite knowing how to begin this conversation. "I noticed you haven't been quite yourself lately, and I was wondering what was going on." I stopped, looking to him for reassurance, an explanation, something reasonable that would dispel the dread that was eating away at my stomach.

He sighed. "It's nothing," he said with his eyes down. "It's all over now anyway," he added quietly.

"What's all over?" I couldn't help asking. "You can tell me anything, remember? I'm your wife…your best friend…" I faltered as I saw his face crumple. "What's wrong?"

He had gone pale and there was a stricken look on his face. "I'm sorry, I can't keep it in anymore…"

He looked at me and I took his hand, encouraging him with my eyes.

"She called me over after morning prayer last week…said there was an intruder in the house and begged me to come and check it out for her. She was scared, pleading with me to come."

I waited for him to continue, but an icy coldness was creeping up my arms. I could no longer feel his hand in mine.

"I went over there and she answered the door,

wearing a really nice dress. She had perfume on and makeup and everything."

"At four in the morning?" I asked, incredulous.

"Yeah." He sighed. "I didn't want to...I really didn't!" He looked up then and my heart stopped.

"I don't know if I want to hear this," I said. "Did you fuck her?"

"Don't say it like that," he pleaded. "I didn't want to. I didn't even cum inside her."

I was speechless for a long moment. "You didn't cum inside her? Where the hell did you cum?" I could feel my voice rising in hysteria. "What do you mean you didn't want to? You must have had a choice."

He recoiled as if I had slapped him. "I'm sorry. It was only once. I didn't mean it."

Only once. My mind replayed the comment. Did it matter? Once, twice, every friggin' night? What was the difference? I was home with two babies, and he wasn't with me. My fantasy of family life was irretrievably broken.

An icy calm descended on me. The anger hardened into a numbness that reached my heart and made my fingers and toes seem disconnected from my body. I looked at him, slumped in the chair, looking pitiful. I couldn't find one ounce of pity for him right then— I only felt contempt. I stood up and walked downstairs, put on my hijab, and went out. The kids were asleep and I needed air, and time to think.

I moved one foot in front of the other, all the way

up the hill toward the main shopping district. Before
I got to the busy part, I turned down a side street and
kept walking. I didn't want to meet anyone, or have
to talk right then. The dialogue in my head was loud
enough to shut out everything else.

What was he thinking? I shook my head. *He knew
she wanted him, he should have been more guarded around her.
He definitely should have kept his dick in his pants!* I almost
shouted out loud in rage and frustration and grief. *What
do I do now? Do I leave him? I have two young girls. Come to think
of it, I haven't had my period yet this month. Damn it all!*

I put my hand protectively over my belly. I couldn't
leave, I couldn't break up the family. My kids needed
a dad. I wanted them to have a dad. In truth, Said wasn't
there much as a father, or as a husband, and it was
getting worse. But I pushed those thoughts away. I didn't
want to look at the reality of the situation. I couldn't give
up on my dreams—they were all I had.

Tears sprang to my eyes as I walked. I didn't own
him anyway, did I? I mean, if he truly loved and cared
for his family, surely, I should forgive a mistake. If it
was truly a mistake, as he said. I shut my eyes and tried
to think clearly. *I am a good wife and mother, I am a good
Muslim too. I'm not a coward, and I'm not someone who gives
up just because things get rocky.* I took a deep breath.

The Voice intoned in my head: *A good Muslim woman
supports her husband and family at all costs. She keeps herself
looking nice and pays attention to him so he doesn't feel neglected.*
Had I neglected him? Had I let myself go with two

back-to-back pregnancies? Perhaps I wasn't trying to be sexy anymore. No wonder he was drawn to other women. I hadn't really made an effort to seduce him.

Another, softer voice whispered that I was angry that he didn't help out much. I was angry that he had led me down this path of marital life and then left to go back to the circus without me. I felt betrayed.

The pain of these voices was too much. I took a breath and silenced all of them. I didn't want to feel. I didn't want to think. I did what I had always done as a child and retreated into my own fantasies. I could make everything okay in my head, spin the story the way I wanted. It didn't even matter what the reality was, because I wasn't living there. I didn't notice the cool breeze on my hands. My body itself floated away, and I felt an inner peace descend on me.

I rounded the corner and headed back down the hill toward our house. I would stay for my own honour and for the family. I would stay because I was a fighter. The feeling in my feet began to return as I breathed into my decision. I could feel the hardness of the pavement and the shock waves that spread up my legs with each step. Something in me had changed though. I could feel it. I was in this relationship alone now, for better or worse. I would never again feel completely wed to Said. The confusion of my feelings was beginning to clear, although I wasn't sure the clarity was any less painful than the fog.

I was wed to my own ideal of love, partnership, and family. I didn't need anyone else for that. I would do it

on my own. Just as in my days of fairy-tale romances
in my room as a kid, I found it easy to create the same
inner reality now. I didn't realize how I was setting
myself up for eventual disappointment, even despair,
if I ever dared to feel again.

I opened the door and went in, took off my coat
and shoes, and went to the kitchen to put the kettle on.
Now that the decision was made and I knew where
I stood, I felt I could mobilize myself to endure whatever
came next. Said poked his head round the doorframe
and asked if I was okay.

"Well, I am extremely upset and disappointed.
But if this was really a one-off mistake on your part,
then I have decided to stay." I turned to him resolutely.
"It should never happen again though." I heard myself
say the words although they seemed to float in the air
around me, without my lips saying them. It didn't even
matter what the words were, I didn't care anymore. The
innermost part of me had left the marriage already,
I was untouchable.

"Thank you, Ailsa." He came and put his arms
around me. I barely felt his embrace, although I returned
the hug. The feeling of being held in a safe space was not
there anymore. I comforted him as though he were a
stranger. Islam does not condone adultery, for either sex
partner, although in reality there was much more
lenience for men than for women. It had never crossed
my mind to be interested in anyone else when I was
married, but maybe men were different. Perhaps that

was why Islam allowed men to have up to four wives.
I mulled over this thought as I turned to him.

"Do you want some hot tea?" I asked, turning back
to the kettle, which was now boiling furiously. The cold
tea upstairs had left my mind. It was as though time had
cracked, and there was no going back.

It's funny how life can carry on normally even after
everything has been turned upside down and shaken.
I don't know what I expected exactly, but it seemed weird
to be doing the same routine with the kids, the same
shopping and cooking and cleaning as before. Inside
myself, nothing was the same. This gulf had opened
up between my heart and Said. I turned to Allah when
I needed strength and support. I had been learning
to recite the Quran and studying Arabic. I gave a talk
on charity at our local Muslim women's study group.

It would not be seen to be my fault that my husband
had desired another woman.

It could not be my fault! I mobilized myself, the fear
pushing me to work harder, be better. I could not let
down my guard. The shame and doubts about being the
cause of this cut like thorns into every pore of my body.
I hated him and I hated the circumstances that had led
me to take the blame for all of this.

One time—only one time—the pain almost broke
through my barriers.

Mourad, Said's cousin, called me. I heard his voice
on the other end of the line and froze.

"Hi, Aishah," he said in a serious tone, "I wanted

to tell you the truth of what happened with Said and my wife."

I was shaking. I could barely respond. "I don't want to hear it," I said as strongly as I could. "It doesn't matter to me, I have decided to support Said and stay with him."

Mourad's voice rose. "How could you do that after what he did?"

"I don't want to know." I hung up the phone, my hand trembling in my lap. It took everything I had to push the terror down. I didn't want to imagine an alternative life, on my own with two daughters. It was terrifying, shameful, impossible. I would die.

The only way to feel in control was to take responsibility. If it was my fault, then I could do something about it. I could pay attention to Said's needs, I could make sure he had sex once or twice a week. He couldn't complain about that.

I became almost cold and calculated about my role as a wife. Make sure dinner was prepared, kiss him when he came home. I excelled at my studies of Arabic and Islam, he could be proud to call me his partner. These were my safeties.

Said was distant too. He seemed to always be finding someone to visit or something to do with his friends. Some days, I barely saw him at all. In a way, I was relieved when he wasn't at home. The kids were young and I was exhausted. We scraped by on the government assistance and child support. I had little time or patience with his needs or demands. I was in awe of my friend who told me how she always pleasured her husband before he went out anywhere, even just to the store for milk. She wanted him to be satisfied so that he wouldn't be tempted to look at other women. I wondered if it worked for her too. I was afraid to know the answer.

In Islam, it is possible for a man to take four wives if he feels he can be a good husband to them and treat them fairly. I had picked up a book on polygamy from the bookstore and browsed through it absent-mindedly. There were the usual proofs and sayings of the Prophet Muhammad and excerpts from the Quran. I found the Arabic scholars long-winded and lacking in feeling. However, there was a chapter telling of these two cousins who had decided to share the same husband. They had both agreed to marry the same man and live together in one house. Each had her own private bedroom, but they shared the family living space.

I was intrigued.

I was also lonely, and the idea of having another woman, a friend, that could help and work with me in the home, was tempting. I had lost faith in my husband ever being a partner for me; perhaps another wife would work. I read the passage a few times. The women were good friends, they helped each other with the chores, they took turns and shared the responsibilities of being a wife, they raised their children together. I craved someone who would understand what my days were like, with whom I could talk things over, share the burdens of motherhood. I no longer pretended, even to myself, that my husband would be any of these things.

Without really being aware of what I was doing, I began to look at every Muslim sister I met in a different light. Would she be a good co-wife? Could I be friends with her? Was she also in need of the support of a husband and family?

Would she want me? the voice inside me asked. *Someone must want me.*

We could help another woman too, I thought. There are women who can't find a husband, who maybe can't have children, or are older. I would be living another great part of Islam, pleasing Allah, working toward heaven. It made sense on so many levels!

"What would you think of having another wife?" I asked Said innocently one day.

"Really? Would you let me?" The unspoken words "after all I've put you through" hung in the air. His enticing smile broke on his face. I hadn't seen that expression for months.

"Well…" I wasn't sure I was giving permission. "I was just thinking it might be something to consider. I just wondered what you thought about it."

"I am always so proud of you, baby. You are the best wife and Muslim a man could ask for!" Said beamed at me. I felt a rush of emotion. I couldn't remember the last time he had looked at me that way. The thought of having another woman seemed to have awakened his desire.

"Come here," he whispered, holding out his hand, "I want you." He led me to the bedroom. His desire felt so strong, I let myself melt in his arms. It felt so good to be touched. I hadn't realized I missed it so much. He lifted my dress over my head, and I wished I had nicer underwear on. I had switched to plain white cotton when I was pregnant and hadn't bothered to go shopping much recently. He didn't seem to notice, and I unsnapped my bra quickly, liking the feel of his hands on my naked body. He pushed me forward onto the mattress; he had always liked that position, from behind. I braced myself, pushing my hips back into him. He was fast and rough, his desire taking over.

"Fuck me harder!" I breathed over my shoulder. I knew that made him crazy. I hardly felt anything in my own body except his desire. He responded eagerly, thrusting deeper inside me. I crawled forward onto my knees, knowing he would follow me. He slapped my buttocks lightly.

"You like that?" he teased. "Tell me how much you want me," he ordered.

"I want you," I replied dutifully, adding some passion to my voice, hoping he wouldn't see through the falseness of my responses.

"Louder!"

"I want you! I need you inside me!" I shouted, writhing under his grasp.

He put his hand heavily on my back, pushing me down. I felt his heaviness on top of me. He entered again, pulling my head back by my hair.

"Oh, baby!" He came in shudders, falling forward on top of me and taking my breath away. I gasped and then giggled, pushing him over. The pretense was complete. I felt only a wave of control as I realized I could win at this game. I could make him powerless to his own need for sex. It was almost arousing in a way, and I enjoyed the feeling. Contempt for the weakness of men swept through me like the waves of orgasm. I smiled seductively.

"We haven't done that in a while." I smiled at him as I snuggled against him.

"Mm…" he replied, already dozy after the exertion.

"So maybe having another wife would be a good thing?" I asked in a teasing voice.

"Definitely!" he replied sleepily.

I didn't feel sleepy at all afterwards. My mind turned over the idea. Maybe it would bring us closer together again? Maybe it would give me some sense of power in this relationship? If I was willing to offer him another woman, legally, within his rights as a Muslim man, maybe he wouldn't ever want another woman outside the marriage. Surely with two women at home, he couldn't possibly want anything else. He would appreciate me for being so giving, such a good wife. I almost laughed out loud.

I am such a good wife, I thought as my eyes began to close too. *I know he won't leave me. I give him everything.*

I awoke early the next morning in a better mood

than I had been in in weeks. I hummed as I prepared breakfast for the girls. They could both eat solid food now, and I was thinking about running a playgroup for Muslim mothers in the area who also wanted to meet in the comfort of a home where we could all be together without wearing our full burkas. I had developed a strong network of sisters, mostly Pakistani, who also practiced their faith strictly. It was common to have many children, and they were welcomed in our gatherings. I loved the relaxed understanding of sharing the same rules, and Said was proud to see me fit in with the religion so well.

One woman and her husband ran a business sewing the loose garments we all wore over our clothes and selling them to the large Muslim population in Manchester. I had acquired a few different coats and burka styles since my first experiments with a headscarf and had even sewn a couple of my own. Umm Abdullah (whose name means the mother of Abdullah) asked me over quite often to help her pack the scarves in boxes for shipping to other stores and locations in the UK. Her first baby had been a girl as well, Amatullah (named for the female slave of Allah), and her second was a boy, the Abdullah she had wanted. It was customary for a woman to take the name of a child they hoped to have and call themselves the "mother" of that child. I was often called Umm Omaima, using the name of my first child. It was taken for granted we would aim to have children. Many of my friends already had three or four.

Now and then I remembered that a few years earlier

I had decided never to have children. It was a hazy
memory, as if in another lifetime. I couldn't quite
connect with the person I had been before meeting Said.
I smiled inwardly when I thought of my past goal
to see my name in lights. Would I have made it in
the performance world? If not, it wouldn't be for lack
of talent, I'd been good at most things I'd tried. My
teachers and coaches had been disappointed that
I chose to end my training.

Somehow, I had always felt I was not good enough.
I had sabotaged my own chance at success by deciding
I wouldn't make it, before I even tried. Perhaps I was
afraid of success more than failure? Afraid of being seen.
Now I had chosen not to be seen, to be covered up.
Was it really a way to get to heaven, or was I just letting
fear run my life? I didn't really want to know the answer.

With Islam, I wanted to do things right. We lived
to make God happy by following his rules. It was
comforting to know that if you followed the commands
in the Quran and the sayings of the Prophet Muhammad,
you would have peace and joy in the afterlife. It was
so much easier to let God make the rules. I didn't have
to think about anything, just follow what was prescribed.
My parents had successfully trained me to be dutiful,
and my teachers were pleased when I performed well
in school. The validation and praise felt good. I didn't
even notice that my own self was being eroded away
until there was nothing left of my own desires. The
danger inherent in this abnegation of my own will was

not yet apparent to me. The world seemed to support this loss of empowerment, and I was too young to know any different.

It was a relief sometimes to pack up the kids and go over to Umm Abdullah's house for the afternoon. She had the Quran playing in the background. The girls loved playing on the bikes and the trampoline in the backyard. We made rice and curry and drank tea. Life seemed normal. Normal in the way that I didn't have to listen to my deeper self or the nagging fears and doubts that floated somewhere just beyond my everyday awareness. Normal was sacrifice and silencing the voices. Normal was denying my own self.

Occasionally I wondered why normal didn't feel good. When I looked around me, most people were living this kind of disconnected normal, and they all seemed fine. Why couldn't it work for me? I had become so isolated in my own world, a dream-like cocoon. I was stuck between the normal world and the truth.

And so, it seemed fairly normal, in that sense of the word, when I found out I was expecting again later that fall. Most of my friends were either pregnant or had young children. It was a sign that you were fulfilling your duties as a Muslim woman, to populate the world with children of Islam. I was used to the feeling of tiredness and nausea that swept over me in the first few weeks, but with two young toddlers, it was harder to find time to rest. I was too overworked to continue my playgroup, and I settled into an even more isolated lifestyle.

My activities outside the home decreased—that way
it was easier to focus on my own needs and those
of my children. Said found it challenging to watch
two young girls, and it seemed he was not interested
in learning. As my friends also had multiple children,
we did not socialize that much. The world closed
in around me, only letting the light in through cracks
every now and then.

I was particularly worried about one close friend.
Said and I had helped her and a new refugee from
Algeria get married. She had two children from a
previous marriage and had recently begun to practice
Islam more strictly. Her new husband had seemed loving
and considerate at first but lately had been stopping her
from going out of the house. She already covered even
her eyes, and her burka dragged on the ground on the
few occasions when her husband had let her accompany
him to the mosque for a talk. I was one of the few
women that he allowed to visit her at home. He was
worried that the women were backbiting and gossiping
"as women are prone to do" and didn't want his wife
exposed to any harmful talk.

I felt honoured to be trusted to visit her, although
I worried about her being so isolated. I was amazed
and impressed that she could be so dutiful as a wife and
mother. My own indiscretions loomed larger than life as
I observed her piety. I couldn't get used to staying in the
house all day, and I joked with Said that I had "standing
permission" to go out whenever I wanted. I tried to keep

my eyes down around other men and to remember not to answer the door without my full hijab on, even just to get the mail. It made me feel special, the fact that no one saw me.

It also felt like non-existence sometimes. Was I ever seen at all?

One of the sisters gave a talk about the evils of TV and seeing various degrees of nudity and violence on the small screen, which led to us all competing with one another to curb our appetite for sin and stop watching anything except the news on TV.

We helped each other to practice more and more strictly, passing out books and pamphlets on various topics relevant to women and the home and family. It was as if, by being more obedient, we could earn some kind of reward.

One of the sisters, Shanaz, who took the role of teaching most often, explained to me that anything that took your heart and mind away from the worship or thoughts of Allah was evil.

"We can only have one love in our hearts," she stated. "If you love Allah, then that is all you can have room for in your heart. You cannot allow anything to take your attention away from your God."

The sisters began to talk more about the benefits of an Islamic state. If we could live in a place that put God's law first, we would end all the problems our Western society had fallen prey to. We refused to vote in any kuffar elections (i.e., in countries of non-believers), as we would not support any non-Muslim representative. We collected money to send to Yemen and other Islamic countries struggling with drought and famine. We praised the places where fellow Muslims were fighting for their rights. I felt lucky that we had a connection to Morocco, a Muslim country.

We were all zealous about our religious and spiritual growth, and it wasn't until I saw one of my friends drag her kids off the street, admonishing them for playing with the non-Muslim neighbours, that I wondered if we were doing the right thing. They were just kids playing in the street. I kept my thoughts to myself though, as I didn't want to be lectured or judged for my lack of piety.

The fact that sacrifice was necessary to the spiritual path was not a new concept to me. I had understood sacrifice from a young age. The taming of my exuberance, my love of colour. The "be a good girl and stay quiet" demands. I had been trained to give up my true joy for years, and now being told that the more I gave up, the more Allah would love me and reward me, if not in this life, in the hereafter, made sense. Hadn't all the great spiritual seekers in the past had to undergo great trials and tests? And after all, God only gives you what you can handle. I had already been tested and found my strength. I would continue to prove my worthiness. I knew how this system worked, it was familiar.

My father had been raised by British parents in Kenya and sent to a boarding school at a young age.

Much of his upbringing was typical of the stoic view on parenting and schooling that we make fun of today: don't ever show your feelings; keep a stiff upper lip; keep your chin up, old chap.

This kind of thinking oozed from my father. My mother too was disconnected from her feelings. We lived in a world of shoulds and should nots with no real way of being present to our inner motivations and desires. Perhaps this was the goal of a society that undervalued feelings, to make us more easily led by those in power.

It hadn't yet sunk in that I had only replaced one system with another.

Arriving home after a rare visit with a friend on a particularly beautiful summer day, I felt immediately that something was off. Said hung up the phone looking upset. He had been speaking to his parents.

"What's wrong, baby?" I asked. I had grown fond of his mother. She was overweight and had high blood pressure and diabetes; she could take a turn for the worse at any time. His father, Taher, was still working, although he was into his seventh decade now. He had worked his way up to being the head gardener for the Saudi King's palace in Tangier.

When we first became a couple, Said and I had both sent the money we made in the circus to Morocco for his parents. They had been living in Said's uncle's house for years, and his uncle had finally decided to sell.

Apparently, that meant Said's parents were being evicted, and Said's father had begged us to buy a small plot of land just outside the city and let him oversee building a house there. In the future, we could add another apartment above the ground floor for ourselves.

"My mom is not well," he said. "I don't know what to do."

"What's wrong with her?"

"Her blood pressure and sugars are up quite high, she doesn't feel good. And Dad has two hernias. I am worried about them."

"Maybe we should think of moving there," I said, more as a comfort to Said than with any real plan in mind.

"Oh! Do you think so?" His eyes lit up. "I've never looked after them much. It would mean so much to me to be able to help them."

"Well…" I hadn't expected the conversation to take this turn. It took a few seconds for me to begin contemplating the real practicalities of such a move.

We could do it. The kids had not started school yet, Omaima was just three.

"I wouldn't want to leave before the baby," I said, putting my hands protectively over my belly. I was due in September, not far away now.

"Of course," Said said quickly, then his expression changed to a dreamy look. "I've always imagined doing *Hijra*."

"Hijra?"

"Holy pilgrimage back to the land of Islam!" he said excitedly. "Like the Prophet Muhammad did back to Mecca. We would be following our faith. Allahu Akbar!" He threw his arms around me.

I smiled dazedly. Had we decided then? We were going? I hadn't reckoned my Saturday being blown off track by this new direction. I had planned on doing some laundry and sitting down with a cup of tea.

The baby kicked inside me, and I felt I could have kicked something myself. That old feeling of being overwhelmed rose up and brought tears to my eyes. There seemed to be no end to the changes and struggles of being a good Muslim. Would I ever be good enough? I felt I was being shoved into a smaller and smaller box. My breath caught in my chest, there was no more room for me to feel.

That Wednesday, as I got ready to go to my morning study group, I glanced nervously in the mirror. Would I like living in Morocco? Could I leave all my friends and my life here in England? I sighed. It wasn't like I hadn't done it all before, left everything and everyone I knew and cared about to change my life. I looked down at my huge belly. How had I ended up here? I was trying to be a good wife, trying to make his dream come true, but now…Morocco?

I picked up my Arabic textbook and my purse.

"I'll see you in two hours, Said," I called upstairs.

"Okay, have fun," he mumbled sleepily. I could hear the girls crawling around in our bedroom. They had eaten and I'd changed their diapers. Hopefully they would survive my short absence.

I arrived at the sister's house a little out of breath. Having babies was not working for my physical fitness. It seemed like months since I'd had time to go for a proper walk. I smiled and sat in the circle, but my head was not really in the learning zone today.

"*Alif, baa, taa,*" we repeated after Aabida, the teacher. We looked at diagrams of the mouth and throat, where the letters were supposed to come from. "*Kaf, qaf,*" she said, demonstrating. The first sound came easily, like our English *K*; the second sounded like she was swallowing the sound as she said it. I tried again, almost choking. We all laughed. It was a nice group of Muslim sisters, two of us were English converts and the others were Pakistani. We had all wanted to learn to read the Holy Quran in Arabic. It seemed to take us a long time to learn the letters. We had begun to put the sounds together and read short words with the vowel sounds written over the Arabic consonants. I did not understand all of the words we read, but Arabic is a mercifully logical language, unlike English, and it's possible to sound out the words with a beginner's knowledge of the alphabet.

"Okay, now we will memorize another verse of the Quran," Aabida said, opening her copy of the holy book. We listened to her recite a line and then tried to copy her tone and inflection. It was still hard to get my tongue around the words, but the poetry was unmistakably beautiful. Over and over we chanted. My body rocked to the soothing rhythm of the verses. After half an hour, we blessed the Quran and finished the lesson with tea and cookies. I relished this time with my friends, other women who were living the same life as me. We all had children or were pregnant, and we all stayed at home. The demands of housekeeping and the duties of being good Muslim wives and mothers kept us busy.

"Said and I are thinking of doing Hijra," I told my friends as we sipped our tea.

"Really? That's so amazing!"

"I don't know how you have the courage, sister Aishah."

"Yes, I don't think I could do that."

I smiled inside with what I took to be praise of my sincerity in my religion and my courage to make sacrifice for Allah. "We have a house there with my parents-in-law, but it doesn't have electricity or running water yet. The people there are nice though."

"Will you wait to have your baby here?"

"Yes, I have to sort out shipping our things, and we may go to Canada to see my family before we move there permanently." I reached for a cookie.

"That is so great, you will have to write and tell us all about it."

"Yes, of course. I will miss you all." My voice wavered slightly. I hadn't known these women that long, about three years, but they were all I had since I had embraced Islam so strongly; my past had been erased when I took the Shahada. Now I would find the strength to give up these new friends, to go to Morocco, and live with my husband's family. I couldn't really bear to feel my loss. I was used to locking away my feelings, so what I was experiencing now was familiar. It even felt good in a way, the pain of sacrifice bringing some feeling of life in my body.

I suddenly felt tired and shivered slightly. "It's getting late and I left the girls at home with Said. I should go and see how they are doing." I put my teacup on the tray and tightened the scarf around my head. Standing up I felt a little dizzy, too long sitting cross-legged on the floor.

"May Allah bless you," I said, thanking Aabida for the lesson and tea. I fastened my veil over the scarf and lowered the burka over my head. I slipped my gloves on, picked up my Quran, and waved to the others. "Assalamu alaikum. See you soon, *inshallah*."

The next few weeks passed quickly. Packing and organizing our lives for an international move required many hours of planning and phone calls.

"Said, I was thinking." We were sitting together in the TV room on one of those rare evenings when the kids were in bed and Said was home; I was folding laundry. "We are shipping a whole container to Tangier. We should maybe collect some extra kids' clothes and toys and things and take them to give to the neighbours and less well off families in Val Fleuri," I said, referring to the suburb of Tangier where we'd be living. "I found out that it costs the same amount, whether we fill the container or not, so we should probably fill it. The people there could use the things, and I know the sisters would help me collect some nice stuff."

"Sure, that sounds like a great idea." Said smiled at me. "You always think of other people. *Mashallah*. May Allah bless you. Your face is lit up with noor, the light of Islam."

I blushed and looked down. "I'll talk to the sisters tomorrow. It will be nice to be able to take some things to that poor family with the sheep, the one that lives behind our house." On our visit to Morocco the previous year, I had looked down onto their roof from ours. They had ten children, the youngest the same age as Omaima. Their house was only one floor, and I had often watched the younger ones playing on the roof while the older sister was doing laundry. They had been so excited to have our young family with kids right next door. They had come over every day and asked to play with Omaima. *It will be good to move there*, I thought. The girls will play outside more in the nicer weather, and the people in our neighbourhood looked out for one another. I smiled to myself. We were pleasing Allah, and things would go better for us.

The generosity of the other sisters over the next few weeks was overwhelming. They brought boxes of toys and children's clothing. It is one of the five pillars of Islam that you must be charitable, so many of my friends were taking this as the perfect opportunity to fulfill that tenet. I did as much packing as I could; we didn't want to pay for the movers' time as well as the transport. A couple of weeks before my third baby was due, we had everything ready to ship.

A huge flatbed truck rolled up outside our house with a container on the back. Two men came to the door and rang the bell while I was giving the kids their breakfast. I put a few scraps of toast on Safia's high-chair tray and told Omaima to sit at her table.

"Said! The movers are here!" I shouted upstairs as I scrambled to put my scarf and veil on over my pajamas. At least the burka covered up whatever I was or wasn't wearing. Said was getting out of bed, but I went to open the door, as the men had already been waiting long enough.

"Hi, come on in," I said a little breathlessly. "My husband is just coming to show you where everything is." The men looked a bit taken aback at my black getup, and they were hesitant to come in. I was getting used to this reaction from people that weren't Muslim. It kind of made me feel powerful, in a way. They couldn't see me, but I could see them. Since women weren't supposed to be seen or be in the midst of men unless absolutely necessary, I breathed a sigh of relief and backed away into the kitchen when Said came down the stairs. The movers looked relieved too, and they stepped into the hallway.

"All the boxes in the upstairs hall are ready to go, and the only big furniture is the sideboard and table,"

I called out from behind the kitchen door.

Said led the way, and I heard boots clumping on the stairs. I peeked out the window from time to time, watching the boxes disappear into the back of the container. I crouched down at the small table with Omaima, not wanting them to see me through the panes. I reached up and drew the curtains across. I was getting used to not being seen, and it felt like second nature to hide with the kids whenever there were men visiting. It felt safe and kind of cosy to sit and drink my tea with the girls, looking at a picture book, staying out of the way.

With three of them working, it didn't take long to clear out all the carefully packed boxes. Said knocked on the kitchen door, and I stood back out of sight as he came in to speak to me about the paperwork. I looked over the forms and made sure the addresses were right. He signed the bottom and took it back to the movers. Our stuff was officially gone. We had kept just the essentials in Manchester. The container would take a couple of months to ship to Tangier, so it would get there just before us, hopefully.

I suddenly felt overwhelmingly tired. I was almost at my due date, and my body felt much heavier and sore with this pregnancy. This was the third time in as many years, and I was feeling the strain.

I had decided to try having this baby at home with a midwife. I had wanted to try a natural, home birth from the time of my first pregnancy, but the reality of the experience had overwhelmed me the first time. The second baby had been much easier, and I had left hospital a few hours after giving birth to Safia. This third pregnancy, although tiring, had gone well, and I felt confident that I could do it without all the hassle of being in hospital. My parents were coming to stay for a couple of weeks, and the plan was for them to help with the other two girls so Said would be free to stay with me.

We passed the last week of my pregnancy just keeping up with daily chores. My parents were staying in a nearby hotel this time, as there wasn't much space with us now. On Saturday I woke up with cramps, and as the morning progressed they began to feel more like contractions. I called the midwife and she said she would check in with me every hour or so. I tried to keep the normal routine for the girls through the morning. Said got up after a bit and went to get my parents.

After lunch the midwife came over with a student, and we talked between contractions as I paced up and down the living room. By three o'clock I was getting cranky, and the pains were intense and close together. My mom suggested that she and my dad take the girls out for ice cream and maybe to the park. I smiled weakly and said that would be great.

"Why did I ever think it was a good idea to have another baby?" I whined to anyone who would listen. I didn't have much time to reflect on that before the next contraction made me sink against the wall. "I think

I might need to lie down soon," I said weakly.

"We can go upstairs to your bed if you like," the midwife said brightly. She was much too chipper for my mood.

"Okay," I growled back as I led the way upstairs. I had prepared the bed a week ago with a plastic sheet and old sheets and blankets. Said helped me to change into a nightie, and I crawled onto the bed, my belly hard and tight. "Ugh…"

The midwife brought in the nitrous oxide and set it up beside the bed. "You let me know if you want to start using the gas," she instructed cheerfully.

Said shuffled around uncomfortably and muttered something about maybe going to pray. I grabbed his shirt and pulled him next to me as the next contraction exploded. "Don't go! I need you here."

He looked helplessly at the midwife, but she just smiled at him and turned back to me as I started moaning. "I think you are almost there! Almost time to push," she said, sounding like a sports coach. "Would you like to use the gas now?"

"Yes," I hissed, as I was gripped by pain again. Everything inside me wanted to push, and I grabbed the closest thing to me.

"Ow!" Said yelped. "That's my beard!"

I grabbed the mask frantically as the next pain hit and clamped it over my mouth and nose.

"Breathe in deeply," the midwife instructed. "That's it, you're doing great!"

I clutched the mask with one hand and Said's shirt with the other as I started to push.

The one advantage of having done this twice before is that it actually does get easier. It didn't seem to take long at all before a baby girl was plopped onto my chest, all sticky and warm. I sighed and held her close to me as the midwife busied herself with checking out the umbilical cord and tugging it gently. I felt something warm and slithery, and then she held up the placenta to show me.

"There you go! All done," she stated triumphantly, letting the student midwife prepare and cut the cord. They wrapped up the baby in a blanket and helped me into some disposable pants and a huge pad. I lay back contentedly, very glad to be able to relax in my own bed. Said went to call my parents and then came back to kiss me on the cheek and gloat over the new addition to his growing family.

"Are you disappointed it's not a boy?" I asked him tentatively.

"I love her, I love all my girls," he said smiling at me. "Are you happy?"

"Yes," I smiled back, "I am."

Omaima and Safia exploded into the room, followed by my parents.

"Mama! It's a baby!" Omaima squeaked excitedly. Safia looked confused as she saw the new baby in my arms. I held out my arm to stop them jumping on my still tender body.

"Come here," I said quietly. "Carefully, don't hurt

the new baby. She is still very delicate."

"I want to hold it! Can I hold the baby?" Omaima bounced up next to me and Safia crawled up as well, peering over her excited sister's shoulder.

"Sit here next to me, habiba," I said directing her wiggly arms and legs into a sitting position. "Hold your arms out. There you go!" I placed the baby in her arms, and she gazed transfixed at the small hands and feet.

"Was I this tiny, Mommy?" she asked, incredulous.

"Yes, I guess you were when you were born." I smiled. "You have grown so big, I almost forgot."

"What's her name?"

I looked over at Said. He had had the final say in naming our children so far, although I had suggested the name Omaima for our firstborn. We had usually picked out both a boy's and a girl's name, to cover the bases.

"Her name is Hind," Said said. "She was a famous convert to Islam. I'll have to tell you the story about her."

"Tell me the story about our names too!" Omaima said. "Here, Mommy, the baby wants you again." And she helped as I brought the baby to my chest.

"Did you want to hold her too?" I asked Safia, who was still sitting by my feet sucking her fingers. She shook her head. "You look tired, sweetheart. Are you ready for bed? Did you have something to eat with Granny and Grandpa?"

"We had tea and sandwiches and ice cream." My mom jumped in with all the details. "Maybe I can give the girls a bath and get them ready for bed?"

I nodded gratefully. I didn't want to have to get up yet. I still felt exhausted from the birth, and I needed to try and breastfeed the new baby, who was fussing more now.

"Thanks, that would be great." I gave her a small smile. "Maybe Said can help me diaper Hind and get sorted out here." The midwife and her student had packed up and were ready to leave. She said she'd be back tomorrow to check in with me and the baby.

"You did a fantastic job. Congratulations." She smiled at everyone and swept out.

I marvelled at her energy and enthusiasm. I felt like I'd been in a train wreck. I sank back into the pillows gratefully. As I held her close, baby Hind wriggled and found my nipple. It was so much easier the third time around, I barely thought about breastfeeding, it all happened without effort now. Only the twinges in my uterus as she suckled reminded me that this time around, it would be more challenging for my uterus to contract. My mind drifted to the upcoming move, which was one step closer now. I was glad to be through the pregnancy phase. The physical recovery could start, and I could move on to the next hurdle. I didn't take much time these days to savour the moment. Each one seemed so full of other people's needs, I didn't want to stop, afraid I would be overwhelmed by the gathering swell.

Chapter
Seven

THE DAY FINALLY CAME WHEN it was time to leave. We had packed our last suitcase, and Said had loaded it into the car. I had fastened the three car seats into the back seat and done a final check of the house. I had bought diapers and snacks and packed toys and books so I could get to them easily. The three-day drive to Tangier was never easy, but this time we were going for good. It was exciting and scary at the same time. I looked at Said and grabbed my purse, with all our ferry tickets and information in it. I had flipped my veil up over my burka so I could see better, but as we closed the door of our house for the last time, I lowered it over my face. A couple of the brothers had stopped by to see us off, and I got in the car quickly so they wouldn't feel awkward having a woman around while they were talking to Said.

The girls were all buckled in, and I was anxious to get started, as we had to make the ferry over to France by the afternoon. Said shook hands and came around to the driver's side. He looked like a sheikh in his white kandora and short trousers. His sunglasses made his dark curly hair stand out, and I flushed with pride that he was my husband. The girls were fussing already, and I appeased them with reading a story as we pulled out of the driveway and headed off.

I had always liked travelling, and over the last couple of years I had gained tricks for travelling with young children. I had lots of snacks, I bought disposable diapers instead of trying to use cloth ones and keep them in a bucket until our destination. I let Said drive and I entertained the kids, and when we stopped to give Said a break, I took the girls for a walk away from the car, so he could sleep for a short time. I talked to him to make the time pass more quickly, and in some ways, our times travelling were some of the best. He told me about his older brother leaving to fight in the Sahara, and about his sisters, who joined the circus when he was only ten. He shared intimate details about his life and experience growing up in Morocco in the late sixties and early seventies. I listened, fascinated. His life was so different from mine. Some parts sounded magical, and some things brought out my sympathy. I felt awe and compassion, in a way that felt like love. I was enamoured of him and eternally grateful that I could be part of his life now to support him and help him. Me converting to Islam meant so much to him. He would speak of it and tears would glisten from the corners of his eyes. He felt that his life was worthy because he had helped me to come to the right path. At these moments, the hardships of my daily routine faded away. I felt I could endure anything for Allah if I stayed in this feeling of gratitude.

The journey seemed to blur, three days and nights of driving, eating, and keeping the girls from screaming in the car. Said and I would exchange looks and focus on our destination in an effort to keep our minds off the fussing and crying from the back seat. The ferry crossings between England and France and again between Spain and Morocco were a welcome time to stretch our legs. The girls were happy to be out of the car, and it was exciting to go on deck and watch the waves. It seemed like a dream when we finally pulled up next to our house in Tangier. Said's sister was watching from the flat roof, and when she realized it was us in the car, she called out and came running down the stairs.

"Du du, a ta, a ta!" Her voice came out awkwardly, although her excitement was obvious. I smiled and kissed her on both cheeks. Her grip was surprisingly strong, and I flinched as she squeezed my stiff shoulders. Her noise had alerted Said's parents that we had arrived, and they came out to greet us. I struggled to free the extremely wiggly girls from their car seats. They stood next to the car, shyly taking in the excited adults around them. Said's mother kissed me a number of times before moving on to the kids and Said.

"*Marhaba! Marhababik,*" his parents said. Said's father did a little jig in front of the girls that made them laugh.

"Come in, come and eat." His mother wanted to usher us upstairs to the kitchen right away, with her usual Moroccan hospitality.

"Just a minute, Ma," Said said. "We will bring in our things first." His father grabbed a bag and shuffled into the house. The last time we were here, the house was only one level with the kitchen on the roof. Now the house towered three storeys high, and the neighbour's house had been built up on the opposite side of our road. It felt much more constricted, I could feel the city closing in around us. The sounds of people and smells of cooking drifted out of the other houses. An older lady hobbled past with a black plastic bag from the local corner shop. She smiled and nodded at us, peering at the girls curiously.

Said's father led the way up the stairs. "Look how we have built your apartment!" he said. Each step was wide enough to accommodate a luscious looking green plant, all in huge terracotta pots. Even in my exhausted state, I couldn't help feeling awe at the beautiful tiles and whitewashed walls. At the top of the first flight of stairs was a thick wooden door leading to our new apartment. The bathroom was still unfinished and mostly housed three big barrels that Said's father had filled with water for us to use. I noticed the toilet and bidet were in as well as the bathtub and sink, although there was no running water in the house yet.

The door to our apartment opened up into a huge living space. Moroccan-style sofas edged the back wall, and a beautiful carpet ran the entire length of the room. A coffee table sat in the centre covered by a white, plastic lace tablecloth. The scent of jasmine wafted in the open windows. It was inviting and the girls ran to sit up on the sofas. There was one main bedroom off the living room, and two tiny rooms with a hall that led to a small balcony. A couple of mattresses lay on the ground in one of the small rooms, and a double bed was made up in the main bedroom. There were no wardrobes or cupboards; I guessed this was because people didn't have as much stuff in Morocco. A couple of hooks on the back of the door were usually enough to hang a dress or two and a jellaba and scarf. A set of drawers was propped on the far side of the main bedroom for underwear or important papers and things. It was also indicative of the way my life would be here, busy with cooking and cleaning and children. Any "free" time could be spent chatting with the other women in the late afternoon on the steps of our house, as the street ran right along the front of the houses. The communal space was most important, the way the sofas enclosed the living room showed how much this was a part of the life here. Private space was almost non-existent. My individualism took a step further inside. Here it was most important to fit in and be a part of the family.

My father-in-law had commandeered a very small patch of ground in front of our house as a garden and had somehow coaxed tomatoes and fennel and even sunflowers to grow there. He really did have a magic touch with plants. Said had told me that he often left for work at four thirty in the morning and didn't get home until after dark, around seven. He did this six days a week. He was close to retirement age and was extremely lucky to look forward to a small pension from the Saudi palace, as Morocco had no state pension. It was common for extended families to live together in one house to pool resources and help look after more vulnerable members.

Said's sister came in carrying a big silver tray with tea glasses and a silver pot, the enticing aroma of mint wafting in with her. She set the tray on the table and instructed her mother to begin pouring us tea while she went to get the snacks. This was all done by hand signals punctuated by grunts and guttural sounds, which Said also seemed to understand. We all nodded enthusiastically at her, and she hurried off upstairs to get the food. I helped Safiyya to cool the tea for the girls, and they hopped excitedly by the table waiting to taste it. Hind, who was almost six months old, was beginning to fuss; I held her on my lap. Safiyya motioned that she would take her, but I smiled and shook my head, pointing at my boobs. I sat back and leaned against the tiled wall so I could nurse Hind more comfortably. I couldn't quite believe we were finally here. For good.

I allowed my eyelids to close for a second as I sat and
listened to Said talk with his parents. I still couldn't
understand much of the Moroccan dialect, and for now,
I was just happy to be in the background. Hind suckled
contentedly, and I sipped the aromatic mint tea. The
girls hung excitedly around the table where Fatima,
Said's sister, was keeping them supplied with *baghrir*,
a special type of pancake with a thick layer of hazelnut
chocolate spread rolled up inside. It was getting late in
the afternoon, and the adhan rang out from the mosque.

Allahu Akbar, Allahu Akbar.
Ashhadu anna la ila ill Allah.
Ashhadu anna Mohammadan rasul Allah.
Hayya alas salah.
Hayya alal falah.
Allahu Akbar, Allahu Akbar.
La ilah ill Allah.

The first couple of weeks in our new home passed in a
whirlwind of unpacking, visiting Said's extended family,
and getting used to life without running water and many
of the other comforts of life in England. The mattress
was harder than I was used to in the UK and Canada.
Here they still stuffed the cloth with sheep's wool and
straw, and this sat on top of the wooden bed frame.
I found my black burka and veil cumbersome and
quickly adopted the local women's way of dressing:
leggings and undershirt with a dress over top made

of stretchy knit material. Most women wore a smaller white cotton headscarf around the house, knotted around the back of the neck and around your hair to keep it out of the way while cleaning and cooking. I also asked Said to get me a *mendeel*, a woolen cloth that was worn around the waist as a combination of apron and blanket, also useful as a baby blanket or to tie one of the girls on my back. His family laughed at me for being such a "village girl," but I kind of liked the wholesome, practical style as opposed to the "city" women, who wore bright dresses and jewellery that seemed wholly nonsensical when I spent most of my day bent over washtubs or chasing toddlers.

Safiyya prepared many of our meals upstairs in the communal kitchen, and I appreciated the help as I was still getting used to my new role of Moroccan housewife. She was an excellent cook and seemed to relish the opportunity to impress us with her delicious dishes that ranged from traditional Moroccan to French cuisine. She had worked most of her life as a cook for a French family, and her food was delicious. She had learned much although both she and Said's father were illiterate. I was amazed at how they could both work such long, physically demanding hours. I was no match for her at all!

Said's father went every morning to get French baguettes and croissants for us, and the girls loved the *pain au chocolat*. Milk came in small cartons, and we usually needed three or four of these to make the milky coffee and hot chocolate for the girls. When I went upstairs to join the family for breakfast a few days after our arrival, I caught Said speaking with his father in hushed tones, looking upset.

"What's wrong?" I asked.

"My dad keeps asking for money for the food he gets for us, the croissants and milk. It's stressing me out. We don't have that much money left."

"Well, tell him not to bring all that stuff every day. We don't need fancy bread all the time." I couldn't help my voice sounding a little edgy; money was a touchy subject between us. The expense and stress of moving to another country had drained our small resources, and the reality of living in Morocco where there were no government social supports was starting to sink in. I had not fully realized how much we had relied on the system in the UK to support our needs. It was all very well to make Hijra to a Muslim country, but I was having my doubts about Allah being able to literally provide for us.

Said's mother looked worried. She asked in Arabic what I was saying. She could tell I was upset but could not understand why. Said shuffled uncomfortably and tried to explain. I could tell it was not going over very well, as his mother pursed her lips angrily. Said placated her by kissing her forehead.

"Why don't we just have regular bread for breakfast for a while?" I suggested.

The girls, who had been increasingly fidgety during this exchange, finally made their presence known by running in and out of the door to the roof.

"Come on, girls, we are going to have breakfast now," I called impatiently. "Come and wash your hands again, and try to sit nicely now." Keeping the girls' hands clean to eat was a greater problem than you might think in Morocco. Taher kept pigeons on the roof, for food and to sell. The birds wandered freely in and out of the kitchen area, and the girls were constantly entertained by chasing them around the roof. I sat Omaima and Safia firmly down in the corner of the sofa and wiped their hands with a wet rag. Nothing was wasted here; old cloth was cut up for use as cleaning rags or to wrap up food in the fridge. Fatima had a whole pile of neatly cut up cloths to use during her period, as sanitary pads were quite expensive.

Safiyya placed a big plate of olives drizzled with olive oil in the middle of the table, and Said broke off pieces of fresh bread and passed them around. We had already bought the milk, so steaming cups of milky coffee were set down for Said and Fatima and me. Said's parents preferred the traditional mint tea.

"Bismillah," I said, pointedly looking at the girls. "Thank Allah for your food."

"Bismillah," they chimed in, making Said's parents beam with pride.

We all dipped our bread into the olive oil and picked up the olives themselves. It is hard to explain how delicious this simple meal can taste when everything is fresh and you are hungry.

"Are we going to go shopping at the market today?" I asked Said.

"Okay, we can do that." He turned and said something to his mother. "Ma will come with us and help get the best deal. You have to bargain for everything."

I smiled and nodded in her direction. I still felt overwhelmed hearing only the Moroccan dialect. I wanted to understand and be able to communicate more. It was frustrating to only be able to say things indirectly through Said. I was never quite sure that he put things across in the way that I meant them. In any case, his mother usually advocated for me when I wanted to buy something, so it was just as well she was coming. As if she read my mind, she said something to Said and looked pointedly at me.

"What did she say?" I asked.

"She wants you to make sure you dress the girls up to go out. It's important to have your children looking their best out in public, or people will think we don't look after them or that we are poor."

"What's wrong with being poor?" I asked.

"People pity you, and you are looked down on, as second-class citizens," Said answered vehemently. "Just make sure they look nice, in dresses, and you, put your best jellaba and scarf on."

"I don't see the point, if we are just traipsing around a dirty old marketplace," I grumbled under my breath. Said glared at me when his mother looked the other way, and I dutifully fell silent. An hour or so later, I presented myself and the girls.

"How do we look?"

"Very nice, sweetheart." Said brushed my lips with his. "I'll tell Ma we are ready to go."

The girls and I made our way downstairs. Said knocked to tell his mother we were ready, and she came out wearing a red jellaba and a cream scarf over her large frame. She was wearing actual shoes, which looked out of place, as I realized I had hardly ever seen her in anything other than the plastic sandals everyone wore around the house. She carried a small change purse, and as she came out into the entryway, I could hear Fatima calling out to her and making frantic signs.

"What does Fatima want?" I whispered to Said.

He chuckled. "She wants us to get her some candy."

Said nodded vigorously in her direction, and she smiled and waved.

I had still not tried driving in Tangier, and I was glad Said was behind the wheel as we wound our way through crowded, narrow streets. The main market was down in the old part of the city, which was built long before cars. We found a parking spot in the main square, and I got the two older girls out of their car seats with firm instructions to behave and stay with me the whole time. I had left Hind at home with Fatima, as she wasn't walking yet and I didn't want to have to carry her the whole time. Said's mother confidently led the way into one of the alleyways. The stalls were crowded on both sides, and it was hard to take it all in. Most people bought food at the market almost every day. Everything was fresh, and there was not much freezer or storage space in the houses here. You would buy what you needed for the day and go home and cook it right away. The girls stayed close to me, and I felt kind of sorry for them as they wouldn't be able to see much at their height.

We headed down a side row, which seemed to be a clothing area. All the stalls looked the same, with leggings and socks in bins at the front, while hanging behind the vendors were cute children's outfits and coats. Safiyya stopped at one particular stall and introduced Said to the vendor, who seemed to know her well. He stooped down to kiss the girls and gave them each a candy. Said looked at me and pointed to the outfits hanging up.

"It's almost Ramadan. My mom says we could pick something out for the girls to give them at Eid."

I looked around. Matching skirts and tops, or leggings and sweaters, were paired together in sets. It looked kind of cheesy to me, not at all what I would have picked for the girls, but "when in Rome" came to mind and I sighed in resignation. I tried to look enthusiastic about picking something out. Safiyya was obviously trying hard to please me and the girls. I smiled and nodded at a couple of outfits, and we held them up to check the size.

"These are good." I nodded to Said, and the bartering began.

Safiyya haggled and argued with the vendor for

a few minutes, bringing up his family's friendship to our family, and then seemed to lose patience. She told us angrily to walk away. A bit bewildered, I followed her with the girls holding my hands. We only got a few paces before the man came running after us, begging us to come back and promising that he would lower the price. Safiyya beamed and walked back, looking to Said for the money to pay. He was chatting with a friend and seemed a bit put out at the interruption, but he handed over the money and rolled his eyes at his friend.

Safiyya proudly took the bag with the kids' clothes, and we headed in the direction of women's wear. Said called out that he would just have coffee with his friend around the corner while I shopped for some leggings and undershirts for myself. I scowled after him. I didn't like shopping at the best of times, and being left to fend for myself with his mother, whom I barely understood and who seemed to have very different ideas of what kind of clothes I should buy, made me irritable. I think she could tell I was unhappy, because her face took on a worried look. I hurriedly smiled at her and obligingly picked out some warm leggings and undershirts, as the damp rainy months could feel quite cold here. I pointed at her and then at the leggings and tried to indicate she should buy some for herself as well. She shook her head but I pushed the money Said had given me into her hand and nodded vigorously. She picked out some under garments as well and seemed pleased. On the other side of the aisle was a stall with some candy and snacks, so we bought some for Fatima. The girls were getting tired, and I pointed at the yogurt drinks, wanting to give them a snack.

It was surprising how much they could fit into the cramped alleys of the marketplace. We rounded the corner to find a couple of picnic tables outside a café stall. Said was sitting there with his friend, and they moved over to let Omaima and little Safia climb up beside them with their snacks. Said proudly patted them on the heads, and his friend expertly helped Omaima with her straw. My mother-in-law and I waited on the other side. I looked around at the other stalls, wishing I had the time to explore the market more. I knew Said wanted his mother to be happy with our shopping excursion but did not want to spend too much money. I resignedly turned back, and in a few minutes Said called me over to help gather the girls up. I nodded modestly toward his friend without looking directly at him, and lifted Safia up on my hip. She was looking tired, ready for a nap.

"We should probably go home," I said quietly to Said.

"Okay then," he whispered back. "Omar! It's been wonderful to see you, my brother!" he said in Arabic, holding out his hand to his friend. "Come and visit us soon." His mother added her voice and asked that he say hello to his parents and family from us. I realized I was beginning to understand some common phrases. With more kisses for the girls and praising Allah, we

finally backed away and headed back in what I hoped
was the direction of the car. Everything looked the same
in the market, and I felt a bit lost. We emerged into
bright daylight, and I recognized the main square we
had started from.

I put the kids in the car and we headed for home.
I wasn't sure how I would ever be able to come out
shopping on my own; it seemed completely overwhelming.
I sank back in my seat and put my hand on Safia's arm,
needing to feel the comfort of just holding my children.

The days began to blend into one another as the
weeks passed. We had enrolled Omaima and Safia in
a local *hadana*, a nursery. They went in the morning and
afternoon with a break for lunch. I kind of enjoyed the
walk back and forth to take them and pick them up.
It was a welcome relief from the seemingly never-ending
chores at home. I had never thought of myself as lazy,
but housework was taken to a whole new level here than
I had experienced in either England or Canada. We still
had no running water in the house, and for now, Said's
mother and I got up really early once or twice a week
to hand wash all the clothes and sheets using a hose
running from the neighbour's house.

Today was one of those days, and the alarm went
off at four thirty. I rolled over groggily and turned off
the clock, groaning as I hoisted myself up to a sitting
position. My body had not accustomed itself to the
hard mattress yet either, and even though I was only
thirty, I was finding my joints stiff and achy in the

morning. It was January, and until the sun came up later, it felt cold and miserable. I reached out for my leggings and undershirt and pulled them on, followed by a dress and my woollen mendeel, which stopped the cold water from splashing all over my clothes. I tied my hair up and wrapped a scarf to hold it out of my face.

I leaned over and prodded Said.

"You should go to the mosque and pray Fajr," I whispered.

"Mm hm," he mumbled, rolling over.

"Go," I prodded. "You'll feel better to go and pray."

"Can you put the kettle on for me, baby?" he asked.

"Alright," I said, getting up. "I'll put it on but then I'm going up to do the washing with your mom."

"Okay," he answered.

I filled the kettle from the water barrel in the bathroom and lit the burner over the gas bottle. Part of me was glad to leave the rest to him and head upstairs to the early morning peacefulness on the roof.

I put a sheet down on the floor and loaded all the dirty laundry onto it. As I gathered it up, it seemed like a huge pile. How did we get so many dirty clothes so quickly? I grunted as I hoisted the bundle onto my back and trudged upstairs to the roof. Safiyya already had a bucket of water heating and the washtubs all lined up. I really appreciated her kind heart.

"Good morning," I said, smiling as I dropped the huge bundle onto the roof. She looked worried by how much there was but quickly pasted a smile on her face and set to work sorting the clothes into colours and whites. We sprinkled Tide powder into the tubs, and I held the hose to fill them up with water. Two huge tubs for washing and as many smaller tubs as we could gather for the rinsing. She packed the clothes to soak in the soapy water and we added some of the hot water too, so our hands didn't have to freeze quite so much.

She set the washboard up on the side and leaning over from the waist started scrubbing the clothes. I watched as I held the hose, still filling the tubs. I was impressed with her skill, as she deftly scrubbed and twisted the clothes, dumping them into the first rinse tub. The tubs were full and I hooked the hose over the edge of a large barrel, which we filled up for use during the week. I stooped over the smaller tub and began to swish the clothes around and wring them out, dumping them into an empty bucket, ready to be hung on the line. We worked in silence for a while, as the sky slowly began to turn lighter just above the horizon. I enjoyed the feeling of working together and was starting to feel some pride in our two lines of clean clothes flapping in the early morning breeze.

I stopped to look over the wall at the men returning from morning prayer. In groups of twos or threes they walked slowly back to their houses, shaking hands and talking quietly. I checked the water level in the barrels; seeing they were all full, I took the hose and carried it gingerly downstairs, pulling it along as I went. I set it to fill our barrels downstairs, as Said and his dad came up the stairs.

"Hey, can you watch the hose for a bit? I'm still helping your mom with the washing." I handed him the hose and traipsed back upstairs before he had time to complain.

Said's father nodded hello as I passed him on my way to the roof. He sat down on the foam seat in the kitchen and put his feet up. I stepped back out into the cool morning air. The sun was coming up properly now, and the last clothes were in the rinse tub. Safiyya was emptying the dirty water into the corner where a drain emptied out onto the street below. I motioned to her to go and sit down and I would finish. My hands were raw and red from the combination of cold water and the detergent. I twisted the last few things to squeeze out as much water as I could and carried the bucket over to the last empty line of the four wires strung up across the roof. Turning my face to the sun as it appeared over the horizon, I took a deep breath. I was exhausted but also satisfied with a good day's work.

I was ready to eat. I felt like I could devour a huge plate of fried eggs, and hot coffee sounded like heaven. I was grateful to see that Safiyya was preparing the food, and I went downstairs to see if the girls were awake yet. Not quite nine o'clock in the morning, and we had already done so much!

We had been in Morocco for a few months now, and I was beginning to feel settled. While the girls were at nursery school, Hind spent quite a lot of time upstairs with her grandmother and aunt, leaving me able to cook and clean without too much interruption. I had, by now, insisted on having my own gas burner and small oven downstairs. Sharing everything with Said's parents had been too much for me to bear. Everything I did was not right. My loaves of bread were a strange shape, not the flat round ones common here. I liked to have the kids' toys and crafts out in the living room instead of having all our personal items hidden away. I didn't wash clothes right, I didn't clean the floors right, I didn't know how to plump the pillows right. I didn't want net curtains in my apartment. I realized I would never fit in and be the perfect daughter-in-law. Having my own space was necessary for self-preservation.

My sister-in-law would tell on me if I left the house to go and get milk by myself, or if I went for a walk. They said they were worried about someone taking advantage of me because I didn't speak Moroccan. I appreciated their concern, but I was going crazy in the house all day. The only times I could go out were when I walked the girls to their school.

Walking back from the nursery I had a view of the whole neighbourhood where we lived. Most of the houses were not finished. Only part of them was whitewashed, and most had bits of metal sticking up in the corners of the roof, bricks lying around in piles. It was usual to start building one floor and move in but keep building upwards as you had more money. Often, people put a garage on the ground floor. This could be rented out as a shop or some other business. Moroccans

were the most enterprising people. One man had started
a business typing up letters for people who were illiterate,
which was almost half the population, even then, in
2003. Another had put in a small sink and started a
barber shop. There were a couple of chairs and a table
outside on the street, and the area was already becoming
a hub for men to meet and discuss their affairs. A young
boy of ten or eleven came out of the house next to the
barber shop with a tray set for tea. The men thanked
him and sent him on another errand to get some bread
and cheese from the corner store on the next street.

Unfortunately, for many kids, school was not an
option. Boys commonly began working at a young age,
helping out older relatives or apprenticing for a few
dirhams, or coins, a week. Girls were needed at home
to help their mothers with younger siblings or with
laundry or sewing if they took in work. The youngest
of the ten children living next to us was sent out with
the family's few sheep every day to graze them on any
land that wasn't built up yet. I marvelled at how even
a four- or five-year-old could do this kind of work.

Said was busy these days, trying to secure a job.
I hardly saw him.

Often, I would go up to the roof at the end of a
long day, when the kids were asleep. The breeze would
caress my cheeks, and I would feel free for a few minutes.
One particular night, as I looked at the stars, tears
sprang to my eyes and I struggled to breathe. I had
complained that morning to Said about not having any

money left. I was trying to have faith, but it was so hard.

"We have to start making money soon," I said impatiently.

"I am trying my best!" he said, rebuking me. "I've been getting to know these brothers that are interested in having a herbal medicine shop in the market in Tangier. I think there may be an opportunity to make a business with them."

I knew his mother had asked him for money that day too, and the dark circles under his eyes showed the stress he was under.

"A business would be good, if you are sure you can make it work. Maybe we could ask the brothers in England for a loan," I suggested.

Said winced and a frown creased his forehead. "I hate asking them for charity."

"You helped them a lot though," I reasoned.

He sighed. "Okay, I'll ask them."

I shifted my position, trying to get comfortable on the sofa. I had been feeling extra tired the last few days and wondered if I was getting sick. I wanted to go to bed, but Said was home this evening for once, and I didn't want to waste the opportunity to see him.

"Do you want me to make us some tea?" I asked, running my hand up his arm.

"Okay, sure." He smiled at me. "That would be nice."

I got up to make tea for my husband. He had been wearing his beard shorter since we moved to Morocco.

And he wasn't so strict about reading the Quran and studying either.

"Are you happy we moved here?" I asked.

He nodded. "Very happy. I need to be near my parents now. They are getting old, and I haven't spent much time with them."

"Are you happy with me?" I asked as I brought the tea back to the sofa.

"Of course I am," he replied. "You are the best thing that has ever happened to me!"

I leaned into him and turned my face up to kiss him. I loved these moments more than anything else, sitting cosily with my husband, feeling loved. All the hardships of the day melted away as I sipped my fragrant mint tea. I was happy just to sit here next to him, with my feet tucked up underneath me. He flicked on the TV and looked through the channels. I watched absent-mindedly, my eyes drooping closed despite my efforts to stay awake.

He nudged my shoulder. "You should go to sleep, baby, you're tired."

"Mm hm…" I mumbled dozily.

"I have to go up and say goodnight to my parents anyway." He straightened up and I lifted my head. I sighed and took the tea tray into my tiny kitchen and got ready for bed. I would have loved to take a hot bath, but we still had not connected our house to the town water supply. So, I washed my face in cold water and brushed my teeth quickly. Our bed was cold and on rainy days in the winter, it could feel damp when you first got in.

I hoped Said would come to bed soon, so I could snuggle next to him for warmth. I had put three or four blankets on the bed, and they weighed down on me. Maybe tomorrow I would take the girls to the bathhouse, the *hamam*. Safiyya would come with me and help wash the girls. My muscles were aching with all the clothes we had washed that morning. It would be worth the few dollars it cost, just to relax for an hour in the warmth of the steamy room.

I awoke with a renewed sense of vigour and anticipation. My skin prickled with excitement at the thought of sitting naked in the steamy heat of the inner chamber of the bathhouse, the girls sliding around happily on their bums and me leaning against the wall in blissful peace and relaxation for an hour. February was cold and damp in Tangier, and some days it felt like you could never get warm, no matter how many layers you put on.

Safiyya was supportive of my plan. I packed a bag with clean clothes and four towels for the girls and me. We could buy soap and shampoo there, from the lady that ran the place. The soap was homemade and looked like brown glue, but it made the most amazing lather, and it was easier than carting stuff from home. The girls were waking up now, bleary-eyed and sleepy, their curly hair sticking up in all directions. Safiyya and I quickly got them fed and ready to go, and we headed up the road to the hamam. It was still early, but the street was busy with taxis and cars and people walking

purposefully to work. We picked our way along the
muddy edge of the road and turned down the lane
to the bathhouse. I hoped it would not be too busy, being
a Saturday morning.

The lady smiled as we came up to her desk to pay
and buy soap. "Good morning," she said in Arabic.

"Good morning." Safiyya did the talking and I
handed her the money. I smiled and herded the girls
into the outer change room. We took off our shoes and
clothes; I hung them up and pushed everything under
the bench. I made sure the towels were on top and easy
to reach, as it felt cold when you came out, and I didn't
want the girls to get sick.

"Mama, can we go in now?" Omaima asked,
hopping from one foot to the other in excitement.

"Yes, I think we are all ready," I replied, grabbing
the soap and our buckets on the way in.

The outer room was a comfortable temperature,
but our destination was the innermost room, closest
to the hot water trough, which was built over a fire pit
under this part of the building. It was dim as we got
farther in, but I could make out a few other women
already reclining inside. We sat the girls near one of the
side walls, and I went to fill our buckets. You could take
as many as you needed, and the water was very hot, so
it was necessary to mix it with cold water from the tap.
I gathered a couple of hot ones, and cold too, and then
brought an empty bucket to mix the two together for
the girls. We each had dippers, which we used to dip

the water and splash over ourselves.

I threw a few bowlfuls of water playfully on the girls and left them to scoot around and enjoy the warmth before I washed them. I sat down and leaned back against the wall. *Ahhh...* I let my eyelids droop as I felt the cold and tension melting away. Little Safia slid over next to me, and her skin felt soft and smooth on mine. I put her on my lap and absently stroked her back as we relaxed into each other. My mother-in-law reached for Hind and pulled her over to wash her. Hind protested at having to sit still, but Safiyya was firm and held her arm as she ladled warm water over her head.

I sighed and roused myself and called Omaima to come and sit near me. I lathered her hair and scrubbed the suds all over her body. I took out one of the round combs they use in Morocco and pulled it through her hair, trying not to hurt her too much when it got stuck in the tangles.

"Let me scrub you, habiba," her grandmother called to her as I finished with her hair. Omaima scooted over to her *aziza*, and I began the same routine with my second daughter.

"Close your eyes tight!" I warned. "I don't want you to get soap in your eyes."

After a preliminary washing, we let the girls relax as we turned our attention to ourselves.

"Shall I scrub your back?" I asked Safiyya. She turned and handed me the loofah. I scrubbed in circles all over her broad back and rinsed it off with water.

Then, handing her back the loofah, I sat down again to wash myself.

I squeezed out my hair and twisted it up out of the way. It had grown quite long since I had been married, although it had lost its old thickness. I poured warm water over my body. It felt so good, I didn't want to stop. My hands rubbed what was left of the soap over my breasts and belly. I looked down and noticed my belly was rounder than I remembered, and I wondered how long it had been since I'd had my period. My breasts were tender and enlarged; maybe it was that time of the month soon. I had kind of lost track of the weeks and months since we had moved to Tangier. Every day passed much the same as the last, and I had not been paying attention.

My mother-in-law saw me lingering over my belly. "Are you pregnant?" she asked. She made a gesture with her hands of a big belly, and my eyes widened.

"I don't know," I gasped. I looked at my three children. Hind was now only a year and a half old, and the older two still seemed like babies themselves. I shrugged back at Safiyya and smiled sheepishly. Now that I thought about it, I hadn't had my period in a couple of months. "I guess I might be, yes," I said, nodding. I leaned back against the wall, suddenly feeling a little dizzy and light-headed. Could I manage another baby?

My mother-in-law cried out in joy and congratulation. "*Binti!* Habiba! Daughter, I am so happy.

We will have a big *aqiqah* for the baby when it comes.
I will invite all the neighbours!"

Her eyes were shining and I couldn't help but feel
some excitement at how happy that made her. I had
to admit, it was nice to feel important, just for being
a mother. I smiled back at her, acknowledging her idea
of hosting a naming party. At times like these, I almost
did feel accepted as one of the family here in Morocco.
We finished washing ourselves and the girls in a much
more convivial spirit, and collected our things to go out
and get bundled up for our walk home. I felt my mood
had improved with the warmth and relaxation of the
bathhouse, and I hoped the girls would be in a quieter
mood when we got home, content to maybe watch
some cartoons and have a snack and leave me to relax
for a while.

I thought about it on the way home, and by the time
we had reached the house, I was convinced I was
pregnant. I knew the signs, I just hadn't been paying
close attention, with all the excitement and stress of
the move and getting used to living in another country.
I invited Said's mother to come in and sit with us for
coffee, and she happily accepted. I found it odd that
she felt the need to be asked before coming into our
apartment to visit, but maybe it was another way the
Moroccans had learned to cope with the often-crowded
living conditions and no personal space.

When we entered our apartment, Said was up
and waiting.

"Have you had breakfast yet?" I asked.

"No, I was waiting for you to get back," he replied, getting up to kiss his mother's cheek and move over for her to sit down. "Come here, my little munchkins!" He opened his arms to the girls and they crawled up beside him.

"Can we watch cartoons, Baba?" Omaima asked.

"There you go, habiba." He changed the channel for her and turned to speak to his mom.

I smiled. It was heartwarming to see them all enjoying time together. I went into my small kitchen to warm the milk and make the coffee. I had a few eggs left but no bread.

"Omaima," I called out, "can you run upstairs and ask Jido for a loaf of bread, and ask if he and Aunt Fatima want to come down for coffee too." I heard Said repeating my request and sending her upstairs as I cracked the eggs into the pan with lots of sizzling olive oil. It had taken me a while to get used to the amount of oil everything was cooked in here. Frying was the norm, and with my newly queasy belly, I felt my hunger pains turning to nausea. I held my breath and poured some of the now steaming milk into a cup with a touch of espresso coffee. I swallowed a mouthful gratefully and managed to put the olives on another plate with some soft cheese.

"Said," I called out, "can you come and get the tray?" I put the cups and the coffee on one tray and handed it to him. Taking the plate of eggs and the other one of olives and cheese, I followed him down the short corridor into our living room. Fatima came in with two loaves of bread, warmed up and wrapped in a tea towel.

"Du du. DU du du." She signed to ask if we needed anything else. Said shook his head and motioned for her to come and sit next to him. Her smile widened and she looked closely at the food I had laid out. Nodding in approval, she broke pieces of the warm bread for the girls and then everyone else and handed them around.

I poured the coffee. "Is your dad coming?" I asked Said. Fatima motioned that he was out at the mosque, and as if on cue, we heard him coming up the stairs, chanting quietly to himself.

"Allah, Allaaahhh, Allah," he sang in a wavering voice. He stopped at our door and knocked while entering, looking pleased to see us all sitting there together. "How are my girls?" he asked the kids, and they grinned up at him with their mouths full of bread.

"Coffee?" I asked him, picking up the empty cup still on the tray.

"Yes! Thank you." He pulled up a chair on the far side of the round table, as the sofa that angled around two sides was full.

I really did like the communal feel of eating together, which we had adopted since moving to Tangier. The food seemed to go further than when it was all portioned out on separate plates. Eggs were cut with the bread, and it was polite to push some across to someone else if you noticed they hadn't eaten much. Safiyya and

Fatima made sure the girls got enough to eat. I could see the children's eyes beginning to droop, and Hind curled up next to me on the sofa. I let myself relax for a few moments, these precious times where everyone was well-fed, clean, and happy. I lived for these moments.

I sighed and sank back into the cushions, holding my coffee mug in both hands. My mind wandered to my belly, and I reached down to feel it. Another baby. I glowed with pride at my ability to procreate so prolifically. Said had said he wanted seven children. It was our responsibility, as Muslims, to have many children and to teach them to be faithful to Allah. I didn't have as much time now to read and study the Quran and the sayings of the Prophet. I missed my sisters in Manchester and the study circles. Life was busy with chores and child care. Still, we had actually moved to live in a Muslim country! We had performed Hijrah, or holy pilgrimage, from a land of unbelievers to a place that had Islam at the core. The older girls had begun to learn Arabic letters and were memorizing parts of the Quran in their preschool. Said glowed with pride when they recited a line or two of the last *surah*, and I had supported their Islamic education by buying them small scarves to wear to school.

Today, being Saturday, was a day off, and so far, it was going well. Fatima got up to wash the dishes for me, and after breakfast Said's parents went upstairs to their own apartment. I had a few rare moments with Said.

"Baby, I have some news…" I ventured tentatively.

We hadn't talked much lately, and I knew he was stressed about finding more permanent work.

"What is it?" he said, absently glancing at his phone.

"Well," I took a deep breath, and hearing my tone, he looked up, "I think I'm going to have another baby."

"Oh!" He sounded more surprised than I expected. "That's great."

Somehow, I didn't feel elated by his response. "Are you happy?" I questioned.

"Yes, yes, of course I'm happy." He came over and kissed me. "Of course I'm happy. You are the mother of my children."

Blushing, I put my head on his chest and let him hold me for a moment. "What are you doing today?" I asked.

"I'm meeting the boys in town. I am also meeting with my friend to try and open a shop in the market."

"Oh, okay."

"What's the matter?" The defensiveness was obvious in his voice.

"Nothing." I shook my head quickly and smiled. "I just wondered if we could go out to the café near the sea sometime soon. I don't get out of the house usually, and it's hard for me. I am used to being able to go around on my own."

"I know, baby. Be patient. Maybe I'll take you to pray in the big mosque next Friday."

That wasn't exactly the outing I was thinking of, but anything where I got to spend time with him would be better than nothing. "Sure," I smiled, "that would be good."

I don't know if it was the pregnancy hormones or the fact that I really hadn't been out of the house much for a few weeks, but in the following days I was extra sensitive and moody. I wanted to snap at his mom every time she called the girls upstairs to give them candy. Just hearing Fatima's voice calling out to see if I was around drove me nuts. I knew she couldn't hear, and her eyes were not that good either, but a part of me wanted to hide instead of going over to tap her lightly on the arm and have her tell me some stupid gossip about someone in the family. Said's dad offered to buy milk for me every morning, which I appreciated, but even that was making my skin prickle in resentment, as it seemed like a ploy to make sure I didn't go out.

When Said did come home in the evening, I was shrewish and not inclined to be the dutiful wife. He tried to reignite our connection by asking for a blow job or sex, which backfired completely. I was tired and unhappy and beginning to wonder if our move to Morocco had been a good idea.

"You need to get out of the house, baby. You've been working too hard here. I'm going to take you to the big mosque tomorrow for Friday prayers. Maybe you'll meet some other women." Said smiled in a paternal way. "I've heard some women have study circles here too.

Maybe you'd like that?"

"Sure, whatever," I growled. I really wasn't in the mood to make small talk to a bunch of Arabic women and to sit through a long talk by the imam, most of which I wouldn't understand, but I said, "I guess that might be good" and tried to sound grateful. I had grown so accustomed to being on my own in the house with the kids that I was nervous to meet new people.

"Okay, good." Said looked relieved. I was positive he just wanted me to meet other women so he wouldn't have to spend time with me himself or try and understand my feelings. Still, I had no other option for an outing, so I shut up and tried to make the best of it.

The next morning, after feeding the girls and getting them dressed, I took them upstairs to spend a couple of hours with Said's mom and Fatima. Safiyya was overjoyed to have them with her. I was always amazed at her capacity to enjoy the girls at all hours of the day or night. She was always welcoming them with open arms, and a pile of stashed away candy. I couldn't imagine ever feeling that way. I mean, I loved my kids, but I couldn't imagine being able to dedicate my time and attention to them in such a selfless way, all the time. Still, it was nice that their grandmother felt like that, even if she did spoil them.

I stepped out of the house with Said, feeling lighter than I had for weeks. We drove to the main mosque in Tangier. The streets were quieter than usual, being Friday morning. Morocco followed the Islamic traditions, and Friday is the Muslim holy day. All the men who are able are required to attend prayers at the mosque, and any women who would like to go are welcome also. In study circle I had learned all the etiquette for attending mosque. I knew I would not be in the same room as Said and the other men. I pulled my veil straight as we parked the car. Said pointed out the women's door around the back.

"I'll see you after prayers, habiba." He squeezed my hand.

I walked nervously past all the men filing in for prayer, keeping my eyes down, and tried not to stumble on the uneven cobblestones. A couple of women entered the back door in front of me and I followed them in, ducking my head as I passed through the low doorway. It took a few seconds for my eyes to adjust to the lack of sunlight inside, but as they cleared, I saw the rack for shoes along one wall, and further on, there was a tap for making ablutions.

I put my shoes on the rack and searched my memory to determine whether I had lost my Wudu, my sacred cleanliness, since this morning. I had not been to the toilet, and I had not farted. I figured I was good to go, and I really didn't want to have to wash here in front of anyone and with all my hijab on. I entered the carpet covered prayer space and moved quickly to one side to make the obligatory two prostrations for the mosque. I glanced around nervously after that, realizing that the imam still had to give his sermon. There were only a few women there, and they mostly looked older than me. Younger women were often too busy to attend Friday prayers. No one really paid me much attention, so I walked over to the ledge at the front of the room and picked up a copy of the Quran. It was peaceful and quiet here, and it was nice not to have the girls crawling all over me for a few minutes, so I settled down with my back to the wall and leafed through the pages. I had learned all of the last chapters of the Quran and could read and recite them in Arabic, although my understanding of the words was sparse. I picked out one I knew and read through it, my lips moving but barely making a sound.

I had gotten through about three surahs when the imam started speaking. I looked up from my recitation and tried to listen. The introductory words I recognized as being the ones said before any spiritual speech. After that, I played a game with myself to see if I could understand the gist of what the talk was about. I could always ask Said later and see if I was right. It didn't take too long for my mind to wander though, and I found the rise and fall of his voice lulling me almost into a trance. I came to with a start as I realized the adhan was being called and it was finally time to pray.

I stood up and approached the other women to line up. I had learned in England that you should touch your shoulders and feet together with the people either side of you, so that Shaitan had no chance to come between you. Here in Morocco though, I found the women were not so keen to be that close. We lined up loosely, forming only two lines across the front of the space. I could see a little through the screen, and the men filled the huge main room of the mosque.

"Allahu Akbar," the imam said, starting the prayer, and I lifted my hands and bowed my head as he recited.

The prayer was over quickly, and I turned to shake hands with the women next to me.

"Are you from Morocco?" one of them asked.

"No," I answered in my limited Arabic. "I'm Canadian."

"Oh!" the two of them cried jubilantly. "You are Muslim now? We are so happy for you!"

With tears in their eyes, they embraced me and kissed both my cheeks. I was somewhat accustomed to the elation of other Muslims when they found out I had converted to Islam, but it was still a nice feeling to be so welcomed and praised for my beliefs. I smiled shyly and answered a few of their questions.

"What is your name?" I understood one of them to ask.

"Aishah," I replied. I had sort of taken on the name Aishah; it was close enough to my birth name of Ailsa.

"Oh!" one of the ladies cried out again. "There is another Canadian Aishah here in Tangier. She comes to visit me, you will have to meet her!"

I nodded and smiled, wondering if it were true that another Canadian woman was in Tangier and had the same name. Would I like her? Would she like me?

I would so love to have a friend who spoke English and understood me. I asked the lady, by motioning with my hand, to write her address down in my notebook and the date of her next gathering. I was excited to meet some more sisters. Said's idea of coming to the mosque was better than I had thought.

Stepping back out into the sunlight, I hovered shyly near the door, waiting to see where Said was. I still felt unused to being out in public in Morocco in my full hijab. The black burka I wore was not typical of what the women wore here. My mother-in-law had told me to wear the Moroccan version of the jellaba and veil, but I had stubbornly refused. Wearing the Saudi style burka had been a symbol of piety in the UK, and I was loath to give that up just to blend in. But here, in the busy town centre, I felt conspicuous and out of place, and I looked around for Said, hoping he would hurry. I finally spied him near the main door, talking to a group of other men. He always seemed to attract a crowd of eager listeners, and I knew he could be focussed on chatting with them for a while. I waited for a few minutes and when he still didn't look over and notice my wave, I held my breath and crossed over nearer to him and the other men. I knew he wouldn't want me to hang around near his friends and would probably make his goodbyes and leave with me. Sure enough, he gave me a sideways glance and nodded. He shook hands with his friends then walked over to me, and we climbed the stairs up the hill to where we had parked.

The day was heating up and it was about noon when we were finally heading home.

"How did you like the mosque?" Said asked hopefully.

"It was nice," I answered. "I met some ladies and they invited me to a sisters' circle. They said there was another Aishah here from Canada! Can you believe that?"

"Oh! That's great." He smiled. "See, I told you you would make friends here."

"Yeah, I guess. I hope I like them."

Safiyya had cooked lunch and was just finishing baking the bread to go with it when we arrived home. Omaima came downstairs to meet us and showed us the piece of dough she was kneading.

"Look, Mama, Aziza let me help make the bread!" She poked at the ball of dough excitedly.

"Oh, that's amazing! I can't wait to taste it!" I said.

Safiyya was standing on the steps near the large bread oven with an oven mitt on one hand. The Moroccan loaves were shaped as flat, round bread that was denser than the bread I was used to. It was easier to break pieces off and use them to scoop up whatever we were eating. Knives and forks were hardly ever used, and I liked eating with my right hand almost more than the very British way I had been taught as a child. It was improper to use your left hand, as that was the hand you washed with after going to the bathroom. Having no toilet paper was something I never really got used to. I always hated not being able to dry myself properly, although washing with soap and water made sense.

"Come and sit upstairs with us," Safiyya said, motioning for us to go up and get comfortable. "I'm almost done here."

We went in to their apartment, and Said kissed his father on the forehead and wished him a prosperous Jumua. The two younger girls came galloping out of Fatima's room then, gleefully holding a piece of gum she had given them.

"What about me?" Omaima asked, coming in then as well.

Fatima extended her hand with her piece. She reached for her arm and pulled her in to hug her as well, although Omaima squirmed out of her grasp after giving her a quick kiss on the cheek.

Fatima laughed and pointed at the girls, making a "she's crazy" motion with her finger circling by her ear. We all laughed.

I didn't want to admit how much the outing to the mosque and the anticipation of meeting another Canadian Muslim woman had refreshed my outlook on life in Morocco. Said would take the fact that I was happier as proof that he was being a wonderful husband. I didn't want to give him the satisfaction of inventing that story. Somehow, without me catching it, he would convince me of how wonderful things were and that my patience and piety were paying off. I was happier now than ever before. Wasn't it wonderful that I had found Islam and married him? And he always made it sound so reasonable! It was infuriating.

That week passed much the same as before. I was well into my pregnancy now, and I found the daily chores took up most of my energy. The day of the women's evening, I took it easy and lay down in the afternoon while the older two girls were at nursery school. Out of the books I had brought with me from England, I picked up the one on polygamy in Islam. I hardly ever took the time to read these days, and I missed using my brain to study. I quickly skimmed through the introduction and got to the part where two cousins talked about sharing a husband and how that worked so well for them. I was intrigued when they described having a friend to go shopping with, how they helped each other around the house and had more time to enjoy their own interests, since their "services" as a wife and mother were shared.

My imagination was piqued. How nice it would be to have someone to share the housework, to laugh with and talk with over coffee. Even to have a night alone in bed to sleep properly! I cringed as I realized how being with Said now had become more of a burden than a pleasure. I remembered back when we first met, how we jumped on each other whenever we could. There was nothing better than to spend a few hours in bed making love and snuggling. Just this morning, Said had burst into the bedroom after having a shower, naked and obviously posing, awaiting my approval of his admittedly well muscled and toned body. I had smiled weakly and made obvious groaning noises as I hauled myself out of bed and sidled past him to the bathroom, with only a cursory pat on his stomach. I had not wanted to arouse him then, it would only mean having to take extra time to pleasure him before beginning the morning chores. Sighing, I turned back to the book. Now, my idea of bliss would be a few hours to myself.

The following chapters extolled the benefits and rewards of living a polygamous lifestyle in Islam. How it helped women have a place in society, gave them status, reduced the desire for men to have mistresses. If a man actually could marry more than one woman, he also had to provide for her and treat her with all the respect of a wife. It seemed like the perfect solution. My pregnancy exhausted body felt relief at the thought of a way to share the work of raising a family. I laid the book down and closed my eyes for a few minutes before having to head out to pick up the girls. Maybe I would mention my idea to Said. Although we had toyed with the idea of polygamy when we were still in the UK, it had not gone anywhere. The fact that it was illegal to marry more than one person at a time there had made it hard to properly consider entering into such an arrangement. Now that we lived in an Islamic country, it was possible, and I found myself considering the potential benefits again.

I rushed through the afternoon chores and made semolina porridge for the girls' supper. I was excited to meet the other Aishah. Would we connect? I hadn't realized until now how much I missed having a friend. Said had told me so many times that he was my best friend. I had been devastated to find that most of my friends did not make the effort to keep in contact now that I was not living in the same country. I don't know what I had expected. We were all busy with babies and husbands, but I felt more alone here than I remembered ever feeling in my life. We didn't have a computer, and using the phone line for long distance calls was expensive. I used the telephone only to talk to my parents once a week or so. The isolation and abandonment I felt, being pregnant here in Morocco, brought me to my knees more than once. I turned my head away from the girls and wiped my eyes on my sleeve as I remembered how Said's only response, when I was sobbing on my knees with exhaustion, was to pull me to my feet.

"This is your life now, get up and face it, you have no other choice." He had said it kindly but with firmness. There was no room for disagreement or discussion. "Allah doesn't test you beyond what you can bear. Come on, you are a strong woman."

I wanted to be strong, I wanted to survive, I wanted to please him and Allah…but God, I wanted to surrender control, just once, feel supported and held. His hugs no longer felt like the safe haven they had at first. Now they seemed a determined plea for me to keep going, to be strong for him and everyone else.

I wiped my eyes fiercely and turned to take the dishes to the kitchen. Said should be home soon to take me to the sister's house. I skipped bath time today and got the girls into their pajamas early. Thank goodness

they were tired from being out at nursery school all day.
I herded them all into the bathroom and lined them up
in front of the sink to brush their teeth. Omaima and
Safia could brush their own by now, but I was impatient,
so I grabbed the brush and did it for them. They
protested mildly at this affront to their independence,
but they soon realized I was not in a mood to be swayed.
So, they stood and opened their mouths and kept quiet.

Fatima had offered to sit with them and put them
to bed in a little while. I was grateful, although doubtful
that she would actually do things the way I wanted.
Still, it was a small price to pay for an evening out with
other women.

Said still had not come home, and I was edgy and
irritable. Where was he? He wouldn't forget, would he?
I tried not to think about it and went to get changed.
Maybe I should just pretend he couldn't take me out,
so I wouldn't be disappointed if it didn't work out. Deep
down, I knew I was just fooling myself, I cared very
much. These little things had assumed huge proportions
in my mind. Whether he arrived home on time to take
me out became a measure of how much he loved me.
My heart dropped. Did he even love me anymore?
He seemed to be happier when he was out with his
friends than hanging out at home with me and the girls.
I had hoped that things might be different here in
Morocco. Said would become the head of the family
and take his roles as husband and father more seriously.
Where was my heroic knight who becomes the noble

king of his realm? This wasn't the way the story was
supposed to go.

I sighed and tried to pull myself together. This
train of thought was not going anywhere good. The
dissonance between reality and my fantasies was
becoming more and more disturbing. He'll be home
any minute now. As if in answer, Fatima came in then,
asking where Said was. I gestured impatiently that he
wasn't home yet, and she shook her head disapprovingly.
I scowled behind her back. She was right, he was late,
but I hated that she could express what I guiltily hid
away. Why wasn't it okay for me to be angry too? The
inside of my skin prickled with electric energy. I wanted
to jump out of my body. It was an intolerable feeling.

I was all ready and the girls were settled, watching
cartoons on TV. I took a deep breath and warmed up
some leftover mint tea for me and Fatima. She accepted
the tea happily, and when I produced a package of
cookies, her face broke into a smile and she settled
on the couch with the kids. I sipped my tea and gazed
in the direction of the TV, but thoughts flooded my
mind, fuelling my anger and resentment. Why was it so
hard for him to remember the one day I was invited out?
I bet he wouldn't have forgotten an invitation to his
friend's house. Oh, and by the way, how many times had
I sat for hours at some stranger's house, drinking tea and
trying to converse with some woman I didn't know,
while he and his friend went around Tangier? He always
assumed I'd had a splendid time, trying to keep my kids

happy most of the day on only cookies and tea, with no toys or opportunity to go outside. Sometimes, finally, in desperation, the women we were visiting offered us a room to take a nap for a couple of hours, just so they could get on with their day and not feel they had to entertain us. I had still not adjusted to the Arabic way of visiting.

My mind was showing no signs of stopping its onslaught, when I heard the door.

"Anybody here?" Said called up the stairs.

"Yeah, we are in here," I replied a little sharply. Of course we were here, where else would I be? "I'm ready to go."

"Oh, okay…" He looked longingly at our tea glasses. "Do we have any dinner ready?"

"No," I snapped. "The kids and I had porridge. I suppose you could see if your mom has anything upstairs. But I was hoping I could go now. The sister said come at seven and it's seven thirty now. You can come home and eat after you drop me off," I suggested, trying to make leaving now seem more reasonable. The prickly energy was returning unbidden to my body and I needed to move.

He looked at my face and nodded. "Come on then, I guess it's been a while since you went out to see some sisters."

He kissed the girls and waved to Fatima, and we left.

I was quiet as we drove through the streets of Tangier. I still didn't know my way around much past the area where we lived. The streets winded and twisted around each other, sometimes ending in unexpected dead ends, where a house had been built in the way of the road. Some of the older parts of the city were only accessible on foot. Old, worn stairs cut into the stone wound between alleyways that branched off at various intervals. They all looked the same to me, and I didn't get the chance to explore much. I doubted whether Said or his family would let me go wandering around by myself anyway. My Moroccan was still rudimentary, and it was obvious from my accent that I was not Arabic.

I gazed out of the car window. The whitewashed walls of the houses, the many colourful jellabas the women wore. The men wore jellabas too, only theirs were more muted colours of tan, grey, or cream.

"Here we are." Said pulled over to the edge of the road. There was a gate with some vines growing around the edges.

I looked at him. "Do I just go in?"

"Sure, there is a bell there on the wall. Ring that."

"Will you wait and see if it's the right house? Please?" I didn't realize I was so nervous until now. It had been weeks since I had been out to visit. I had lost my usual extrovert nature.

"Okay," Said answered, looking at his phone. "Go on, I'm just seeing if the brothers are at the café."

I slid out of the car and closed the door. The bell on the gate rang somewhere inside and I heard footsteps.

The bolt of the gate slid back and a young man was standing there.

"Um," I stuttered, unprepared to explain why I was there "Women...today..." I struggled trying to find the words in Arabic.

He smiled and opened the gate. He pointed up the stairs. "Welcome, sister, the women are upstairs."

Chapter
Eight

AS I GOT TO THE top of the staircase, I heard
women's voices. Turning immediately into a small
living room, I saw there were eight or nine other women
already there.

"Assalamu alaikum," I said in the general direction
of everyone, and looked for a free space to sit down.
I fumbled with my veil, and it took me a few minutes
to see the faces around me properly.

"Welcome, sister," an older woman said in Arabic,
and turning toward her voice, I recognized her as the
woman I'd met at the mosque. "How are you?"

"I'm fine, thanks to Allah," I answered shyly. "Thank
you for having me," I think I said, although after the
thank you I wasn't so clear in my words. "Aishah, other
one, here?" I asked.

"She's coming, she's coming," the woman assured me. "She is from Canada too!" The women seemed as excited as I was about getting us together. I pulled off my black gloves and tucked them in my purse and adjusted my burka so I could sit comfortably.

"You're pregnant?" Another lady motioned with her hand over her belly.

"Yes." I smiled.

"How many children?" This was an inevitable question in Morocco. Women seemed to be measured by how many children they had, how many were still alive and how many had died, whether they were boys or girls. I was often asked if I would keep trying for a boy when they heard I had only girls so far.

"Three girls," I answered.

"Oh! Wonderful!" everyone cooed. "You want this one to be a boy?"

I shrugged and smiled. "Whatever Allah provides."

"Oh, yes, of course, praise be to Allah!"

The older woman was shuffling through some papers and looked ready to begin, so we turned toward her expectantly. I sighed inwardly, preparing myself for a long hour or so of listening to Arabic that I didn't understand.

"In the name of Allah, the most merciful, the most kind…" She began the long introductory speech that the Prophet Muhammad used before all of his teachings. I heard the mention of the wives of the Prophet and vaguely understood the gist of the topic was about women. The sister's voice droned on, and my eyes were just beginning to flutter closed when the door of the gate banged shut and there were footsteps on the stairs.

"Assalamu alaikum," a slight, energetic woman said, hurrying in. She smiled to the group and settled herself on the floor, apologizing for being late. I guessed she was the Canadian woman everyone had told me about. Her skin was pale but with a pink undertone that betrayed her nationality. She wore a black burka and veil like mine, and she smiled as she caught my eye.

The rest of the women nodded and respectfully turned back to listen to the talk. I barely understood anything else as the talk progressed, and my attention wandered to looking around at my other companions. There were a couple of young women, who seemed to be university age, looking studious and demure. An older lady sat in the corner, her legs straight out in front of her, as I had learned was common among the older Moroccan women. They had been accustomed to sitting like that for hours doing needlework or picking through a plate of lentils to get the small pebbles out, or similar chores. Another two or three ladies sat upright on the sofa, with their hands in their laps and their veils pulled down to reveal their faces. I sat cross-legged opposite the newcomer.

"… and praise be to Allah for his kindness and mercy." The speaker finished and looked up. I breathed a sigh of relief and shifted my legs. I pretended to understand the question and answer session that ensued but found I could not understand enough to contribute anything relevant. After some discussion, our hostess called a young girl in and asked her to make tea. This was the signal we had all been waiting for to relax and talk amongst ourselves.

"You are from Canada?" I asked the latecomer in English, hoping I had guessed correctly.

"Yes!" She smiled broadly. Our hostess noticed us and quickly shifted over to make the formal introduction, proudly taking charge of the fact that she had brought us together.

We both acknowledged her and then continued our conversation in English, as she was busy pouring and serving the tea.

"You have children?" I asked, realizing the irony of asking the same question that I had tired of so quickly myself.

She nodded. "I have seven children, two girls and five boys."

"Wow! I have three girls, and one more on the way." I pointed at my belly. "And are you married to a Moroccan as well?"

"Yes, I've been here for three years now. You'll have to bring your girls and come to visit me!" she said quickly as we were passed tea glasses. It was difficult to converse much more than that, as the other women, noticing we were speaking English, wanted to know what we were saying. We smiled at each other, acknowledging our secret connection, and turned to participate in the group

discussion as best we could in a language not our own.
I felt a flame inside, a warmth of connection that
I hadn't felt for a long time. That feeling that someone
else "got" me, understood where I was coming from,
and could share my perspective. I drank my tea quietly.

The women's voices merged around me in an
indistinct medley of sound. My mind was elsewhere.
I had so much I wanted to share with my new friend,
with someone who could understand. I was starved for
friendship and sharing. The heaviness of everything
I had been through so far in Morocco, in my marriage,
as a mother, swirled around in my head, making
me sleepy.

I quietly texted Said that I was ready to go and
hoped he wouldn't be too long. I had recently got a flip
phone for this purpose and still marvelled at the idea that
we could be in touch from anywhere. I wanted to get
home, to my bed, to think things over. I reached over and
touched Aishah's arm, pushing a piece of paper with my
phone number on it into her hand. Getting up, I thanked
the hostess and said goodbye to the other women. Said
was soon pulling up outside and I climbed in, pasting a
smile on my face as I told him about the evening. I felt
reserved about sharing with him too much. I didn't want
him to know I had been happy for a couple of hours.
He always managed to use these revelations against me,
and I instinctively kept the details to myself.

"I'd like to go and visit Aishah soon," I stated.

"Yes! Of course, you must go and see her." Said

seemed relieved that I had met a friend. I understood.
He was from here, he wanted me to love it as he did, to
love his family as he did. I could also tell that he wanted
me to be happy in a way that didn't require effort from
him. It was an impossible paradox.

As my belly grew over the next weeks, so did my anxiety
about birthing a child in Morocco. I definitely didn't
want to go to the government hospital in Tangier. I had
heard stories of them rushing the women in and out,
of it being dirty, and no one I had talked to had had
a good experience there. I called my mom to talk over
my options.

"Can you come over when I'm due?" I asked. I really
wanted to feel comfortable and have someone on my
side, so to speak. "You could even deliver the baby!"
I was only half joking. I had already had a home birth.
I was pretty confident I could do it again.

"Gah! I can't do that!" Mom shrieked through
the phone.

"Why not?" I laughed but was surprised at her
response. Having a baby was a natural thing, and I had
done it before.

"I just don't think I'd feel comfortable with that,"
she said.

"Okay." I was a little peeved. I mean, I was the one
birthing the baby, all she had to do was catch it. "Well,
can you at least come for a bit? I don't really feel very

supported here, emotionally or personally. I mean, Said's parents are nice and all, but they don't understand what I need."

"Yes, I think I could come, probably just on my own——"

"That's awesome!" I interrupted, relieved. "Thank you!"

I breathed a sigh of relief as I hung up the phone. I didn't have to do this alone. Now I just had to find a clinic or midwife here that was willing to deliver the baby.

My mother-in-law was over the moon that we were going to have a baby in Morocco. She had already begun planning the aqiqah, the ceremonial naming party. I had overheard her talking with a few of the neighbours, arranging cooking rotas and borrowing pots. Normally for a girl baby, one sheep was sacrificed, and for a boy it was two, but Safiyya had cornered my husband a few days ago and said that we definitely needed two sheep to feed all the guests, never mind the sex of the baby. For her, this was her one chance to throw a party and show off to the neighbours. She had wanted to have a Moroccan wedding for me and Said on my first visit to Tangier, but I had been five months pregnant with Omaima then, and I had not felt like celebrating the marriage when I was on the way to motherhood. Moroccan weddings were elaborate affairs that often lasted for at least three days, if not longer. There were different themes to each night's party, and different outfits for the bride. It seemed overwhelming. All-out parties and celebrations were not a part of my experience. As a Quaker, I had grown up savouring the quiet and solitude of that religion, where simplicity and reverence of the small daily pleasures were cultivated.

North African culture couldn't be more different: lavish parties with flamboyant clothes, music and dancing, and rituals where whole communities came out to celebrate things like births, marriages, and death. I was in awe of the ability of the people here to celebrate so fully. It felt inclusive in a way that I had not experienced before.

I was excited to be the focus of this party. It made this birth special for me. I had been through three others fairly recently, and I was in danger of taking it all for granted. Said had found a small clinic with a midwife who was willing to deliver my baby there, provided I needed no extra medical assistance and everything proceeded normally. I felt confident I would be fine; the pregnancy had been okay, my mom was due to arrive next week, and I was just waiting now.

As he struggled to carry out all his mother's requests for the party preparations, Said began to look harried. This was her one shot and she was going all out. We had one hundred plates of sweets made up and wrapped for the guests. She had ordered chickens and two sheep for the main courses. We were to have the first night for men and the second night for women. This was on top of the tea and cakes we were to have on hand for any visitors who came around in the first week to offer their congratulations. I tried to stay out of the hustle and bustle. I couldn't understand the nuances and significance of all the fuss. I felt sidelined and a little helpless but busied myself with my other girls and keeping up with daily chores.

I hadn't been able to sleep lying down for the past couple of weeks, and I shifted uncomfortably in bed. I couldn't wait to have the baby now. I sighed and levered myself to sit on the edge of the bed. Everything felt like an effort, with the baby inside me draining my energy and the three girls straining my every last nerve. Not that it was their fault, I just wasn't in the mood to deal with them much. As I struggled to the bathroom, I remembered with some excitement that my mom was due to arrive today. She hadn't been to Morocco on her own before, and she had seemed somewhat nervous to travel by herself.

I called out to Said, "You remember you are picking Mom up from the airport this afternoon, right?"

"Yeah, what time?" he mumbled as he rolled over in bed.

"I'll check, but I think it's about three o'clock," I replied, feeling anxious and excited and relieved all at the same time. I wanted someone here whose priority was to care for me. My mom and I had had our difficulties, but in the end, she was still my mother.

My mother-in-law had offered to cook dinner for us. The gesture softened my resentment toward her for

taking over the party plans and the celebration of my
fourth baby. I could see that she wanted to be at the
centre of the fun and excitement. To be fair, she had
missed out on many opportunities to celebrate. Her older
children had left home young, before marrying or having
children, and she had lost touch with them after they
left Morocco. I wondered if leaving the traditional way
of life in Tangier and suddenly being thrown into
European culture and society had led her two daughters
to turn their backs on their family. No one ever talked
about it, but it seemed that a deep hurt prevailed in
the family. Said had also left home young, and although
he had visited, he had not given her cause for celebration
until we had moved here with her grandchildren.

My heart did ache for her. How must it be to have
your children leave home and never come back? In
the end, who did we really have? Said and I were drifting
apart. I was so busy with children and home, and he had
immersed himself again with younger acrobat friends
who were still in Morocco hoping to get a job in Europe.
Most of them weren't married yet, and they idolized
Said for his experience in the circus world. The illusion
of an integrated extended family only went as far as the
surface. In truth, I felt more isolated here than I had ever
felt. Maybe he did too. Maybe even his parents were
disappointed; I wasn't the daughter-in-law they had
imagined. Only the girls, being young and unaware,
seemed to thrive in this pretence of community. They
were too young to know any difference. In their eyes,

everyone loved them, and that was enough. The paradise that I had thought we were joining here in Morocco was merely a veneer. I had begun to see the cracks.

I sat sipping my coffee by the window, a notebook open on my lap. My mom had requested a synopsis of my daily routine, so she would know how to help with the girls while I was laid up with the new baby. I smiled. It wasn't easy to write down what I did every day. Wake up, diapers and toilet time for kids, breakfast, walk the older girls to preschool. Then the cooking and cleaning started: make bread dough, put the yogurt pots to set, plan lunch, tidy up. Collect Omaima and Safia from school for lunch; they had two hours between their morning and afternoon sessions. It was nice to be able to have a hot lunch with them and check in. It was a long day for three- and four-year-olds, sitting in the cramped benches. After lunch, walk them back, stopping at the corner store on the way to pick up a couple of cookies for them to take for snack time. The afternoon usually passed quickly as well: laundry, shopping at the small market up the road, or sewing filled it up until it was time to bring the girls home. I usually made zucchini bread with yogurt or something easy with mint tea at that time, as it was too much to cook twice in a day. The Moroccan tradition was to have tea around five o'clock and then a late dinner around nine. I found I didn't like eating a meal so late, so I just skipped the dinner part and made tea the last thing. I also put my kids to bed by around eight, which was unheard of here.

My mother-in-law shook her head at my strange need for routine, her tongue clacking her disapproval. In her understanding, kids should be allowed to sleep when they wanted to. When we had family visiting from the village, the adults sat and talked and the children just played around until they were tired. Any woman seeing a child nodding off would just tuck them up in a shawl on the sofa near them and let them sleep there.

I did like the way the children were treated as part of the family, without being given undue attention. I balked at having my girls around all the time though, and I did think it was important to brush their teeth and have them rested for school the next day. It was a difficult merging of values and traditions, and I felt like the odd one out. I was curious to know how my new Canadian friend managed it. I had contacted her, and we had arranged to visit after I'd had the baby.

"Guess who's here!" Said called from the stairwell.

"Mom!" I waddled heavily to the door. "How was your trip? It's great to see you." It was good to feel her arms around me. There really is nothing quite like a mother's hug. She was larger than me, with a heavy bone structure, and so even now, as a mother myself, I still felt like a child in her arms. She had tied a colourful scarf around her hair, as a gesture to the local custom of dress. I appreciated her sensitivity but made a mental note to help with the styling of the scarf next time we went out.

Said brought her suitcase in and set it down. Mom took in the room with bright eyes and smiled with gratitude at Said. He had resumed his charm now that my mother was here, and I knew it had worked on her.

"Shall I make tea?" I asked them.

"Yes, make tea for your mom. I have to go out and see some friends." Said shifted his weight uneasily as he stood by the door. "It's nice to see you, Mom. I'll let you and your daughter catch up." To me, he said, "I'll be back later."

He always managed to make what he said seem logical and polite. I could find no fault in his words, but the lack of real warmth in his voice made my skin prickle. I quickly nodded and shut out the feelings that threatened to spill over into my consciousness. Turning to my mother, I smiled and said I would put the kettle on.

A couple of days later, I was woken by severe pains. I could tell today was the day. My mom had adjusted quite well to our house and routine, just in time! I got up, as the pains were fairly regular and wouldn't let me sleep any more.

Mom and I got the girls up and dressed. By now the pains were making it hard to stand up straight.

"Baby," I whispered to Said, who was still asleep. "I think I'm going to need to go soon."

"Go where?" he asked sleepily.

"The clinic! I'm in labour." I tried not to sound exasperated. "Are you going to come with me?"

"Oh." He rubbed his eyes and opened them. "Well, I've seen it all before. My mom could go with you. They don't usually like men in these places anyway."

My face fell but I answered steadfastly, "Sure, I guess that works. Can we go soon though?"

"Okay, let me get up then. Is there any coffee?" He pushed himself up to sitting and stretched his naked body provocatively.

"Yeah, um, I'm having a baby today, so I don't think you are getting anything in that department." I had to laugh at his efforts to look sexy. There was no way in hell I was going to respond the way he was insinuating. Why would he joke like that with me now? This was supposed to be my time.

"Huh?" he looked disappointed. "You never have time for me anymore."

"Really?" My voice wavered. "You expect too much of me. I can't do everything with the kids and still take care of you too." Just then another pain hit, and I scowled. This conversation was not going the way I expected at all. My mind jumped to the book I had read on polygamy a few weeks ago. "Maybe you need another wife to do that, if I'm not enough." I was not being reasonable at this point, but the pains were coming more regularly and I was not in the mood to be reasonable. "Anyway, get dressed, we need to go soon."

"Yeah, sure." His voice was quiet and cold. It sent shivers of dread through me. I hated when he was like this. I turned away to hide my tears and went to get my bag of baby things.

I returned the cold tone. "I'll be ready whenever you are. My mom is good with the kids here."

He was already in the shower, with the water running. Whatever. I turned to go to the living room and speak to the girls. I tried to find a smile for them, I loved them so much.

"You guys have to be good with Granny, okay? You can see the new baby soon!" My voice was a little higher pitched than normal, but having to stay positive for them helped me regain control.

"You feeling okay?" Mom asked. She rolled over on the sleeping mat we had put in the small bedroom off the kitchen.

"Yeah," I lied, "these pains are just getting more intense. Said is going to take me to the clinic now. I think his mom is coming with me. You okay with everything here?"

"We will be fine," she answered, picking a book up from the couch.

She knew I was upset, and I was grateful that she did not push the point, as I wasn't in a space to go into my relationship concerns right now. "Okay, girls, kiss me. I'll be back with your brother or sister soon."

The girls hugged me, not really aware of the occasion, and Said helped me down the stairs. His mom was waiting in her jellaba and scarf near the car. "Help her into the car. Drive quickly," she dictated to Said. She fussed at Said the whole way to the clinic, telling him to hurry, then to slow down and be careful. Her frenzied energy was too much for me to take in. Safiyya had always been an emotional and highly strung person.

I sank back in the seat, glad to have someone else advocate for me. It was beginning to take all my concentration to deal with the pains.

When we arrived at the clinic, the midwife led me into a pretty room with four or five beds and cots next to them, decorated with either blue or pink ruffles. She welcomed my mother-in-law then turned to me and pointed to one of the beds.

"You can lie there, dear, and let me know when you feel like you want to push."

I nodded obediently and sat on the bed to remove my burka.

"Men are not allowed to stay," the midwife said to Said. "We will call you when the baby comes."

Said smiled at me and looked relieved. "I'll see you later, baby. I know you'll be great."

I nodded dazedly and lay down on the bed, pulling the covers over me. I didn't have the energy to respond, I just wanted to concentrate so I could keep from screaming and crying with the labour pains. Safiyya looked at me with compassion as she sat in a chair across the room. She had never had the opportunity to watch her daughters give birth or get married or any of that. Perhaps her effusive desire to help was a small attempt to reclaim these small joys that were taken from her, when her own daughters went to Europe and America and never came back. I didn't want her help though, I didn't want her, I didn't want anyone. Pulling the covers over my head, I breathed, shutting out the world. I kept

my eyes closed as the pain washed over me in waves.
It seemed like forever and yet not long at all until I
recognized the beginning of the transition stage. My
body began to push without my conscious direction,
and a wavering cry escaped my lips.

"I think it's time to push soon," I heard the midwife's
voice next to me. "Come into the other room with me."

My mother-in-law and the midwife helped me
hobble, moaning, into the birthing room. I somehow got
up on the table. The contractions were coming intensely
now. I could feel the head crowning, and I let out a
piercing scream as the head came out. The rest of the
body slithered out with the next contraction, and I was
shaking and crying with relief and shock.

"It's a girl!" I heard her say. "Everything is good,
you rest now."

She took care of the rest quickly and efficiently, and
before I knew it, I was back in my bed in the other room
with a heavy pad on my stomach and my baby girl next
to me. I took out my breast to feed her.

"No, no! You mustn't feed her now, you must rest,"
the midwife ordered.

As my baby rooted for my nipple, I stubbornly let
her suck. I wanted to feed my baby!

"Keep the pad on your stomach, it helps your uterus
to shrink down again," she told me sternly, obviously not
used to having a woman disobey her commands.

I heard clattering on the stairs, and then Said appeared
with the other girls.

"Mama! You have a baby!" All three of them crowded around, trying to touch her.

My mother-in-law intervened. "Give your sister some room. Here, let your mother have something to eat."

A hot plate of chicken tagine had appeared, and as the scent wafted through the room, I realized how ravenous I was. Struggling to sit up a bit, I passed the baby to my mother-in-law and tasted the food.

"Can I have a bite?" Omaima asked.

"Me too!" Safia and Hind looked at the plate expectantly.

"Here." I gave them the mandarin orange to share while I tore off a piece of chicken.

"I want some chicken too." Omaima reached for the plate.

Said laughed. "Let your mother eat."

I finished a few mouthfuls and gave the plate to the girls to finish. "Here, share the rest, nicely."

I looked up at Said. "I want to come home now. She won't let me wash here, and I want to get cleaned up and relax at home. Can we go?"

"I guess, if you are sure you are ready," Said replied. "Let me just pay her first." He took out a big roll of cash and went into the other room to pay the midwife. She came back into the room to say goodbye. She had a big smile and gave the girls an orange each.

Her parting words were directed to me. "You did very well, dear. Look after your family."

I stood up shakily. It had been a long day. We packed my bag. I had a huge pad on to catch the blood still coming out in gushes when I moved. I threw on my burka over top. I didn't care what I looked like at this point, I just wanted to be back home.

It turned out that the hard part was yet to come.

Chapter
Nine

I WAS TOTALLY UNPREPARED FOR THE social customs of birthing a baby in Morocco. That evening, the very day of the birth, I had the first of many visitors to see me and the baby, mostly people I had never met. Said's aunt from the village came first; following the custom of the village elder women, she carried almost everything she owned on her person. Money was tied up in a corner of her scarf. She wore two or three layers of clothing. Undergarments with a stretchy cotton dress over top served as both warming layers and pajamas. Over the top, she had put on her nice "going out" dress, followed by her mendeel, the woven woollen cloth worn around the waist that served as both an apron and a blanket. On her head she had a couple of layers of scarves, with a few wispy white hairs poking out behind her ears. She had lost probably half of her teeth, and the effect of her smile along with her prominent chin hairs was slightly alarming.

She climbed right up on the bed with me to see the baby and made herself at home, leaning back on the pillows to gaze at my daughter, whom we had begun to call Hajar.

"Beautiful, beautiful, *jameela!*" she muttered, more to herself than to anyone else. Said looked at me and motioned with his hand to say that she was a little crazy in the head. As if I hadn't noticed. I smiled uncertainly at her and she patted my boob with her work-worn hand.

"You have good milk?" she asked in Arabic. I nodded, not really sure what to say to that. "Good girl." Her face shifted then, as if she was remembering something long ago. "I had many babies when I was young…" She faded off, and I smiled at her again. I needed to breastfeed the baby, which usually made the pains worse again as my overstretched uterus rebelled against shrinking down to its rightful size for the fourth time in five years. I needed some privacy.

"Said, maybe you can get your aunt some tea?" I called out desperately.

"Come on, Auntie, Mom has tea ready. Let's leave Aishah to feed the baby." I smiled gratefully at him and set myself up for the hard work of feeding. The pains brought back the feeling of being in labour. I was thankful my mother was around to occupy the other girls. They were reading stories in the other room, and I breathed a sigh of relief at having a few moments alone with Hajar.

The next few days were a whirlwind of looking after the baby and a constant stream of visitors. I barely saw Said, who was kept busy running errands on his mother's orders, to prepare for the aqiqah, the naming ceremony. Safiyya came down to peruse my apartment and suggest the best configuration of tables and seating to accommodate the fifty or sixty guests expected on each of the two nights. The first evening was for men only. My mother and I would be required to stay out of sight, and I planned to put the girls to bed and then stay in the bedroom with them and my mom until the men left. I knew this wouldn't be until after midnight, as the parties in Morocco are renowned for being long and extravagant. The second night was for the women and, I thought, for me.

The smells of cooking pervaded the small balcony outside Said's parents' apartment. Safiyya and a few other women from the neighbourhood were sitting around on stools, stirring huge pots of meat and vegetables. A couple of women were kneading dough and shaping the round loaves that would be baked fresh for the evening's festivities. I nodded to the ladies, feeling I owed them some kind of acknowledgement for their hard work. Sitting inside, I chatted pleasantly for a few minutes, hoping I would not say anything impolite.

The women were hard-working and pleasant in general. I had grown used to the slightly condescending air with which they talked to me about cooking and housework and parenting. I had often elicited bemusement and ridicule when I voiced any ideas on these subjects that went against their cultural norm and the "right" way to do things. I had to admit that their ability to pull off a two-day feast of this magnitude was well beyond my capabilities.

My mother was still new to the segregation of Islamic social events, and she found it difficult to accept that she and I had to stay hidden away in a back room while the men enjoyed feasting in our living space. I sometimes reminisced about group gatherings from before I became Muslim. I had enjoyed the company of men, many of my best friends were male. As I cuddled my newest baby in the corner of the bedroom, watching the peaceful breathing of my children, I was aware of the disparity of my feelings. Partly I was happy to be hidden away, not having to make an appearance or an effort to look good or be polite. But in a rebellious corner of my being, I felt overlooked and unappreciated. Was the fact that I had birthed this baby not the sole reason for all this fuss? It seemed incongruous to be totally ignored for the celebrations.

My musings were interrupted by my husband. "Baby, give me Hajar, the brothers want to see her." He sounded impatient and in my emotional postpartum state, I could feel the tears rising in response to his uncaring tone. "Put her in the basket, with the pretty blanket. Make her look nice," he continued.

I nodded, not trusting my voice to speak without wavering. "The blanket is over there," I said, pointing.

He arranged the blanket and the baby quickly and took her out to the admiring men.

"Oh, she is beautiful, praise be to Allah," I heard them all saying. "You are so lucky to have four beautiful daughters," they continued to my husband. "It is a blessing to have pious daughters, it will take you to heaven." As is the custom, they tucked small offerings of money in the basket.

Said thanked them, revelling in the attention and praises of his friends and neighbours, as if everything was of his making. I curled up in the blankets and closed my eyes. Tiredness mercifully took my tears away.

As I nodded off, the words of the Prophet swam into my awareness: "The best kind of woman is the one who pleases her husband if he looks at her, obeys him if he orders her, and does not subject her honour or money to what he dislikes."

If I cannot be this for my husband anymore, maybe it is only fair that I offer him another wife who can. The thought pervaded my mind these days as I went through the motions of tending to my children and my home. Said was definitely not my first priority anymore, although I paid lip service to the fact when he asked me if I still loved him. His existence seemed to drift on the edge of my reality. We were no longer partners and lovers, we were separate satellites orbiting the same sun but never quite touching.

The second night proved to be even more distressing, as everyone was tired and grumpy after the men's night, and yet the cooking had to be done all over again. Said was busy all day running errands, and I was having trouble breastfeeding as my milk was still only just coming in. I was achy and sore and tried my best to stay in my room with the baby. Safiyya was bustling about upstairs, I could hear her footsteps going back and forth in the large, tiled kitchen. I marvelled that she had the energy. She was so determined to prove herself and her family as being capable of throwing this lavish party for her friends and neighbours. I felt a small pang of guilt about turning down her offer of a large Moroccan wedding ceremony a few years ago. It was probably more important to her than it had been to me. I was only beginning to understand the importance of appearances in this culture.

As the time of the guests' arrival drew near, I looked forward to sitting and enjoying the food with the women and placed myself at one of the tables we had set up in the living room. Neighbours and guests began to trickle in, and the seats filled quickly. I was surprised to see so many people. I had been to parties in Morocco before, but I hadn't thought we would have so many guests.

The first plates of food began to arrive from upstairs. The smell of chicken and olives and freshly baked bread made my mouth water. I was just about to break up

a loaf and hand it around my table when I caught sight
of my mother-in-law beckoning to me from the doorway.

I gave the loaf to the lady next to me and went to
see what she wanted.

"Come upstairs and sit with us," she whispered.
"There is not room for all the guests if you stay here."

I was taken aback. "Um, okay, Ma." I faltered
slightly, wishing I understood. Wasn't this evening
supposed to be for me to enjoy also? I went over to get
baby Hajar and nodded to the other women, indicating
I was heading upstairs to help.

"Please enjoy," I said to them in Arabic.

Upstairs, I sat in a corner with the baby and felt
sorry for myself. Everyone was busy and the sun had
gone down, leaving the balcony upstairs in semi-
darkness. The glow of the gas cooking rings showed
up brightly in the gloom. The sliver of the moon
was hanging forlornly in the deepening blue of the sky.
It felt empty, just like me.

A while later, one of the women brought me a plate
of the bony chicken pieces left over from downstairs.
I picked at it hungrily, wishing I could enjoy it, but the
feeling of resentment left my stomach tight, and I barely
tasted the food. I dozed off and on in the corner, trying
to ignore my aching back and the cold draft on my feet.
Hajar slept peacefully in my arms, the warmth of her
body soothing me somewhat.

It was much later that I awoke with a start and
realized it was over, most of the women had left, and

Safiyya and Fatima were quietly washing the last of the dishes. They had worked incredibly hard for the last two days. A pang of guilt shot through me. I got up and stretched my legs.

"*Shokran busuf*," I said, thanking them. My words seemed inadequate somehow. I crept downstairs and saw that my mother and the girls were already asleep in the back bedroom. I sank thankfully into my own bed.

So that was a naming ceremony? I thought sleepily. *Not what I expected at all.* So many of my experiences here in Morocco were strange to me. As I drifted off to sleep with Hajar, I wasn't sure I'd ever feel at home. Said was still out, and I wondered if he would be gone all night. Perhaps he had known the women's night would go late and he had decided to stay with a friend. I was too tired to worry about where he was now. My eyes closed. The day was finally over.

After my mom returned to Canada, the stifling heaviness of routine fell back on my shoulders. Hosting the two-day party had seemed to take all the life force from my mother-in-law. She was pale and often complained of not feeling well. Said didn't seem to notice that much, and I was too busy, so on the day that it happened, we were all taken by surprise.

It was late winter, and the worst of the cold and damp were over. When the sun came out there was a steamy freshness to the landscape, and rare greenery sprouted up everywhere. Sometimes, we paid the little girl next door to collect snails for us to eat. A whole bucket cost us only a dollar or so. Omaima would sit with her grandmother and use toothpicks to pry the meat out of the steamed snail shells. It was one such day, when I was feeding the baby and the other girls were upstairs, that I heard Omaima call out, more panicked than usual, "Mama, Mama!"

I put the baby down on the floor on her blanket and scurried out to the steps.

"What's wrong, habiba?" I called, worried she had hurt herself. I heard her start to cry.

"Aziza! Aziza!" she cried out desperately.

I raced up the stairs. "What's wrong?"

My heart stopped as I took in the scene. My mother-in-law had fallen sideways on the bench, her eyes were unfocussed and her mouth slack and drooping to the side in a grotesque way. I rushed forward.

"Ma...MA! Can you hear me? What happened? Can you sit up?" I tried in my panic to lever her back to an upright sitting position, but her dead weight was unwieldy. I finally gave up and told Omaima to get me a wet cloth from the kitchen. The coolness seemed to revive her slightly, and she blinked her eyes and tried to speak.

"Said...," she managed to croak out in a slurred voice.

"Okay, Ma, you're okay. I'm gonna call Said now, we will get the doctor to come and see you. Don't worry." I tried to soothe her, as I could see her eyes wide in fear as she realized she couldn't talk or move her left arm properly.

"Omaima, sweetheart, can you go downstairs and see if you can find my phone next to my bed and bring it up here for me?" I tried to issue the instructions as calmly as I could, hoping she could carry them out without me having to leave Safiyya alone to get it myself.

Omaima silently nodded and trotted off to find my phone. I was thankful for her obedience. I could hear the baby starting to fuss as well. Where was my father-in-law?

Omaima came in with the phone and I smiled at her gratefully.

"Thank you, habiba, you were a big help. Do you think you can go and sit with the baby now for a few minutes until I can come and get her? And if you see Safia downstairs, ask her to go to the mosque and call Jido to come home right away."

Omaima looked at Aziza worriedly but nodded again and went back downstairs.

I reached for the phone with my free hand, trying to keep my mother-in-law from rolling off the cushion with the other. I dialed Said and prayed he would answer.

"Hello?" His voice came through the speaker, and I almost cried in relief.

"Said! You have to get home quickly." I gulped, trying to get the words out in a sensible order. "Your mom...she...something's wrong." I looked at her, still dazed and unable to sit up. "We need a doctor!"

"What happened?"

"Omaima called me upstairs, and she was lying on

the sofa, she fell over, and I can't get her up. Please just come quickly!" I was close to panic.

"Okay, stay with her, I'll get a doctor and come now." He rang off and I caught a sob rising in my throat. I took a deep breath.

"Let's try and get you lying down better," I said to Safiyya, trying to keep my voice soothing. I levered her onto her back and lifted her legs up onto the sofa. Her left arm and leg seemed to be completely dead, and I wondered vaguely if she had suffered a stroke. I thought I remembered something about that being one of the signs. She seemed to be in a safe position, so I went to get a blanket from her room. I noticed then that her dress was wet, and I became aware of the smell of urine. Poor thing, she must have wet herself.

I returned with a blanket. "Here we are." I tucked it around her and felt a bit helpless as I realized I couldn't do much else for her until I had someone to help me lift her. She was a large woman, and with half of her body being dead weight, I couldn't think through how to do anything else.

Safia came upstairs with Taher, whom she had called back from the mosque.

"What's going on?" he asked.

"She needs a doctor." I struggled with the right words in Arabic.

He sat next to her. "What's wrong? Are you okay?" He said it gruffly, but it was obvious he was worried about her. She looked at him mutely, unable to speak.

He patted her head. "Said's coming now, he will get the doctor, you'll be okay." His blind faith in Said's ability to fix everything was astounding. I felt the weight of the responsibility Said's parents placed on him here, and for a moment I could understand his reticence to take on the role, although the understanding did not excuse him completely in my mind.

"Can you sit with her for a few minutes?" I asked him. "I need to check on the kids."

"Yes," he said. "Said is coming, right?"

"Yes, I told him. He said he was going to bring a doctor." I turned and almost ran down the stairs. My phone rang and I had to go back to answer it, where I'd left it on the upstairs table.

"Hello, baby, are you coming?"

"Yes, I'm on my way now. I have the doctor with me. How is she?" he asked.

"Your dad is with her, she wet herself, and she still can't talk." My jaw hurt from clenching.

"Okay, we are almost there." His voice was strained and I could tell he was struggling to hold himself together. His mom was the one person in his life he felt he owed something to. She had loved him unconditionally, even when he had hurt her by his lack of attention. He had even told me that she had kept him beside her to sleep until he was twelve years old. This had seemed a little extreme, but the ways of Moroccans were foreign to me.

I heard the door slam, and holding the baby,

I rushed out to the stairs.

"Is she upstairs?" Said asked brusquely.

I nodded and let him lead the way, the doctor and
I following behind. Taher looked relieved to turn things
over to the doctor and moved out of the way. Safiyya was
lying on her side where I had left her, her eyes looked
a little more focused, but her mouth was still alarmingly
slack, and she tried to talk but could only grunt wordlessly.

"Hey, Ma, you're going to be okay, the doctor is just
going to look at you." Said comforted her as the doctor
got out his blood pressure cuff. Said turned to the doctor.
"Do you know what's wrong with her?"

"I think she has suffered a stroke. I need to check
her blood pressure though," he replied curtly. "Hold
her arm there, and let's sit her up for a minute." His
nose wrinkled as the stink of urine wafted up, but he
pretended not to notice, and they got her sitting upright.

I got some more pillows propped around her as they
worked on setting up the blood pressure cuff. It took a
few minutes, and the doctor had a worried look on his
face as he took the stethoscope out of his ears.

"Her blood pressure is still extremely high," he said.
"She needs some medication as soon as possible to bring
it down, or she could have another stroke. I'll write a
prescription for you, and then you should get her cleaned
up and lying down quietly for now. I'll come back and
see her tomorrow." He spoke to Safiyya. "You need
to stay calm and not get angry or upset. Okay? And
no salt or sugar. Try having some soup or something

if you can swallow alright tonight." He packed up his things and wrote out a note with three or four different medicines he wanted us to get.

"I'll come back tomorrow and check on her," he said again, speaking to Said. "Get her these and I'll bill you then. If she takes another turn for the worse, you would have to take her to the hospital to get help there."

The Moroccan medical system was purely pay-per-use, and if you happened to need emergency attention when you had no money, it could be really difficult. I had seen the neighbours asking for charity, from time to time, when a family member needed surgery or fell ill. I wondered if we would have to ask for charity now.

"Thank you, doctor." Said shook his hand. "May Allah bless you."

I motioned to Said to stay for a minute. "Can you help me to change her dress? I don't think I can manage to do it on my own." I gave Hajar to Fatima, who had been hovering nearby. She didn't understand what was happening except that her mother wasn't well. I shook my head at her as she tried to ask me what was going on. I didn't have the patience to explain to her right now. I turned back to Said. "Help me get your mother changed before you go out to the pharmacy."

With Said helping to lift her, I pulled the dress up over her head. I got a wet towel and some warm water from the kettle to wipe her down. The sofa was damp as well, and we managed to get the cover off the cushion by scooting her down to the other end.

"Wait," I said. "Put that sheepskin under her. That will help, in case she has another accident." Safiyya looked at me helplessly, and I felt for her. It must be awful to lose control of your bodily functions like that. Even worse, not be able to say anything to the people around you. "It's okay, Ma, don't worry, we will take care of you," I said soothingly as we settled her at the other end of the sofa with a blanket tucked around her and a new dress on.

I sighed. "Okay, Said, I guess you can go and get the medicine now."

We didn't sleep well that night, any of us. When someone close to you gets sick, it changes everything. Said was distant and unsettled, he shifted in bed at every sound. Twice he got up to check on his mom upstairs. I had the baby to feed. The next morning, we made coffee upstairs and sat together, just sharing space in silence. Safiyya was more present and could speak a little, although the slurring was pronounced. Fatima did what she could to help. She got blankets and made tea with no sugar for her mom.

"So, what now?" I voiced the question we were all wondering. "When will the doctor come? Do you think she will recover any more?"

No one had any answers. We all looked at each other, shifting uncomfortably and trying to make small talk for Safiyya. I excused myself to go down and sort the girls out for school. Said called the doctor, and Taher and Fatima carried on with cleaning up the dishes and trying to act normal. The practicalities of nursing my mother-in-law were beginning to sink in to my stunned and now exhausted awareness. The task was huge. I could barely manage the girls alone; Hajar was only a few weeks old. I shook my head and concentrated on what I was doing, getting ready to take the older two girls to nursery school. Maybe the doctor would have good news, maybe she would get better quicker than we thought. Maybe... My mind blanked out.

"Come on, Omaima and Safia, let's go!" I put Hajar on my back, using the cloth to tie her securely on. I was proud of myself for mastering this way of keeping the baby close. It actually was way better than the fancy carrier I had used with my first baby. "Hind, you will have to walk with me today too, habiba. Aziza is sick. Hold hands, everyone."

We passed Said in the staircase going out.

"I am going to get the doctor now. Will you be back soon?" he asked. "I want you to be here to hear what he says."

"I'll do my best." I gave him a squeeze on his arm as we passed. "It will be okay," I whispered, although I had my doubts.

I was grateful to have the walk to clear my head. Just to get out of the stifling atmosphere of the house made me feel lighter and more positive. The girls trotted along happily enough, and thank Allah the older two had somewhere to go and be occupied for a few hours. I kissed them goodbye and waved to the teacher. I told her that their grandmother was sick and I had to hurry back to check on her.

"May Allah bless her," the teacher said, and smiled understandingly.

I shifted the baby to a more comfortable position on my back. As I made my way back to the house, I felt proud, in a way, that I could fit in to this lifestyle. Not everyone could, or would even want to try. I had talked on the phone recently to a Muslim sister back in the UK. She had said, "You live without a washing machine? How can you deal with that?"

I had laughed at her quietly, in my head. *You are so spoiled and you don't even know it! You would never have survived living at the time of the Prophet Muhammad.* It was judgmental to think that, but I wanted recognition of the hardships I was facing. The hardships that had just become so much greater.

I crossed the main street, holding Hind's hand tightly. The cars did not stop for pedestrians, and there were no discernible rules of the road. It was every man or woman for themselves, so I suspended my thoughts and concentrated on the traffic. Hind danced up and down when we got to the other side. "Can we get a biscuit from the shop?"

I sighed. "Sure, I guess so. We need milk too." I figured a treat wouldn't go amiss today of all days. "We need to hurry though to see the doctor and Aziza."

I looked toward the house to see if Said was there with the car yet. There was no sign of him, so we turned off the path and went in the dark doorway to the corner shop.

Really, to call it a shop is being generous. The few planks nailed up on the wall were scantily stocked with packs of biscuits, tins of tuna and sardines. A few bags of flour sat in the corner next to a table and chair, where an aged man was sitting.

"Assalamu alaikum," we greeted him, and he nodded gruffly. I turned to address Hind. "Which biscuit do you want?" She picked one of her favourites, a package of individually wrapped, chocolate covered wafers. I gave the shopkeeper a dirham. "Shokran," I said, thanking him.

"How's your mother-in-law this morning?" he asked as I turned to go. I started. How did people know what was going on, even before I did sometimes?

"Um, I'm just going back now. The doctor was coming to see her again today," I replied in my rudimentary Arabic, not really knowing what to say. "Oh, and I need two cartons of milk also." I fished again in my purse.

"May Allah give her strength and a quick recovery," he said with feeling. "Tell her I send my regards."

"I will." I smiled, although he wouldn't see my face under my veil. I was touched by the strong sense of community here. Back in England, I hardly spoke to my neighbours, let alone cared to find out about what was going on in their lives. Hind and I stepped out into the bright sunlight. I put my hand under my veil and held it out to get some air. The mustiness of the shop made it hard to breathe.

"Oh look, Baba's back!" I said to Hind. "Come on, let's see what the doctor has to say about Aziza today."

My heart was racing as we climbed the stairs. I could hear voices but not any clear words. I stood back in the doorway, aware that I was in the presence of a non-related man, as the doctor stood leaning over Safiyya. Said nodded to me grimly and gestured to me to come in.

"She has definitely suffered a stroke," the doctor said, standing up and putting his stethoscope around his neck. "She needs to be on blood pressure medication and diuretics from now on, and no salt or sugar in her diet. She needs to eat very plain food, and not too much, as she doesn't want to put on any more weight."

"Will she be able to regain the use of her left side?" I asked, looking sideways at Said to see if he disapproved of me speaking out.

"It may come back after a while, or it may not." The doctor shook his head. "It's hard to say at this point. Also, she needs to stay quiet, no anger or stress."

I wondered how well that would work. I had never known Safiyya to stay calm for even one day, in the whole time we had been here. Small things made her angry, and she often obsessed about them for ages. To be fair, she was as giving with her love and attention as she was with her anger, but neither of those states would help her maintain her blood pressure.

"You can call me if you need me again." The doctor packed up his bag. Said saw him out and I went to take off my hijab.

I felt dazed and emotionally drained. The last couple of days had stretched my already tired "new mom" brain. I didn't know how to feel or what to do. I had no idea how Said was holding up, we had barely spoken to each other. He came up the stairs then, his feet treading heavily on the tiled steps. His eyes were dull, and black circles made them look even more sunken. He looked as if he had aged a decade in only a few days. I went over to him and put my head on his chest. He wrapped his arms around me and we just stood there, not speaking. There was nothing to say that would help lift the heaviness.

He pulled away first, and I could see he was struggling to hold back the tears that filled his eyes.

"Maybe we should bring her down here," I suggested quietly. "It would be easier to watch her and help her if she was close by. She can see the kids playing around her too. I don't know if I can keep running up and down the stairs all the time."

Said looked at our living room. "Yeah, I guess that might work. We could put a bed over there for her."

"Okay, help me set it up, and then you can talk to your parents and we can figure out how to get her downstairs." I felt better focusing on doing something.

The morning passed quickly in logistical arrangements and ended with Said and a few friends helping to bring Safiyya down to our apartment to recuperate.

We quickly realized that half dragging her to the bathroom every couple of hours to relieve herself was not practical, so I improvised with a large plastic tub that she could sit on and I could empty out. This only required us to help her from the bed to sit on the tub, which was difficult enough. If we had felt lighter, it probably would have made us laugh. Her left side was completely non-functional, and we didn't always get the angle right to lower her down to a seated position. Once we missed the bin entirely and the three of us ended up on the floor in a heap of twisted limbs.

It turned out that having the girls around was stressful for Safiyya. She kept calling me to see why one or the other of the kids was upset or crying. I also had not factored in that my father-in-law and Fatima would come down looking to me for breakfast and meals. Safiyya had always prepared their meals upstairs, and they missed her mothering and presence. I felt I was a poor substitute as my cooking was nowhere near her standard, and my knowledge of Moroccan customs was still lacking in many respects.

Fortunately, a neighbour came over every morning for an hour or so to help me cook and tidy up. She talked to Safiyya and helped to cheer her up. She and I decided to try giving Safiyya a sponge bath. I had spent some time thinking about how we could manage this without having to move her too far.

"If we put some plastic tablecloths on the mattress and have her head off the end, we can put the bin to catch the water and use a cup to wash her hair." I tried to explain my idea with my rudimentary Arabic and lots of gestures.

The neighbour looked dubious, but I plowed ahead and got everything set up. She held Safiyya's head as I poured cups of water over it to wet it. I massaged the shampoo in gently. I could feel compassion rising in me as I wondered what it must be like to suddenly find yourself helplessly dependent on others to look after you. I let the warm water run slowly through my fingers as I brushed the soap away from her face. I hoped she could enjoy the feeling of being washed and cared for. My own feelings of inadequacy, at not being what I thought she really wanted for a daughter-in-law, faded. I could feel my own power rising as hers declined.

The "bath" was fairly successful in my eyes, although there was a lot to clean up, and all of us were exhausted when we finally had Safiyya dressed again and tucked back into bed. I put the kettle on for tea and asked the neighbour to stay and drink it with us. She looked at me kindly but shook her head, saying she had other things to attend to. She motioned with her hand for me to follow her as she put her scarf around her head and walked to the door. Out of earshot of Safiyya, she explained that she could not keep coming over every day to help me. Her own family needed her, and it was too much work. I offered to pay her something for her time, but she shook her head firmly, as if she had already made up her mind.

I kissed her cheeks and thanked her for her help, my heart sinking. What would I do? I was already at breaking point. My day seemed a never-ending list of chores and care work. I hadn't slept well in weeks, with the new baby and now Safiyya, who got us up once or twice in the night to pee. I felt too heavy to carry on, too tired even to cry. Said had been locked in his own world of grief at his mother's illness, and maybe paralyzed at his own impotence to help or provide for his family. I had no energy for him, no desire to make him feel like a man, like he was needed. We did what we had to do to get through the day, and we slept next to each other at night without really feeling anything.

I climbed up to the roof for some air—my refuge, the place where I could look out at the world from what felt like my prison, and imagine what it would be like to be free. I wanted to sob, to let all the emotion of the last few days out, but I was dried up and worn out. I felt older than my thirty-one years. Was this all there was to life? More and more trials and obstacles in front of you, weighing you down until you finally couldn't take it anymore?

As if the universe, in some twisted fit of ironic humour, was listening to me, I saw a police car drive up to our house. Two big men in uniform got out, and I was startled when I saw them helping Said out of the back seat.

"What the hell?" I gasped and ran downstairs. I raced into the bedroom and grabbed a scarf as the men came up the stairs. Going to the door, I stood there, hoping to ask what was going on before Safiyya could see Said with the police.

"Good morning," I managed to say to the imposing policeman standing in the hall facing me.

He looked down at me and quietly but with a steely undertone replied, "Good morning, ma'am. We need to come in and search your house. If you could excuse us, please. We also need to take any computers you may have here."

"Oh, um, sure…whatever you need." I glanced at Said questioningly. "What's wrong?"

Said's face was pale and drawn, and he looked ill. His eyes flicked up to mine, and he shook his head, almost imperceptibly. I tore my gaze away from him and stepped back to let the officers into the house.

"Come here, sweethearts." I crossed over to the sofa and pulled the girls to sit with me. They sensed my seriousness and sat quietly. "Baba and the men just need to look at our computer," I said by way of explanation, hoping the girls would not question me any more at the moment.

The police unplugged our computer and set it by the door to take with them. Said stood helplessly as they searched through our bedroom and the rest of the house. They looked through papers and drawers, sometimes questioning Said as to what everything was. He answered in short phrases, his voice sounding faint and apologetic. I tried to catch his eye as the police were looking around. What the hell was going on? I looked over at Said's mother, who had been resting on her makeshift bed on the side of the living room.

"Said, Said," she called. "What do these men want? Why are they here?"

A sob escaped his lips before he could stop it. He reached up to wipe his eyes, and only then I saw his hands were in handcuffs. "It's okay, Ma, they just need to check something on the computer. Everything is going to be okay, don't worry." He looked pleadingly at the officers as they came back into the living room after searching the house. "Please, my mother is very sick."

"Good afternoon, ma'am, may Allah help you recover quickly. We just have some business with your son, it won't take long." They politely kissed her hand and backed away. Addressing the kids and me, they added, "We need to ask your husband a few more questions about something we are investigating. Sorry to bother you."

I nodded mutely, noticing at the same time that Safiyya looked extremely pale. I was too shocked to say anything. The girls squirmed uncomfortably next to me. Said wouldn't look back at us as they left, taking the computer and some papers with them. I let out my breath. I hadn't realized I'd been holding it.

I gathered myself quickly. "Well, come on then, habibas, let's make some tea for Aziza. She might be ready for some after her nap."

Doing something seemed like the only way to stop the panic from rising in my chest. I could see Safiyya was shaken, and I was worried she would have another stroke.

I had no idea what Said could have done to provoke what seemed to be a full-on investigation and interrogation. My mind raced to find something that would make sense. It just seemed crazy.

"Hey, Ma, don't worry, Said will be back soon. I will make some tea for you, don't worry now. They just need his help with something, I'm sure." I sincerely hoped she hadn't noticed the handcuffs on his wrists. "Omaima, can you run upstairs and see if Jido and Fatima want to come down for tea?" I asked, thinking that a distraction was necessary. Safiyya was breathing heavily, and the colour was still absent from her face. I went over and brushed her hair back. "Don't fret, Ma. You know it won't help you get better. Here, watch the baby while I get the tea," I said, placing Hajar next to her.

None of us spoke about Said or the search party as we sipped our tea. The girls were unaware of the grave nature of being interrogated by the police here in Morocco. There were rumours of an underground prison for political prisoners, from which no one ever came out. A sister's husband had been jailed for five years for celebrating Eid on the day that Saudi Arabia proclaimed as the holiday instead of the day after, which was set in Morocco. Torturing a person to gain a testimony was not uncommon either, and I flinched with the thought of what Said might have to go through.

We pretended things were normal, as much as we could. Safiyya was still pale, and I could see Taher's hand shake as he picked up his tea glass. No doubt Safiyya had filled him in on what she knew of the police visit. Fatima was unaware of it all, and we were grateful not to have to try and explain to her what was going on. Her sign language was fairly efficient for daily concerns but was woefully lacking in scope to explain anything outside of her ordinary experience.

I cleared the tea things and let the kids play for a bit before bedtime. I didn't know if Said would be back tonight or not. My mind spiralled near panic as I tried to think through how to deal with Safiyya on my own. She was too heavy for me to help her change position much, and I worried about her falling if I tried to help her onto the pee bucket.

"Don't worry about me, Aishah," she said, as if reading my thoughts, her words only slightly slurred. "I'll be okay."

"Don't be silly, Ma." I was impressed at her stoic effort to cope. "We have to get you to pee. I'll ask Fatima to come and help me lift you."

"Fatima is useless for that," she said hurriedly.

"I'm not sure we have much choice though," I pointed out a little tensely. "I can't do it alone."

"Okay," she admitted. "You better ask her to come down now and help me. She goes to bed early, and you can't call her once she is locked in her room."

"Yes, you're right, I'll go and get her." I got the bucket placed next to her bed, and her new nightgown laid out. "I'll be right back."

I walked upstairs feeling heavier than I ever remember feeling. I stopped my brain from going any further into the future than the next step. My hands were shaking as I reached for the handle on the door upstairs. As I pushed open the door I took a breath, which caught about halfway down my chest. I saw Fatima's back as she headed toward her room and ran after her to tap her on the shoulder.

She started and turned around, peering in the fading light to see who was there. I waved at her and made a "come here" motion, along with swiping my finger down my chin, which was her sign for her mother. I had to do the gestures a couple of times for her to grasp what I wanted.

"A Ma?" She nodded vigorously to say she understood and pushed me back downstairs.

Safiyya looked tired, and her lips were compressed with unspoken words as we came in to help her with her bedtime routine.

"I have only two children," she said emphatically, "Said and Fatima, and now I don't know where they took Said…" Her eyes glistened with tears, and her lip trembled.

"Don't worry, Ma, he'll be back." I tried to sound reassuring as I helped her out of her nightgown.

"Here, try and swing your legs down so we can help you onto the bucket to pee." Fatima grabbed her arm enthusiastically and hindered the process more than anything else, but at least she was there with me. I almost laughed as we tried to turn Safiyya in the right direction to sit down on the bucket. It felt like some drunken dance, and none of us could get it right. I smothered my snort, knowing she would think I was laughing at her, and we managed finally to get her sorted and back onto the bed. With relief, I put the new nightgown over her head and threaded her useless arm through the sleeve. Fatima helped lift her legs up and we settled her into bed and tucked her arm in with the blanket. Sighing heavily, I patted Fatima on the back to thank her. That would do for a few hours at least.

I went around to the girls' room. Once they had their pajamas on and teeth brushed, I sat down, pulling them in close for a story. I needed to feel their little bodies next to mine. I wanted the pressure just to know I was still here, in my body. So much of today felt unreal.

"Once upon a time," I began, "a long time ago in a faraway place…" My voice seemed to come from that far-off place too, as I lost myself in the story. The three older girls snuggled on each side and on my lap; the baby was thankfully asleep in her basket. I didn't want to get up, ever. I didn't think I could cope with anything else. I let the warmth of their bodies comfort me and the story take my mind away from the brutal reality that I was alone in a foreign country. My husband had been apprehended, my mother-in-law was an invalid, my sister-in-law was deaf and dumb, my father-in-law was old and needed someone to take care of him, my four daughters were all under the age of five years, and my family was on the other side of the world. I had no income and no one to turn to for support.

"And they lived happily ever after," I said, finishing the story.

Although I wanted to stay snuggled with the girls, I could feel a sob rising. "I think it's time for bed, sweethearts." I nudged their sleepy heads off my shoulders and helped them into their beds. Their eyes were closing as I tucked them in, thankful they were not aware of everything that had happened today. The baby was asleep as well, and I ran up the stairs to the roof. I threw myself down in a corner on some sheepskins and hugged my knees to my chest as the grief rose in a wave. I'd been holding it back all day, and the dam finally broke as I sobbed my heart out.

Once I'd finally cried myself out, my eyes were heavy and tired. Sleep called to me and I longed to lose myself in the blissful escape. I tiptoed downstairs quietly, not wanting anyone to see my puffy, red-rimmed eyes. I didn't want to try and explain myself to my mother-in-law either. I hoped I could sneak through to my bedroom without her noticing.

The door creaked as I went into the apartment, and the light from the street lamps shone through the shutters. I crept through to bed and curled up in a corner

of the mattress. The bed suddenly felt too big, and I
craved the comfort of Said's arms around me. Where
was he? Why had they taken him? What had he done?
He once told me he had run errands for the local mafia
as a young boy; had he been involved with anything
more recent? The questions crowded my mind and
I tossed and turned, the minutes ticking slowly by.

Chapter
Ten

SOMEHOW MORNING HAD COME. I awoke to Hajar crying in her crib at the foot of my bed. It took a few minutes for my head to clear enough to realize what the sound was.

"Aishah!" My mother-in-law called. "The baby is crying!"

"Okay, I've got her," I called back, pulling myself upright and lifting Hajar out of the crib. "Sh, sh...." I took her out to the living room and sat down to feed her.

"Good morning, Ma." I nodded sleepily. "Did you sleep alright?"

"A little." She pursed her lips in worry. "Did Said come back yet?"

"No, he is not back. I think they wanted to talk to him some more yesterday, and he probably stayed overnight with a friend downtown so he wouldn't disturb us," I lied, hoping to allay her concerns. My own fears I kept firmly locked up. Things would be okay, they had to be.

"He should be here with his family," she snapped irritably.

"I'm sure he will be back today," I said as cheerfully as I could. The baby had settled down. "Do you want me to see if Fatima is up, to help us get you sorted out?"

"Don't worry about me, I'm just old and in the way here. You have your babies to look after. I'll be fine." Her words were so ridiculous, I almost laughed. But her voice told a different story, and I sighed. Why couldn't she just say when she needed something? It would be so much easier than trying to guess and being wrong half the time.

"I'm going to change the baby and then get Fatima. You are not in the way at all, we love you very much." I didn't want her to get all depressed too, that was the last thing I needed. While I talked, I changed the baby and tied her securely to my back. One good thing about having four children was that I had become adept at sorting out babies quickly. "I'll be back in a minute," I said.

I need someone else to help me around the house, I thought as I trod upstairs to find Fatima. *This is crazy, I can't keep doing everything. I will kill myself, throw myself off the roof.*

My mind went down that path for a few seconds, imagining everything that would happen if I did that. Sighing, I pulled myself together. *That won't work. Another wife? Maybe, maybe that's the answer, someone who would be on my side.*

All that day, as I waited for any news from Said, I thought about us having another wife. Someone to help me around the house, who was part of the family and so would be obliged to take on some of the duties that had been heaped on my back. I felt generous in offering another woman status as a wife, I could share my husband. God, it would be a relief to have a night off now and then! I felt guilty thinking that, but my fantasies of blissful, married life had been harshly revealed as shadows that disappear when the light of the full moon fell on them. I hadn't had the energy to deal with Said and his desires for a long time. The least I could offer was another woman, my gift to him, I thought wryly. The thought rose in my mind that I didn't really want him anymore. I didn't even know if I was in love with him anymore. We had shared a lot, we had children together, we had the burden of caring for his family. But at the end of the day, I was too tired to do anything but drop into bed, and since his mother was sick, he no longer seemed to care if I was next to him or not.

I was jolted out of my reverie by the sound of my phone.

"Hello?"

"Allo," a man's voice replied. "We have your husband in custody for questioning. We suspect he may have connections to some terrorists operating in Morocco and Europe. He is not available to speak with you, but he asked us to tell you that he may not be released for at least a week."

My hands went numb, I couldn't feel the phone next to my ear. "Um...okay... What should I do?" A tight cord felt like it was wrapping itself around my neck. The realization of how isolated I was, as a woman in Morocco, had never sunk in quite like now. "What can I do?" I choked on the words.

"I'm very sorry, ma'am, I cannot give you any more information." The voice was sympathetic but clear, he had no more news for me. "We will contact you when the questioning is over." I heard the receiver click on the other end. The nightmares I'd heard about "questioning" here in Morocco filled every corner of my mind. What would I do if he didn't come back? Suddenly my fears came erupting out of the box in which I had kept them tightly hidden.

I sank to the floor, pulled the baby around to my chest, and hugged her tightly. I was stuck. Alone. No money. No one to help me. I couldn't do it. I couldn't go on. As I looked at Hajar, my chest shook with sobs. She would be an orphan, grow up with no parents. I couldn't—

"Aishah?" My mother-in-law's voice broke through my clouded brain. "Aishah!"

"Coming, Ma." I wiped my face on my sleeve, untangled myself from the cloth holding the baby to me, and got up. "Just a minute." I went through the bedroom to the bathroom and splashed water on my face. Willing myself to look in the mirror. *You can do this. Somehow, you can do this.* The face looking back at me, blotched and tear-stained, did not look convinced. *Allahu Akbar, alhamdullilah, Allah never gives us more than we can bear.* My lips repeated the *dua* over and over as I dried my hands and went to face my mother-in-law.

I can't say how I got through that week. The days never seemed to end. Maybe the only thing that saved me was the fact that I didn't sit down. I fed people, changed people, washed clothes, cooked, and started all over again. My father-in-law didn't speak, his lips pressed together in an angry grimace that only hardened over the week. He barely ate and the rest of the day he spent in the mosque. Fatima, for once, was a big help. She washed the dishes every morning and sat with her mother in the afternoons. I was grateful for her presence, even though she didn't understand what was going on.

I hadn't heard anything from the police. I hadn't told my family anything yet. I didn't know what to say, there was no news, nothing definitive to grasp on to. Was my husband a terrorist? How? Why? What had he done to make them suspect him? The questions were terrifying and the answers even more so. I had not realized what living in a country like Morocco really meant until now. Would someone even get a trial or a fair legal process here? What would happen to me and the girls? Could I leave? Would I be detained? I knew no one from whom I could get straight answers. I waited.

I had stopped counting the days. I wasn't even sure what I hoped for anymore. I heard Fatima calling from the balcony upstairs. "Duh du du! Eta, Eta!" That was her name for me, and I went to see what she was shouting about. She came barrelling down the stairs and almost knocked me over. "Du du." She pointed downstairs and made the motion of a beard with her hand. A man was at the door.

I pulled my scarf tighter around my head and followed her down the stairs.

She had pulled open the door before I had made it to the bottom of the stairs. I peered over her shoulder and every muscle of my body contracted. I inhaled sharply.

"Can we help you?" I asked, a little breathlessly.

"We are returning your computer and your husband. We have no further questions for him. We did not want to press any charges. Here he is." And they moved aside so we could see into the back seat of the black van outside. Said was sitting, slumped back in the seat, not moving.

"Is he okay? Are you okay?" I called a little louder, not quite sure whom to address my question to. His head lifted slightly at the sound of my voice.

"He's a little tired probably," the policeman offered. "He'll be alright. Come on, man!" He turned and helped

Said out of the van. I saw him stumble slightly getting out. What had they done to him?

I went closer and took his arm. He seemed distant, but he allowed himself to be led into the house. He was quiet and docile in a way that was chillingly unfamiliar. The men followed with our computer and the papers they had taken to search. They set them down then left without another word. Fatima and I managed to get Said upstairs and into the bedroom without his mom seeing the state he was in. I bit my tongue and kept the many questions crowding my mind to myself for now. He looked beyond answering anything right now. He sank into the bed, and I pulled the covers over him. He was pale and shaking a bit.

"Are you cold? Do you want another blanket?" There were no obvious marks on his body, but the colour of his skin was that of a man in shock. "What happened to you?" I couldn't help myself, I had to know. "Why where you kept for a week?" My voice rose at the end of the question, almost hysterically.

He shook his head and closed his eyes, but not before I noticed a tear slide down his cheek.

It took everything I had not to shake him and scream, "What did you do?" But instead I managed to whisper, "I love you," and brushed his cheek. "Sleep for a bit." I closed the door quietly. The sharp click was the only sign of the volcano of relief and anger that threatened to erupt from my body.

Safiyya looked up worriedly. "Is that Said? Why

doesn't he come to see me?"

"He's just really tired, Ma, he should sleep first."

I sincerely hoped she wouldn't ask anything more right now, as I felt I would not be able to answer another question without exploding. Fatima was sitting nearby signing her news about police and vans and things. Sighing, I turned and went to the kitchen. Let them wallow in the drama, I had to make dinner. I couldn't imagine what the police had done to him. I had no idea what he had done to be accused of being a terrorist. I wasn't sure I even knew who he was anymore. Had he done something wrong? Had he been tortured? And the big thing I dared not even think: If he really cared about us, he wouldn't have done something that got him arrested.

I mechanically began preparing the chicken and rice, ripping off the legs and wings almost viciously. I felt so helpless here. I couldn't do anything except cook and clean and take care of kids. I knew I would not get any answers, even if I could find someone to ask. No man here would talk to a woman. Women should be home with their family, not asking questions. I ripped the skin off the remaining breast and pushed the pieces of meat into the pot with the vegetables and water, measured in the paprika, turmeric, pepper, cumin, salt, fresh coriander leaves, then screwed the lid of the pressure cooker on tightly. Checking my watch, I saw I had just enough time to check on Said and go and fetch the older girls from nursery school before lunch. I looked forward to the walk, just to get out of the house and breathe!

I poked my head into the bedroom and saw he was awake, just lying there.

"What did you do?" I hissed. "Why were you gone for a whole week?"

Said turned his head to look at me, and the vacant look in his eyes cleared slightly. "They questioned me about the guy I bought the car from," he said quietly. "The one in Spain. It was terrible, the torture." He turned away.

The knot in my stomach was tighter than ever. He had only briefly mentioned something about the second-hand car he had gone to see in Spain a couple of months ago. I had not wanted to push him to talk, but my skin prickled with the tension of unspoken words. Was that really why they had arrested him?

I knew he had travelled a few weeks ago with this guy that was selling a second-hand car. Said told me now that the police had informed him that this guy had been arrested for terrorism, and the penalty for that was very harsh. I wondered if Said had been accused of terrorism by association? Now that I thought about it, it did seem strange that he had to travel with him to Spain just to see a car. At the time, Said said he thought the guy wanted someone else to come with him as it made the trip less suspicious. I honestly didn't know what to think. Was Said just naive about the ways of these people, or did he know what he was doing? Were the kids and I in danger now? I recalled my mother's letter to me before we were married. She had urged me to find out my rights in a country like Morocco and told me to be careful. I pushed the fear down and concentrated on the present moment. Whatever had happened, it was obvious that the resulting few days of questioning had completely devastated him. Was it wrong that I felt gratified to some extent that he was suffering too? He had put us all through a hell of not knowing. I looked at the clock and reluctantly stood up.

"I have to go for the kids, we will talk later."

I exited the bedroom and said to Safiyya, "I'll be back shortly with the girls. Can you watch the younger ones? The baby is asleep there in the chair." I brought the car seat close enough for her to rock it and made sure Hind was close by too. Throwing my burka over my house dress, I went out.

I had my head down as I rounded the corner between our house and the neighbours', my mind a million miles away, on a beach in the Bahamas or anywhere else but here. Bam! I ran into someone coming out of a doorway.

"Ouch. Oh! I'm sorry," I gasped as I tried to pull myself into the present moment.

"That's okay." The girl was wearing a scarf and an old dress. She looked to be in her twenties. Her dark hair was pulled back under the scarf that was knotted in the traditional style at the nape of her neck. She was a bit taller than me, and her manner exuded the strength of someone who had worked hard all of her life. I didn't remember ever seeing her around before. "Are you okay?"

she asked me, leaning against the broom she had been using to sweep the step and eyeing me thoughtfully. "Are you the Canadian?"

"Um, yeah." It continually amazed me how everyone seemed to know everything about you here. "I'm Aishah, pleased to meet you, um…?" I put out my hand to shake hers, prompting her to introduce herself. I was proud that I could now confidently hold this kind of conversation in the Moroccan dialect.

"Fatima Zohra," she returned as she grasped my hand in a strong grip. "How is Safiyya? I heard she was sick."

"Oh, she is doing better, I guess." I stammered to find the proper words. "She cannot move her left side."

"May Allah bless her and make her strong. Hey, if you need some help sometime, let me know," she said, smiling.

"Thank you, thank you so much." Tears of gratitude welled up unbidden. I hastily wiped my eyes but not before she noticed.

"What about I come over now for a bit? My mother is out at work, and I don't have much to do. I am finished cleaning."

"Um, I guess that would be fine." I hesitated, not quite knowing if it was okay to invite people in off the street to help in our house, especially with Said just home. I wasn't sure if my mother-in-law would approve. "I am just going to pick up my girls from hadana. Why don't you come for lunch? My cooking is not too bad."

I smiled wanly. "I'll knock on your door on my way back, in maybe fifteen minutes?" Perhaps having someone else in the house would be good today, take the pressure off me.

"Okay, thanks, see you then." Fatima Zohra shook my hand again and returned with her broom through the doorway to what I assumed was her apartment. It was too dark to see much inside.

"You sure your mother won't mind?" I called after her.

"No, don't worry, she knows Hajj and Safiyya." Hajj was the respectful nickname given to my father-in-law, who had been to Mecca for Hajj. He had received the trip as a gift from the Saudi king, his employer, at the time of his retirement. "We are neighbours after all," she said quickly. I didn't push it any further, as my understanding of the manners in Morocco was slim and I usually got it all wrong and made people angry. Maybe neighbours did this kind of thing here all the time. Safiyya did have a lot of neighbourhood women in to help cook when my baby was born. It would be nice to have someone help in the house again.

The walk was refreshing and lifted my spirits a little. The girls excitedly explained to me the things they had done in school that morning, and I tried to listen to their chatter. Omaima showed me her carefully saved writing on her chalkboard. I was impressed with her neat cursive script. One thing they did seem to get right here in Morocco was writing. She was only five years old, and her letters looked beautiful. She was a quick learner, and her teacher had said she would be ready for school by next year. I thought of telling the girls their father was back but decided to wait and see how he was doing when we got to the house.

"We are picking up a friend on the way home," I explained. "She's going to have lunch with us and help me with Aziza."

"Who is it?" the girls asked, excitedly. "Do we know her?"

"She's a neighbour, but I don't think you've met her before."

We rounded the last corner and the girls ran ahead. I stopped to knock at Fatima Zohra's door.

"Hello, we are back." I moved to let her come through the door. We walked the short distance to our house. I was slightly anxious as I wasn't sure Said or his mother would be pleased with my initiative. I had to do something though, I couldn't keep going this way much longer. "Welcome to our house," I said as we entered.

"Said, Safiyya, I invited one of the neighbours to come for lunch, and she is going to help me with some housework afterwards."

Fatima Zohra moved quickly to where Safiyya was propped up on the bed and kissed her hand. "Hello, Auntie, may Allah grant you good health."

Said came to the door of the bedroom. "I invited Fatima Zohra for lunch," I told him quietly. "I hope that's okay. Do you want to eat with us?" We often went against the ruling that men and women had to segregate socially. Moroccans had their own etiquette regarding mixing, and often "family" was extended to include uncles, cousins, and even close friends. The girls squealed excitedly to see their dad home and have a visitor at the same time. They bounced over to the sofas near Safiyya and sat down.

Said grunted and shuffled to the bathroom to wash up. I hoped he would make an effort to converse since we had a guest. It was the least he could do after abandoning us for God knows what kind of scheme that led to the whole police thing. I was hoping that having another person to talk to would diffuse the palpable tension and force him to try and be sociable. Well, at least he was up.

I motioned to Fatima Zohra to come through to the kitchen and help with serving the lunch I had prepared. She was efficient and obviously knowledgeable and had all the plates and bread out on the table before I'd even put the tagine in the bowl.

"Thank you." I smiled at her, feeling already how nice it was to have another woman helping. "Come on, girls!" I ran a wet washcloth over their hands as they came to sit around the table.

"Mm, chicken!" Their eyes widened with delight as Fatima Zohra broke pieces of bread and passed them around.

"Wait for Baba," I reminded them. "He's coming to eat too."

They wiggled impatiently as Said traipsed into the living room, looking only marginally better after making ablutions. I moved over to let him sit down. I was no longer as drawn to making the little touches and flirtations that I used to do. I felt numb and exhausted.

"Here, come and sit down." I moved over to let him pass.

He nodded to Fatima Zohra and his mother. "Assalamu alaikum, bismillah."

The girls dove in, dipping their bread eagerly into the broth and picking out the potatoes. Their mouths bulged like little chipmunks. The adults all politely dipped their bread into the edge of the pan. Safiyya broke off pieces of chicken and encouraged everyone to eat. I sat back and watched, glad to have the diversion of a meal to take away the awkward silences that had plagued us all in the last few days. Said seemed more alive as he ate. He glanced often at Fatima Zohra as she ate and helped with the girls. Very faintly I felt jealousy rise, but I was too tired to care much, and I was weirdly relieved that something had broken his suffering silence. As the plate emptied, he seemed to take the role of host more seriously and asked me to make tea for our guest.

I took the empty plate into the kitchen and put on the kettle. *Humph.* I wanted him to rise to the occasion, but sending me to make tea while he launched into stories about the Muslims at the time of the Prophet Muhammad rankled me. I had just tried to talk about serious things and he could barely say a word. He loved having a fresh audience. Eternal showman that he was, he took the opportunity to shine in the spotlight of fresh, adoring eyes. *Fine, whatever.* I took the tea in and set the tray in front of him. He could pour his own tea. It would take years before I understood that this avoidance behaviour was his protection against any kind of intimacy.

"Come on, girls, I'd like you to have a little quiet time before we go back to school."

"Oh, let them stay if they want. Do you want tea?" Said asked the girls, completely ignoring my haughty tone.

"Yes! Please, Baba!" Omaima and Safia answered eagerly, and Hind climbed up in Fatima Zohra's lap and stuck her thumb in her mouth, determined to stay where the action was.

"I'm going to feed the baby." I turned and retreated to the bedroom. At least they were occupied, and I was too tired to even get upset. I lay down on the bed and pulled Hajar close to me, offering her my breast. It was comforting to feel needed and be able to make someone happy, just by being there. She suckled contentedly for awhile, and her eyelids drooped over her flushed cheeks. My own eyes grew heavy, and I dozed groggily for a few minutes.

"Mama!" Omaima bounced into the room, startling me. "Fatima Zohra is going to walk us back to school! She said she knows where it is."

"Oh, well…what did Baba think?" My mind

struggled to wake up fully.

"He told her to take us back 'cause you were tired and needed a nap," Omaima replied triumphantly.

"Um, okay then, if you guys are okay with that?" The irritated feeling had come back, and I no longer felt like sleeping.

"Yeah! She is nice, and Baba gave us money to get cookies!"

"Well, I guess it's all settled then. Don't forget your chalkboards, and I'll see you later. Give me a kiss!" I reached my free arm out to her, and she leaned in to peck me on the cheek. A minute later, Safia came in to kiss me too, and then I heard them heading out with Fatima Zohra. *She is so cheerful! Wait until she has too much to do and is exhausted all the time, she won't be so cheerful then.* My spiteful thoughts crowded in even more as Said poked his head in the door and smiled. Why did it make him happy to have a new person to tell his stories to, I wondered? I felt cast aside.

"I'm going to pray at the mosque, I'll be back soon. Have a nice nap." He looked almost back to his old self.

Fine! If everyone thinks I should rest, I'll rest! I pulled the blanket up over me and the still sleeping baby and closed my eyes. *Let them all deal with it all! I don't care.* I turned over and was asleep before I could form another thought. I didn't want the thought that it must be my fault to win out in my head. I'd rather feel nothing than the shame of failure.

I awoke from one of those deeply refreshing naps

where it could have been ten minutes or two hours. The baby was beginning to stir, but sleepily, and I figured I still had fifteen or twenty minutes before she was awake enough to be crying for me. I slid out of the bed and crept to the washroom. I wasn't quite ready to deal with my mother-in-law yet either. I shivered slightly with the damp chill that got into the concrete walls of the house in the rainy season. It always seemed to be either too hot or too cold and damp here in Tangier. There were very few days that were really a perfect temperature.

I checked the time, I had an hour before the girls finished preschool. Good, time to feed the baby. I hadn't heard Said come back from the mosque yet, but that was not abnormal. He often stayed to talk to the other men after prayers. I noticed the dishes were all cleaned up from lunch as well. Hm, maybe Fatima Zohra had done that while I was lying down. That discovery did not completely take away the slight jealousy I had felt as Said launched into full storytelling mode at lunch. So, I was still not in a great mood when Safiyya called to me.

"Aishah! I was wondering if you had a few minutes?" She pulled the blankets with her good hand as she talked, seeming nervous for some reason.

"Sure, Ma, what is it?"

"I really appreciate what you have done for me, all this," she swept her arm, taking in her bed in our living room, "but I feel I am becoming a burden on you."

"No, no, not at all," I said politely, patting her hand, hoping I was understanding her Arabic.

"Well, I was wondering if you think I could move back upstairs? Now that we have the potty chair, I can pretty much do that by myself, or with a little help."

I thought of her back upstairs and felt lighter already. It was a constant strain to have her watch everything I did, and I knew she disagreed with my parenting sometimes.

"Um, well, sure, if that's what you want." I tried to keep the elation out of my voice. "I can ask Said when he comes back. Maybe you'd be more comfortable in your own place."

She nodded. "Yes, let's ask Said." Settling back against the cushions, she said, "He should be back by now, shouldn't he?"

"Yes, yes, he should be back." I sighed irritably, not really sure I wanted him back. All in all, it had been an emotionally trying day, and the last thing I needed was my mother-in-law pointing out my husband's lack of responsibility. "I'll run up and see if I can see him from the roof." I wanted to get away for a few more minutes of peace before having to deal with the baby as well.

I spied Said over by the mosque, surrounded by a group of men, and watched for a few minutes. His hands were telling the story as much as his words. The men all watched him avidly. He really was a showman, he couldn't help but perform whenever he had an audience. His escapade with the police no doubt made an especially amazing story. My heart softened a bit.

Perhaps the fear had gotten to me a little too much today. At least he seemed happy when he was talking to other people. I wished he would be that way with me, be the husband I dreamt about. For some reason I couldn't quite put my finger on, my relationship with Said had never quite filled the longing in me to be loved, no matter how hard I tried.

He looked in my direction, and I waved to him to come back. He waved back then shook the hands of the men around him. As he turned to walk toward the house, I headed back downstairs.

"What's up?" he called up the stairs, as his boots clumped on the steps.

"Your mom wants to talk to you," I called back. "I think she is hoping you'll help her move back upstairs."

"Why? Did you two fight?" he asked.

"No, no, she just said she felt she would be more comfortable upstairs in her own apartment, and we have the chair for her to use now. She doesn't like to be a burden on us," I added defensively.

"Oh." He entered and turned to his mother. "Hey, Ma, how are you? You know you are welcome to stay here as long as you want."

"I know, but you and Aishah, you have your own things to do, you don't need me in the way here."

"You're not in the way," Said countered, "but if it's what you want, I can get the boys to come and help me move your bed upstairs again."

"Yes, that's what I want. Fatima can help me more

upstairs." She smiled. "I'm glad you are up and about again, I was worried about you, after the police talked to you and everything. You seem better now?" Her voice rose at the end in a demanding curiosity. I realized then that she was worried about Said too.

"Of course, Ma, don't worry, I'm fine." Said kissed her forehead. "I'll see if the boys can come and help me move you tomorrow." Her face fell. No information was forthcoming, and I could tell by the drop in her shoulders that she felt the same rejection I did.

"Thank you, my son." She patted his hand. "You and Fatima are good children."

I marvelled at her ability to forgive.

A couple of days later I was feeling just a tad more relaxed as I surveyed my living room restored to its original purpose. Not having my mother-in-law watching every move I made gave me some much-needed breathing space, even though her presence had seemed supportive in some ways too, especially in regards to Said.

"Should I get that girl from next door to come and help again tomorrow?" I asked Said. "Maybe make bread and clean upstairs for them a little bit? I could really do with having another woman around the house that could help properly."

"Sure, ask her to come again. She seemed nice, and good with the kids too."

Sure, "nice and good with the kids," I thought. She was a big help, so why did I feel like throwing something at her? Why did it take having another woman in our house for Said to be in a good mood again and spend time with me and the girls? I didn't actually want to know the answer. I really could use some help, so I decided to suck it up. Maybe it would be a good thing. Maybe I should talk to Said about having her come regularly. Deep down, I think I wanted an ally, someone to share the burden of running a household.

Fatima Zohra began to come and help most mornings. She instinctively knew how to make Safiyya feel comfortable, in a way I never could. They spoke the same language, she did the chores in that Moroccan way that I just couldn't master. Said smiled and chatted when she was around, seeming to enjoy the chance to tell the stories about early Islam that I had already heard countless times and grown tired of. Did it make sense to feel redundant and relieved at the same time?

On one of those rare mornings that Said was around and I had made us breakfast and coffee to share, I decided to bring up the subject.

"So Fatima Zohra has made a big difference around here, helping with your mom and stuff," I started.

"Yes, yes, she has been great," Said agreed, stuffing his mouth with fried egg. Amazing how he had recovered so quickly from the week with the police, I thought, looking at him. It was almost like I had been the one who was tortured.

"I was thinking maybe we should talk about having a maid or someone to help more permanently," I continued.

"A maid? Why?" Said stopped chewing and looked at me.

"Well, your mom is not going to get better, not really." I hesitated. "And I can't handle the kids and your parents all the time. Fatima Zohra is a big help, but I think we can't rely on neighbours forever." I wanted to add "we can't count on you either," but the rest of my words lingered as a thought in the air between us.

"Hm, well, I think I would have a problem with a woman being around the house all the time," Said said.

"Why? What do you mean?" I was getting confused.

"Well, I'm not supposed to look at women, and it's hard if she is right there in the house all the time."

"What? Really?" I looked at him dubiously. "Seriously, you would find that hard?" *What the absolute fuck*, my inner voice continued, *after all you've put us through?*

"Yes," he shifted uncomfortably, "I would."

"Oh, well…" I didn't know how to articulate what I wanted to say, the feelings were so jumbled up. "You don't seem to look at me that way much anymore… not really." The confusion was real. I mean, he did want certain sexual favours and things, but it no longer felt like any kind of marital connection. *Maybe it never was*, my inner voice whispered. I could feel the familiar pricking of tears behind my eyes. I didn't want to dissolve into tears every time we talked, he definitely wouldn't want me then.

"Baby, I love you, you know that," he said, "but you're busy with the babies. I still think you're beautiful." Of course, he knew the right words to say. I wished I could still believe them.

I sighed. It didn't fill the hole in my chest to hear him say those words. I didn't feel beautiful anymore. I felt old, and tired, and worn out. Nothing he could say could change that. I found my brain jumping to solutions rather than acknowledge my true feelings. "Well, we could get another wife?"

He laughed. "Really? You'd let me do that?" His eyes sparkled in a way I hadn't seen in months.

"Um, I guess…" This was all going a bit too fast. "I was reading this book about polygamy a while ago, and it seemed like it wasn't all bad." I faltered, not quite sure I wanted to be having this conversation. "You seemed to like Fatima Zohra, and it was nice to see you enjoying telling her Islamic stories and sitting with the girls the other day."

"You're amazing, you know that?" He leaned over to kiss me. "I'm so lucky to have a wife like you."

I basked in the praise. Part of me wondered if doing this together could also bring back some semblance of closeness. "I want to be part of it though," I said. "We have to do this together." The fear of being left in the dust of a new wife was real.

"Sure, of course," he agreed quickly. "You have to like her for sure. We'd do it mostly to have someone to help you around the house," he added. "It's not like I'd be in love with her."

"As long as I am first in your heart, always."

I wondered if this could really work. Was it fair to marry someone without really loving them? And then, what if he did love her but just didn't tell me? What if he didn't really love me either? The confusion hung over me like moonlight on a foggy night.

"Let's not tell my parents," Said said after a thoughtful silence. "It would probably just upset my mom, and we don't want that." Even in Morocco, having multiple wives was not accepted by everyone. In fact, many people actively looked down on the old Islamic practice.

I nodded. "Of course. We should keep it secret for awhile. You have to talk to Fatima Zohra and see if she likes the idea anyway." It didn't bother me that other people wouldn't agree. I knew from my research that the most pious Muslims practiced polygamy and that it helped many women who wouldn't be able to find husbands have an acceptable place in society. It made me feel good to know we could help someone like Fatima Zohra. Perhaps I felt proud that I could be so generous. And besides, she was pleasant and helpful, and she and I could talk about some things. She made an effort to understand my rudimentary Arabic. *And you're lonely*, The Voice reminded me. *You want someone for yourself. Said can no longer even pretend to love you the way you want.*

Said cleared his throat. "Um, yeah, well…I was

thinking you could talk to her first. You know, break
the idea to her, woman to woman. Show her that you
are on board with the idea." He fidgeted with the remote
control as he talked.

"Oh, sure, I guess I can, but you have to talk to her
at some point." I was not very happy to be put in the
position of starting this tricky conversation. First of all,
I wasn't at all sure my limited Arabic would begin to be
able to express the nuance needed for a topic like this.
"Maybe we can talk to her together, when she is over
helping out again?"

"Okay, we'll see." Said turned on the TV and began
a methodical flick through the channels, which essentially
dismissed me and the whole conversation. I got up to see
to things around the house and left him sitting there. The
whole idea had left me with a sour taste in my mouth.
I went to the bathroom to tackle the dirty diapers. The
stench of urine and the overwhelmingly distasteful job
drove the thoughts from my mind, and by the time I had
hauled the basin of diapers upstairs to hang on the line,
I had worked out some of my frustration.

The topic didn't come up again for another week
or two. Life was busy and Said had resumed his habit
of going out a lot.

"We should take the kids to the beach someday
soon," I suggested. "School gets out next week, and
it's so hot!" The great thing about living in Tangier
was that you were always close to the beach. The
Mediterranean and the Atlantic oceans met at the tip

of North Africa and provided many and varied beaches and scenic areas.

Said glanced up from his phone. "I guess, yeah."

"We could try taking your mom out too. She hasn't been out of the house for weeks."

He looked thoughtful. "I guess we could try. She has been doing better, and it might lift her spirits."

"How about Sunday?" I wanted to nail down something concrete.

"Sure, okay."

"Okay!" I instantly went into my organizer mode. "I'll plan for Sunday. You won't forget, right?"

"Sunday," he repeated, not quite smiling but as close to it as I'd seen for a while.

Later that day, I stopped by Fatima Zohra's basement apartment on my way to pick up the girls.

"How are you? How is your mother? Your sisters?" I kissed her cheek between each enquiry, doing my best to copy the long greeting rituals of the local women. "Said and I are going to try taking Safiyya and the girls to the beach on Sunday, and I wondered if you'd like to come along."

"That sounds nice." She looked pleased. "I'll check with Mama, but I'm sure that will be okay. Do you need help getting ready?"

"If you can come early that morning to help get everyone in the car, that should work."

The most difficult task would be getting Safiyya down two flights of stairs. We had been working on her mobility, and she could shuffle her left leg along on the even surface of the tiled floor upstairs with one person supporting some of her weight. We had not attempted stairs. I was determined we would find a way though, even if we had to almost carry her.

"See you Sunday morning then?" I asked. She nodded, and I waved goodbye.

Sunday morning Fatima Zohra arrived even earlier than I had asked her, the moon was still visible, low in the sky. She looked fresh and pretty in a different jellaba and matching scarf. I marvelled at the way Moroccan women could make going out anywhere into a fashion show. My own garment was dark and not showy at all, and I had never particularly worried about matching the colours. *I don't need to compete with her*, I reminded myself. *I am the first wife and I always will be.*

It was refreshing to have another woman helping me get everything ready. Fatima Zohra took charge completely, sweeping in and adeptly getting the girls, groggy from sleep, up and dressed. She had all the towels and blankets packed and was organizing the food to take before I could catch up with her at all. I couldn't help feeling incredibly grateful and yet somewhat inept and useless, as her efficient and dominating presence slowly spread throughout the house. She noticed and responded to Said's wishes with the knowing of their shared culture, something I could never hope to match. I tried to keep up and stay out of her way at the same time.

"Let's load the car and then help Safiyya down

the stairs," I heard Fatima Zohra directing Said with
a familiarity that irked me somehow. I did not want to
offend her at the beginning of the day though, so kept
my feelings to myself. I could not deny that I also felt
hugely relieved, not having to do everything alone. I
allowed myself to imagine her being part of our family,
a second wife, and found I was not completely for or
against the idea. The stronger emotions of jealousy
and inadequacy were drowned out for now by my
overwhelming fatigue. *Let her help*, I thought to myself.
Let her have Said every other night too if necessary. With a touch
of guilt, I caught myself thinking that the break from
cooking and tending to his needs might even be nice.
Said had not been a very caring husband of late. He
was happy to get himself off without giving me much
of a thought. His idea of being a great spouse was
parading his body in front of me naked from the shower
and shaking his dick in my direction, with a "Don't you
want a piece of this?" kind of look.

I giggled to myself, thinking about it, because the
answer was usually, "No, I'm good, thanks!" I had never
actively said no to him, but my body language had
become more avoidant of late. The guilt was layered
on top of the jealousy as I thought about it. It never
really crossed my mind to think about what I wanted
in the bedroom. I had been attracted to Said because
at first, he had made me feel desired, beautiful, and sexy.
I liked that he seemed to get turned on around me and
want sex all the time. I thought that meant he loved me.

Now it just seemed to be annoying. I didn't want to be desired, I wanted help with the kids and the housework. I was too tired to think about anything more romantic. There were days where I felt like a slave, cooking and cleaning all day and expected to dress up and be alluring for my husband at the end of it all.

I turned to Islam for answers to these problems. There were many books written on the subject of marriage and being a good Muslim woman. All the scholars and books on religion said to be good to your husband, give him what he wants, make him happy and not inclined to look elsewhere for pleasure. I shuddered, remembering my friend in England who always offered her husband a blow job before he went out of the house so he would remain pious amongst all the infidel women. I felt both disgust and admiration for her. Where she found the strength to offer that, when she herself was not even allowed out of the house, confounded my sense of righteousness.

I picked up the baby and climbed into the van with everyone else. I would let Fatima Zohra help make this day possible and even enjoyable. What other option was there really? Said beamed in the rear-view mirror as he pulled out onto the road. He was revelling in being the head of such a beautiful family; I could tell he felt proud and important. His mother looked proud too and smiled humbly, the guest of honour.

"We are almost there," I said loudly, trying to calm the now eager and wiggly girls. "Stay in your seats, you will get out in a minute and see the ocean."

Later that evening as I reflected back on the day, I noted how much better I felt having someone helping me all day. Said was in a good mood, the girls loved having another lap to climb on, Safiyya seemed more relaxed with another Moroccan woman around who understood her needs better than I did. All in all, a successful outing. I breathed deeply and let out a sigh. Maybe it would be better to have another wife around all the time. I decided to sleep on the question of how to proceed. Maybe I'd talk to Fatima Zohra about it tomorrow.

The girls were tired out from the day at the beach, and Said had gone out for coffee with his friends. I sank gratefully into bed, relishing having it all to myself. I had still not completely gotten used to the hard mattress, but tonight I was tired, and I didn't care where I slept. Hajar was asleep in the travel cot for now, and it felt amazing to be able to pull the blanket up around my shoulders without having to accommodate her head on my arm. Such small things made a difference when every day felt like a marathon of endurance. Sleep came quickly.

It seemed like much later when I felt Said slip into bed next to me. He reached for me and pulled me into his body. I could feel the hardness of his need, pushing into my back. Sleepily, I pulled my nightgown up so he could feel my bare skin. I was warm and snug and didn't feel like moving, but I knew he liked it when I acted like

I wanted him. I moaned softly and pressed my buttocks into him, hoping he would do the rest and let me sleep.

I felt him enter me, and wriggled a little to let him know I could feel him. "Oh, baby," he whispered as he pumped his way to orgasm, "I love you."

"Love you too," I whispered, too tired to turn around. I pulled his arm around my waist, and his body slackened into sleep. This was as close as we seemed to get these days. Exhausted bodies wrapped together in sleep for a few hours every day. I missed the old times, when we had first met. We had spent hours in bed giggling and sharing secrets, feeling more alive just with each other's touch. It had seemed like the perfect love. Why did it all seem like a spiteful joke now? How does "perfect" crumble to dust in your hands? I should sleep, I told myself, tomorrow was another day to get through and I would rather do it having had what sleep I could. Sighing, I put my thoughts away.

A couple of days later, Said announced, "I am going for tea with Fatima Zohra and her mother. I am going to ask her if she wants to be my second wife."

"Oh!" My hands suddenly got icy, even though the temperature was a sweltering one hundred degrees. "I didn't realize you were ready for that yet."

"You said you liked her." Said's voice took on a slightly defensive tone. "We have talked about this."

"Yes…I guess so." I couldn't find a reason to argue the point, I just felt like I'd been slapped and didn't know why. "I just didn't expect you to ask her so soon." I had talked around the subject with her before, but neither Fatima Zohra nor I had come out and said anything definite. For some reason neither of us had really been serious in our talk. We had giggled a little at the thought of being co-wives, but somehow the idea hadn't become reality yet. The topic had melted into the background of everyday life, and I hadn't processed the outcome completely at all.

"You need help. You have the girls and you need help around the house with my mother. She can help you." Said was applying his powers of persuasion. He could talk me around to anything in the end. "I want to do this for you. I won't love anyone like you, she won't take your place. We won't tell my parents anything yet either." His tone was reassuring and poured over me like oil on water. I wanted these moments of attention from him to last, I needed them to convince me I was still loved.

I wasn't sure if what he was saying was true or not, but I wanted it to be true. Maybe this was his ultimate gift to me, someone to help me. Maybe this wasn't just about him, or that I wasn't enough for him. How could I be enough anyway? I was stretched so thin I felt I would break. I needed this. I knew Said would not be able to help me the way I wanted him to, so maybe I should just be grateful he was willing to have another wife so I could have the support that way. My brain ran on and on, incessantly making rationalizations for why this was a good thing. My hands remained cold.

Said kissed me and left. He looked so handsome. He had dressed in one of his dress white candoras with short, white trousers underneath and some leather sandals. He had put gel in his hair to style the unruly, black curls, and I noticed he had put on a nice watch and ring. He looked like a sheikh, his beard combed and curling down. He always did like to put out a good appearance.

It's funny how I liked that about him, his appearance, his public presence, and yet his inner spirit did not match the looks. When we were first married, I had been shocked to find he sank into bouts of depression that sometimes carried on for days. He was usually only roused out of these states by something new or exciting in his life or a chance to help someone and gain adoration. At first it was me. Now, it was Fatima Zohra. I sighed and turned around, no sense wasting time wondering what was happening. I got the brush and began vigorously brushing the carpet. The physical exertion gave me a vent for my confused feelings.

"Mama, can we go outside and play with the neighbours?" Omaima asked.

"I guess so. Who are you playing with?" I asked absently.

"Maryam," she answered. "And Safia and Hind are coming too. Her mom has cookies."

"Oh, that sounds nice." I was thankful to have the girls taken care of for a bit. I could feed the baby in peace. "Come back before *Maghrib* prayers, before it gets dark," I warned them.

"Okay." The girls slipped on their plastic sandals, and Omaima shepherded her younger siblings down the stairs.

When they were gone and I had checked on them through the window to make sure they got to the neighbour's house, I sank down on the sofa, feeling unusually tired and defeated. Picking up baby Hajar and pulling out my breast for her to feed felt comforting. Someone needed me. After a couple of tries she sucked contentedly, and I could feel my body respond to her, relaxing into the letdown of milk and the softening of her body next to mine. I could feel tears close to the surface, although I had no idea what, exactly, I was unhappy about. Nor did I know what I would wish for even if I had the opportunity of something different.

A few minutes after the girls left, Said came back. "How did it go?" I asked, both interested and dreading the answer. "What did she say?"

"She and her mom agreed," he replied, without elaborating.

"So? What does that mean? Are you going to marry her?" I couldn't help the questions rolling off my tongue in quick succession.

"Well, she agreed, so I guess we can start the process if we want." Said looked uncomfortable as he talked. "It takes a while, I've heard. We have to take our case to the court for approval. It's expensive too." He looked at me expectantly. He had come to rely on me for answers to life's difficulties, and I rose to the challenge. It gave me a sense of purpose and gave my life meaning.

I had no idea how the court system worked in Morocco. I doubted the process was simple and straightforward—nothing seemed to be simple here.

"What do we have to do to take our case to the court?" I asked, my mind jumping as it always did to the practicalities of implementing a plan.

"Well, I can talk to a friend of mine who is a lawyer here," Said began, "and I will ask the brothers who have multiple wives for advice also. I don't know how it will go just yet, but I believe we have to show our financial records to prove I can afford another wife."

"Oh, yeah, I guess that makes sense." I wasn't sure how we would convince any judge that we had enough money. Perhaps the fact that I was from Canada and my parents owned property could help somehow.

"Well, I do like her, and if you want to do that, then I think we should go ahead." I looked him in the eyes, wanting to feel the connection, wanting him to thank me for my understanding and generosity. I wanted to be lauded as an amazing Muslim wife.

"I'm glad you feel like that," Said answered, pulling me to him. "You are an amazing woman." And with that, I felt better. He had accepted my offering, and I maintained my status as the first wife.

And so, from that moment our connection and collaboration as a couple took on a different direction. I think our relationship had always thrived on working

together to overcome obstacles. In some ways, we had
created difficulties just so that we could pull together
to surmount the problems. Or he had created difficulties
so I could overcome them. Recently, I had felt more and
more that I alone was facing the challenges, so, with as
much enthusiasm as I could muster, I embraced the
opportunity to be in some kind of partnership with Said.
I tried so hard to be involved that I didn't allow myself
to really think what this change would mean for me, as
a woman. Once I had started the process, I felt myself
almost dragged along by the momentum.

Fatima Zohra became a more frequent part of our
family. We didn't tell Said's mother and father, as Said
did not want to distress his mom. She had stabilized
somewhat and life had begun to reshape around looking
after the kids as my priority. Said's sister had finally risen
to the challenge of cooking for her parents upstairs, and
this freed me up more to get on with my affairs
downstairs. I could feel myself settling into life a bit more
comfortably again. The older two girls were doing well
in nursery school. Fatima Zohra and I often did some
housework together in the morning and then shared
coffee, and I found my Arabic was improving a lot as
we tried to converse about more difficult topics like
thoughts and feelings.

Almost every week, Said would go to the court in
the centre of Tangier and proceed with the paperwork
to allow him to take Fatima Zohra as a second wife.
None of us had realized how challenging the process

would be, and there were many times where we looked at each other in disbelief and frustration at the bureaucracy that was endemic in Moroccan law. Each time we hit a roadblock, one of the three of us would talk the others around, and we would keep going. One of the big problems was proving that we had adequate financial means to support another wife. Said's business ventures had not gone particularly well. He had had ideas of buying a car to use as a taxi; he had wanted to start a pizza takeaway restaurant; we had even discussed shipping clothes or Moroccan goods to Canada to sell. For all these plans, though, there was never anything much to show for it, and we had to rely on some support from our friends in England to survive our first couple of years in Morocco.

Said's most successful venture was a herbal medicine shop with a couple of the brothers he had met here. He had actually seemed to make progress in learning about the medicines, and his shop had been open for a few months. Often, he came home with no profit from his day at work though, always telling a heart-melting story of some person who needed some herbal preparation but had no means to pay. Said loved being their saviour and recipient of the effusive gratitude they bestowed. I think, for him, that was even more sustaining than food on the table. It didn't do much for us as his family though.

Personally, my trust in any of these plans had declined with each new failure, and I had developed the habit of hiding a few dirhams here and there in

the house, in case of emergencies. Said had begun
to rely on my ability to do this.

He came home one evening almost in tears.

"I can't do this," he said, sounding defeated. "My
friends have not valued my time and effort at the shop.
They want to pay me only minimum wages for my work
instead of making me a partner in the business. I can't
support my family on two thousand dirhams a month!"
His voice had risen almost to cracking point, and he
looked as if he was about to burst into tears.

"Don't worry, baby. We have made it this far, we will
make things work. Maybe I could go to work."

"Where? What could you do here?" he asked.

"Well, maybe Omaima's new school needs English
teachers." My parents had offered to pay for schooling
that included English language instruction, as they felt
it was important for the girls to learn and understand
their mother's native tongue. For the past month,
Omaima had been attending a private school that taught
English as well has the Moroccan curriculum. "I could
ask there for a job."

"Really?" Said smiled. "You would do that? I love
you so much." He reached out to hug me, and I felt
myself stiffen. Somehow, somewhere along the way, his
hugs had changed from being supportive and comforting,
to being needy. I felt the weight of his arms around me
more than I had noticed before.

Chapter
Eleven

NEVER ONE TO WASTE TIME, on Monday morning I roused all my strength and prepared to go to the English school and ask for a job. I had never taught school before, I hadn't worked outside the home for almost a decade, and my confidence was at an all-time low. The only thing I could think of to recommend me for a teaching job was the fact that I spoke English. Still, we needed the money, and something inside me wanted to get out into the world again. My love of staying home was dwindling as the months and years passed. I felt like I was shrinking, and soon I'd disappear altogether.

The school was a low building, built in a square around a main courtyard that was open to the sky.

As was the tradition in Morocco, there were gardens and plants tucked into the corners all around and vines climbing up and adorning the concrete walls. Omaima and I went through the gate, and I looked for the main office. Omaima pulled her hand out of mine and ran off to join her classmates. I was left to find my way around on my own.

I found the office, went in, and asked for the director. She was an intimidating woman, with dark hair and stern features. I shrunk inside my jellaba.

"Good morning," I said softly in Arabic and then in English. "I was wondering if you needed English teachers. I am from Canada, and my daughter is at this school in grade one. I am looking for work."

"Ah, good morning," she replied, looking me up and down. "You live here in Tangier?"

"Yes, I have residency here, my husband is from Tangier."

"Hmm, that's interesting." I could see her mind calculating, I hoped it would come up in my favour. "Do you have any teaching experience?"

"Well, not exactly, but I have run a preschool in my home, and my mother was a teacher, so I have some resources through her." I wracked my brain for something else to say.

"Well, actually, we could use an English teacher in the nursery, if you want to try that." I exhaled quickly. Maybe I could really do this.

"Yes! I'd love to do that." My voice was louder now,

and more confident. "When could I start?" I realized
I was not negotiating very well, or at all, but I didn't
want to lose the opportunity.

"You can start tomorrow," she replied. "Come in to
my office, we can start the paperwork now."

"Okay, sure." I followed her, marvelling at how
quickly things had worked out.

"Here is the contract. We can pay you 2,000 dirhams
a month. You will do half a day with the four-year-olds,
and half a day with the five-year-olds. The two classes
swap between the English and Arabic teachers. Ms. Batoul
is the Arabic nursery teacher, I'll introduce you to her in
a minute. Do you have your residency card with you?"
I handed her my card and she began writing in my name
and details. I calculated in my head that 2,000 dirhams
was about 250 dollars a month, not exactly a goldmine,
but I knew that was a typical wage for Tangier, and at
this point, I would take anything just to have a job.

"My daughter already gets lunch here; is it possible
for me to eat the lunch in the cafeteria also?" I wanted
to try bartering for something, now that it seemed fairly
sure I had the job.

"Oh," the director frowned, "I suppose we can
do that, okay." She nodded in a way that made me feel
she wanted me to know she had done me a favour.

"Okay, thank you very much," I breathed out in
gratitude, and her face softened again.

"Alright, let me show you around the nursery wing.
There is already an assistant for each class, so they can

help you get settled. We have new English books for the kids, so you can work through those." She talked proudly about the program and the school as we looked at the nursery classrooms and the separate playground for the nursery. "This is Ms. Batoul, the Arabic teacher." I smiled and shook Ms. Batoul's hand. Her smile was kindly, and she seemed genuinely nice. She seemed older than many of the female teachers, her chin had small hairs on it, and she was slightly plump. I learned later that women often taught until they found a husband and then gave up working outside the home when they got married. I wondered if Ms. Batoul was one of the unlucky ones that hadn't been able to secure a husband when she was young enough to be a desirable catch. Women who did not marry in Morocco were usually forced to work low-paying jobs with long hours for the rest of their lives, just to support themselves. I felt sympathy for her.

"Aishah will be teaching English in the nursery," the director explained, and Ms. Batoul nodded, smiling.

"Nice to meet you," I said.

We both stared awkwardly for a moment, and then the director looked at her watch and said, "Okay, so maybe you want to stay and see the class a little bit today? Tomorrow, you should be here at eight o'clock to start." She nodded to the assistant teacher in the nursery and swept out of the room, leaving me to get my bearings. I smiled and pulled a chair out to sit down.

"I'll just stay and watch for a bit, if that's okay?"

I looked around, my brain racing with thoughts of what I should plan to do. My heart was still pounding from the adrenalin of my surprise success. I had a job!

I went home at lunch time, after observing the nursery classes. My head was swimming with ideas, and I felt exhausted but too excited to rest. Hajar was two now and old enough to stay with someone else for the day, and the other three were old enough to come with me to school. I couldn't wait to tell Said my news!

I felt the familiar nudge of my inner voice. *You shouldn't have to do this too. He should be bringing money home. Why are you doing everything in this family?* I pushed The Voice down hard. I didn't want to listen. It made me angry at something, I wasn't sure what.

Fatima Zohra stopped by in the afternoon, and I told her everything. She was happy that I had found work, and she offered to help look after Hajar during the days. We talked a little about the upcoming court date. We had finally been given a hearing date, in a month's time. After filing our case, Said had continued going to the court almost every week. It was important to get to know the lawyers and make friends if you wanted to get anything done on your case. I did not understand everything that was going on, but Fatima Zohra seemed to grasp how things worked here, and she told me there was a lot to do. Although she had left school at only nine years of age to live with another family and work as a "children's maid," she had a wonderful grasp of logistics. I could feel the threads of jealousy rising. Was I getting pushed aside? Was I becoming redundant in my own marriage? After working and fighting so hard for this second marriage to happen, I wasn't feeling joyful or happy at all. Maybe working outside the house would make things better.

On the heels of the news about the upcoming court date and my new job, catastrophe struck. A few days into my new job, I was surprised to see Said coming out onto the playground as we were supervising break. He looked upset, and I quickly asked the assistant to take over as I moved closer to him to see what was up. When I got within a few feet, I could see tear stains on his cheeks. Whatever could have happened?

"My mom," he stammered, "she...she passed away this morning." He hastily wiped his eyes with the back of his hands. "I'm here to get you and the kids...to see her before the funeral prayers."

"Oh ..." I couldn't think of the right words. I'd known this day was coming eventually, Safiyya had never fully recovered after the stroke, but the thought of her actually dying was almost incomprehensible. "I'm sorry, baby." I reached out and he wrapped me in his arms. He pulled away a second later, summoning his strength not to collapse in front of everyone. "I'll get my stuff and the girls, we will meet you out front in a minute."

"My mother-in-law has passed away," I explained to the other teachers. "I need to go with my husband. Can you manage for the rest of the day?"

They all nodded. "Yes, yes, of course. You go and

get the girls, we will look after things here. May Allah bless you and the family and take her to heaven."

"Thank you." My lip trembled. I turned to go find the girls.

As if in a dream, I collected the kids and their belongings. We went out the main door, and I saw Said leaning on the car. He looked tired and defeated. He smiled at the girls and hugged them as they climbed into the car.

"We are going to see Aziza," he said. "They are washing her body now, she is going to be with Allah." His voice broke and I could see he was having trouble continuing.

"She died this morning, and we will say prayers for her this afternoon," I continued. My voice was hollow and seemed to be coming from a place far away.

"She's gone?" Hind asked forlornly. "We can't see her anymore?"

"No, habiba, she is going to be with Allah." I patted her absently, not able to rouse myself to do more.

"But I want her here with me! Allah doesn't need Aziza, I do!" Hind wailed, starting to cry. Hind had been close to Said's mother. She had been so young when we moved here, and when I had Hajar, Hind had taken to going upstairs for company and attention. I knew she would miss her grandmother very much. I still couldn't connect my heart to what was going on. I continued to speak without hearing my words.

"I know it's sad, habiba. We will have to remember

all the nice things about her." I turned to look back at Hind, feeling completely unable to help anyone, still stunned by the news. Looking at Said's face, I could see the lines becoming more pronounced in his forehead. He had always had creases there. They used to be noticeable when he laughed and his eyebrows wiggled. The addition of Fatima Zohra to our family had brought back his humour a little in recent weeks. I was worried he would fall back into his depression now. I couldn't deal with that again now too. It never occurred to me that I didn't have to take on everyone else's problems, it was just a habit now.

When we arrived back at the house there were people coming and going. They stopped to shake Said's hand and offer condolences. I didn't recognize half of them, but everyone seemed to know who we were. The girls clung to my jellaba, uncertainty making them shy. I struggled to stay present for the sake of the girls.

"The body is in here, if you want to come and say goodbye." A lady ushered us kindly into the downstairs bedroom. I followed with trepidation, I had not seen a dead body before, but I was determined to be calm and strong for my kids. Safiyya was lying on a mat on the floor. She was washed and dressed nicely, her hair arranged. Only the pallor of her skin and the unmoving stillness of her body gave away that she was not still living. I stood and looked at her. The lady asked if we wanted to kiss her cheek, and I moved forward, brushing my lips softly against her cold cheek. The girls

bravely followed and said goodbye. I moved away and
shepherded the girls upstairs. I was profoundly grateful
for the other women from the community who had
washed the body and were seeing to the details. I did
not feel I could have done all that. I moved robotically
to take off my jellaba and scarf.

"Come here, girls, I'll put cartoons on for you and
we will make tea in a minute." I hoped they would settle
down and stay quiet for a little while. I needed time.

I heard Said talking to the men outside. Looking
down from the window, I saw a gathering of neighbours.
They had a wooden pallet. They had come to walk the
body to the mosque for prayers, and then she would
be taken to the graveyard and buried the same day. It
was the way things were done here. In Islam, funerals
are held quickly and the body buried preferably the same
day. Cremation was not practiced, it was not allowed
in Islam. She would have a small plot in the graveyard,
a white stone marking her place. Safiyya would be
remembered for her smile and her kind generosity.
I turned away, letting a tear slide down my cheek
unchecked. It felt like the end of an era.

The glue that held the family together was gone.
I had never fully acknowledged how Safiyya's presence
filled the house and kept things running smoothly.
Even when she was ill, her presence was felt by us all.
I realized with a jolt that I missed her.

It's funny how the wife and mother often play that
role in a family, keeping relationships strong and bonding

people together in a way that women are often just innately good at. I was getting pretty good at this myself, I realized. Some part of me wondered how much my family was held together by this role I had taken on. This role that had not been truly mine to begin with, but in which I was now fully invested.

I allowed these musings to filter through my mind as the house was inundated in the following days by neighbours, relatives, and friends, coming and going. Some of them brought food, which was gratefully served and eaten. None of us felt like cooking, or indeed doing anything ordinary. Death leaves such a hole in a family.

The girls and I went back to school and tried to carry on as normal, but Said was not the same. He rarely smiled, and he seemed dissatisfied with Morocco, and restless. Even the prospect of another wife didn't seem to rouse his spirits for more than a few minutes at a time. I had never fully realized how much his mother had meant to him. I was glad that he had some true feelings of love for someone—it rekindled a shred of hope that I could mean something to him also.

It came as a shock when Said's father, after forty days of mourning, announced that he wanted to marry again. Safiyya's sisters were in an uproar. How could he forget about his wife so soon! How could he move on and marry someone else! To Said and me it made sense, not emotionally but practically. He needed someone to cook and clean for him. He had spent a lifetime working hard for his family, and he received a small pension. It made

sense that he would also want a companion at home.
After all, Said's sister, Fatima, was more like a child
than a fully grown woman. It made sense, but inwardly
I wished Taher would demonstrate more attachment
to his late wife. The fact that he could move forward
so quickly added fuel to my fears that Said was just
the same. Would he forget about me that quickly? Would
Fatima Zohra take my place in his eyes before the ink
was even dry on the marriage papers?

One evening as Said and I sat talking, I said, "We
should tell your dad that you are also getting married
again. He can't really say anything against you now,
not if he wants to remarry also."

Said nodded. "I guess that's true. It's a good time
to tell him." He stood up and took a last sip of his tea.
"I might as well go up now and see him." He had been
checking in a couple of times a day, to make sure his
father and Fatima were okay upstairs. I nodded and
got up to clear away the dishes.

"Seeing as how our court date is in a couple of
weeks, it's a good time, yes." Until I said the words,
I hadn't fully realized how close the date had come.
We had been so busy with the funeral, I hadn't
considered it at all. My chest tightened as I listened
to my husband's footsteps going upstairs. Soon, he would
be spending every other night with another woman.

My dreams were unsettling that night. I woke up,
sweating, feeling a dread deep down that I couldn't put
my finger on. I busied myself with work and kids. There

was always so much to do, I could almost keep my mind from wandering into unwanted territory. Said and I talked in the days leading up to the court date about what I should say and how I should say it. I had not realized until then how important my part in all of this was. The judge would ask me if I accepted another wife for my husband, and why. Said coached me in how to respond in Arabic.

"My husband has a lot of 'strength' and 'desire,' I am not enough for him. I have four children, and I am too busy to fulfill his needs. I accept his marrying another wife, so she can take some of this burden from me and make him happy and fulfilled." I practiced the words, over and over, so I could make it sound realistic and sincere. I didn't let my mind ask about my own happiness or fulfillment, and the foreign words felt like strangers to my tongue. Said had said many times that he would always love me more, especially because I helped him do this second marriage.

No one could take my place.

She would help me.

It was a good thing.

Fatima Zohra and her mother had already decided to move into the apartment we had created on the ground floor of our house when we added the extra floor for Said's parents. Her mother moving with her would give us the ability to "cover" the truth by saying they were just renting from us. The fact that Said would go downstairs to sleep every other night did not need to be public knowledge until we chose to reveal that. We even kept it from the girls as they couldn't be counted on to keep our arrangement secret.

I tried to get my head around the thought of having every other night to myself. Or the thought that my husband would be making love to another woman when he wasn't with me. This didn't really register as a reality yet, and I wasn't sure I wanted it to.

Fatima Zohra came over almost every day. Now that Safiyya had passed on and Said's father knew he was taking another wife, there seemed no reason to be discreet. She was a big help, and the girls had taken to her well. For this I was grateful. If I could only get past the idea of him sleeping with her.

We had even struck up a friendship of sorts, although our backgrounds were so very different. At the age of nine, Fatima Zohra had been sent to work with a Dutch family. She had been told she was part of their family, though really she was there as a servant, not a sibling. The children were about her age, so she had the difficult task of being both playmate and servant. The family had taken her to Amsterdam for a couple of years. I often wondered as we sat having our morning coffee together what it would be like to be sent off like this so young. I respected her strength, growing up in what my culture would consider close to slavery.

One day she came over and said, "I want to help you be beautiful for him. I will do your hair and makeup. You can wear a nice dress. When Said comes back, he will look at you with desire."

I was surprised at this offer. I had not made much effort in the last couple of years to look beautiful. There was always housework to do, and there seemed to be no point. Maybe it would be fun. The small voice whispered that she was trying to manipulate her way into being close to me so she could later take Said for herself and taste the victory of one woman over another. Would I be able to feel for her the same generosity, real or not? I was flooded by guilt, and I vowed to take her offer at face value and try to appreciate the sisterhood.

I had my doubts about whether Said would even notice the results, but I acquiesced. Fatima Zohra looked in despair at my wardrobe. I had to admit it was lacking in the "sexy outfits" department. She finally settled on a simple Moroccan dress, with braiding around the neckline and sleeves. I took down my hair and she brushed it out. It hung down past my waist, but the thickness and volume had decreased considerably after my fourth baby. We tried curling the ends, and she pinned it up on the sides. I didn't own a drop of makeup, so she brought hers up and put some lipstick and eyeliner on me. I felt awkward being dressed like this. I had not grown up with sisters, and the attention on me was unsettling. Fatima Zohra was one of four girls in her family, and I knew they spent much time together dressing up and primping. I wanted to feel like a sister to her, but I couldn't fully let go of the drive to win more love and attention from Said. I had so little left in my relationship, I loathed to share any of it, even while another part of me wanted to let her take on the burden of Said for awhile. I hadn't noticed until now how heavy it had grown.

I turned to look in the mirror. The result was less than stunning but maybe better than my usual "daily grind" look. "You look beautiful," she said sincerely, and I appreciated her effort. I smiled, and we shared a moment of bonding. It felt odd to bond with another woman in pursuit of the same man, but not altogether unpleasant.

Said was coming home from the shop for lunch soon, and we got the table ready together. There was an air of excitement as we did this. What would he think? Would he be pleased at our attempts to work together? And most importantly to me, would he think I was still beautiful?

"Mama, why are you all dressed up?" Hind asked, as the girls came back down from visiting upstairs.

"She is looking nice for her husband." Fatima Zohra winked and grinned at her.

"You mean Baba?" Hind looked intrigued.

"You look pretty, Mama," Omaima said, looking pointedly at her sisters with a "shut up and get with the program" look.

"Baba is here!" Safia chimed in from her perch on the sofa, looking out the window.

"I'm here," Said echoed, hearing her. He laughed as he came up the stairs. "Where are my beautiful girls?"

"We are here!" They all ran giggling to the door.

"Look at Mama!"

Said looked up and smiled. "You look nice, what's the occasion?"

I laughed self-consciously. "Fatima Zohra wanted to help me look nice for you."

"Oh, that is sweet of her. You do look nice." He smiled at her also and I could feel my stomach tighten. Perhaps I had been silly to let her dress me up. Now she looked like the generous one.

"Are you going to kiss her, Baba?" Safia collapsed giggling, sending her sisters into fits of laughter also.

"Maybe. She is my wife, isn't she? I can kiss her if I want to." He leaned in and kissed me lightly on the lips, sending the girls into more fits of laughter.

"Here, girls, sit down for lunch now. Leave your parents." Fatima Zohra sat the girls around the table, and we joined them.

"Isn't this nice?" Said beamed around at all of us. "All my girls at one table. I have such a beautiful family."

I blushed and glanced sideways at Fatima Zohra. It was nice to be noticed and good to see Said smile. He had been so withdrawn since his mother's death. Fatima Zohra smiled at Said, and I saw a look pass between them. Suddenly I could taste bile in my mouth. Had they planned this whole thing together? Did she do this just to get Said's favour? I wasn't hungry anymore and sat back, sinking into the cushion behind me. Would I be forgotten that easily? I felt ridiculous now and wanted to change back into my comfortable house dress and leggings. It was silly to try and look nice, there was work to be done anyway.

Hajar started fussing then, and I took the opportunity to take her into the bedroom and feed her. I viciously tore off my fancy dress and tied my hair up with an elastic. I wiped the lipstick off my face and tried to stop the tears from coming.

I could hear Said chatting away in Arabic to the girls and Fatima Zohra. *Fine*, I thought, *they can be all cosy and intimate. I don't care.*

Picking Hajar up, I realized she had leaked out of her diaper. *Figures*, I thought. *No point getting all dressed up when all I do is clean up poop.* I peeled off her clothes and carried her into the bathroom to rinse her off. Let him fawn over Fatima Zohra, I didn't care. It would be good to get a break from him every other night anyway. I pulled out some fresh clothes for Hajar and sat down to feed her. My body relaxed as she suckled, her little hand rubbing my breast calmed me, and everything else faded into the background.

A while later Said poked his head in. "Are you okay, baby?"

"Yes," I replied curtly.

"You looked very nice earlier, how come you changed?" he asked.

"I had to clean up the baby, and it didn't make sense to stay all dressed up. You were only looking at her anyway," I couldn't help adding.

"I did notice you, baby, and you will always be the

first. I love you so much, you know that." He moved toward me with that placating almost pleading tone. He could be extremely persuasive when he wanted to be, and even though I knew he was saying the same kind of things to her, I wanted to believe him so much.

"Yeah, whatever. You want to marry another woman, I am not enough for you anymore." I was not ready to be forgiving yet. I wanted more.

"Don't be like that, Ailsa." He used my real name, and his tone became harsher. "I'm doing this for you, you need help around the house. Don't be angry with me."

I looked down and didn't say a word. He always managed to make me feel small and mean. Was this second marriage for me more than him? I had no comeback, and I knew it.

"She wanted to make you feel good," he added, pressing his point. "You should be grateful to her. That was very generous of her to help you look beautiful for me."

"Yes, I guess it was nice of her," I agreed quietly, hating the conflict more than the lie.

Said frowned but didn't say anything more. He checked his hair in the mirror then turned around and said he had to go out for a bit to meet someone about the court date next week. "You know, if you don't want to do this anymore, you just have to say so."

How was I supposed to answer that? I wanted things to be good between us, like our first summer, working together in the circus. Now there were so many other people to consider, I was lost in the equation. I sensed that our time to be a couple was gone forever.

"No, I want to," I said contritely. "It is the best decision." He had done it again, made me advocate for what he wanted. The frustration rose and then tightened like a noose around my throat. I didn't know how to play this game.

"Okay, baby, see you later." He kissed me on the forehead and left.

Sighing, I put Hajar down in her cot and went to see about the dishes and the other girls. There was no time to work things over in my head, and maybe that was for the best. There had been a time when seeing me in a nice dress would have ended in passionate sex and a blissful sharing with each other about our dreams and hopes. Now, it seemed, the best we could do was a companionable pat on the back and continue on our separate ways.

Fatima Zohra got up and said she had to leave as well, her mother needed some help at home. I was glad in a way to be left alone. I wasn't in the mood to be sociable.

"Okay, thank you again for helping me look nice for Said." I smiled at her. It's true, she was trying, and all this wasn't her fault.

"Be good for Mama," she told the girls as she left, "and I'll bring you a treat tomorrow."

She pinched their cheeks and kissed their fingers

in a gesture of affection. The girls giggled happily. They really did seem to like her. Thank Allah for that.

The court day came much more quickly than I was prepared for. We hadn't really had much time to discuss it, except that I had to come and testify that I accepted Said taking another wife and why I thought it was necessary. Since we had both started on this venture together, I didn't feel it was right to share my negative thoughts about it. For the most part, we agreed that it was a good idea and that it would be helpful, both to me around the house and to Fatima Zohra, to be married.

It was a little spoken but well-known fact in Morocco that as a single woman you didn't have much respect or freedom. It was a given that you would rather be married, even if that was as a second, third, or even fourth wife. As a single woman, you were constantly at the mercy of men who tried to seduce you, or ignored you. Fatima Zohra's mother had left her father when she was young; he had been an alcoholic and abusive. Her mother had locked her four girls in the small basement apartment while she went out to work as a maid, doing laundry and cleaning. Fatima Zohra's older sister did get married, but coming from a single parent family with no money made it next to impossible for Fatima Zohra to find a man of her own. She had jumped at the opportunity to join our family.

Said prompted me on the drive to the court. "So, when the judge asks you what you think of the marriage, you say, 'My husband is too strong for me.'" "Strong" in this sense meant he had a big sex drive, and I was not able to fulfill him in this area now that I had four children to look after.

"Yes, okay, I've got it," I answered, then repeated the words in Arabic. He and Fatima Zohra laughed. "Why are you laughing?" I felt a bit hurt.

"It's just funny to hear you say that." Said patted my hand. He couldn't help grinning though, and I sullenly refused to practice any more Arabic. The rest of the drive, there was a somewhat awkward silence. I don't think any of us thought we would ever even get to this day. It had taken months of paperwork and Said going back and forth to the courts.

The front of the courtyard was a sea of people. We pushed our way inside, and Said told Fatima Zohra and me to sit on the garden wall while he went to see where we should go. I was experienced enough now to know this was likely to be an all-day thing. Nothing ever happened quickly in Morocco, especially anything requiring paperwork.

"Here, come up these steps." Said ushered us up a small flight of stairs to an outside balcony. More people were crowded into the space, and we joined the throng. I peered into one of the darkened rooms that opened up along the balcony. I could see a desk inside but not much else. We leaned against the wall and listened to some of the other conversations around us.

"You need your mother or father to sign the papers," one clerk was telling a young couple. "She cannot get married at fourteen without parental consent."

I looked more closely at the girl. She did look young, but she also looked like she was from a village, and she carried herself like a woman already. The young man seemed nervous, but he argued his case to the clerk until he was allowed an audience with the judge in the darkened room. The couple went in, and the door swung shut.

Said was busy trying to find out when our appointment was, so Fatima Zohra and I just stood and waited and watched. A few minutes later, the door opened and the young girl came out crying, her fiancé behind her, looking worried.

"Don't worry," I heard him say to her, "we will just get your father to sign the paper."

They disappeared down the steps, and the next people went in. There still seemed to be many people in front of us. I put a hand under my veil and lifted it away from my face. It got stifling to breathe through the material sometimes. Fatima Zohra didn't wear a face covering, just a scarf and coat. Said had lectured her on not wearing such form-fitting jellabas. She did have big hips. We had gotten a bigger coat sewn for her, and she was wearing that now with a bigger scarf that also covered her upper chest. She had talked about wearing the veil, and Said seemed happy that she was becoming more pious as his wife. I wasn't sure I wanted her to, it seemed to make her on the same level as me. I had noticed myself becoming protective about certain privileges. I wanted to maintain my status as the first wife, the most important one. *I mean really*, my thoughts ran, *Said is only marrying her so she can help me.* I quickly shut out the other doubts that crowded into my mind. Now was not the time to have doubts.

As if on cue, I heard the clerk call Said's name. *This is it!* I thought.

Said looked over at us, and we nodded. He went in on his own first, to speak to the judge on his own behalf. Fatima Zohra and I held hands, and for a moment I felt our shared bond; we were both nervous. A few minutes later, Said came out and beckoned us over.

"He wants to speak to you alone," he told me meaningfully. I nodded gravely. I knew what he meant. I had practiced for this moment, I was ready. My heart pounded loudly in my ears, and I hardly noticed anything around me as I walked into the dimly lit room. The judge was sitting behind a large desk, and he looked up as I came in.

"Assalamu alaikum," he said in greeting.

"Wa alaikum assalam," I answered in the traditional way, bowing my head.

"You can relax." He smiled. "How do you like Morocco?" I found I could understand him quite well, although he spoke more formal Arabic.

"It's very nice," I answered in the Moroccan dialect.

"How long have you lived here?"

"Almost three years." I wondered if he was trying to catch me off guard, or just see if I understood enough Arabic to speak for myself. He asked about my children and family, and then he got to the point.

"So, what do you think about your husband having another wife?" He looked up and his eyes narrowed.

"I think that it is a good thing for the family and all of us involved. My husband is very 'strong,' and I am so busy with the children that it would be better for him to have another wife, as I cannot provide for all his needs." I remembered all the right words, and the implication of what I said was not lost on the judge. The corners of his mouth twitched as I spoke.

"So, you cannot provide everything your husband requires of a wife? And you are happy with him marrying again?"

"Yes," I replied firmly.

"That is an unusual opinion for a woman who converted to Islam from the West." He nodded thoughtfully. "You are sure?"

"Yes, I am sure." My hands were getting sweaty, and I hoped the questioning was almost finished.

"Okay, then I guess everything is in order here." He turned to the clerk. "You can tell her husband to come in, and we will discuss the paperwork." He turned back to me. "Thank you, you may go now. May Allah grant you peace and a long life."

"Thank you, and you." I turned and passed Said on

the way out. His eyebrows raised slightly as he looked at me, and I nodded back.

Fatima Zohra was outside. "So? Everything went okay?"

"Yes, I think so." I took a deep breath.

A few minutes later, Said came out holding some papers. "I have to meet the lawyer at the café later, I'm going to need the money then."

"How much?" I asked.

"About 6,000 dirhams. It's expensive but the only way to get the papers passed."

This marriage had already been expensive, and now there was this final payment to the judge for stamping our papers and making sure they didn't land at the bottom of an endless pile of cases where the poor people did not have the bribery money.

"Okay, I think we can do that."

My stomach dropped again. The money just kept disappearing into this paperwork and not leaving anything for food and our bills. At least I was working now. My income was not much, but it covered the basics.

I prided myself on the fact that I could always be relied upon to come up with some money from somewhere. This was a big amount though. My mind was racing. How would we come up with the equivalent of $1,000 by this afternoon?

"Maybe you should call some of the brothers in England," I suggested, "ask them if they could support your marriage in the name of Allah." Sometimes, quoting the religious reason behind things got you more support.

"I guess I could try that." Said looked down, he didn't like having to ask for charity.

"I don't think we have much choice really," I added quickly, not wanting the task to fall to me.

"Alright, I'll see." Said walked ahead of us down the stairs, he seemed to have forgotten our existence now that he was finished at court. He nodded and smiled and shook hands with some friends on the way back to the car but didn't acknowledge us at all. Fatima Zohra and I tagged along like lost puppies. Honestly, I would be happy just to get home and take off my veil and burka. The heat was beginning to get to me.

We drove home quietly, not wanting to intrude on each other's thoughts. The tension was palpable. Said was obviously uncomfortable with having to ask for more money. He dropped us at the house, and we went in without speaking. Said pulled away in the car; I guessed he wanted to deal with his money issues on his own. Probably better, I thought, sighing. I wasn't sure I had heard the full story of why he was arrested a few months ago, and perhaps his way of obtaining money would not sit well with me. Still, it would have been nice to celebrate our court approval a little.

On the way upstairs, I looked back at Fatima Zohra and asked if she wanted to come up for coffee. She nodded gratefully. I put the coffee pot on to heat as she walked through the door. I was glad she was here to take my mind off darker things.

I wanted to connect but was not sure how to do this. I had no precedent for how to be in this kind of relationship. We were not quite friends, and yet we were intimately connected through sharing the same husband. The tradition was for the new wife and her husband to go away for three to seven days, to consummate the marriage and have some time alone, before the new wife was given her place in the family.

"So, how do you feel, now that you are almost married?"

"Good," she answered. "I'll be glad when it's all finished officially."

"Yes, it will be good to have it all wrapped up."

"Said is taking me to a hotel near here, by the beach, for three days, I think." She blushed slightly at the thought.

"Oh?" I hadn't heard this part of the plan. I could feel myself tighten up. Why didn't I know this? "That will be nice." I hadn't had any kind of honeymoon. After Said and I married at the mosque in Manchester, we just drove back to our flat! I smiled stiffly at Fatima Zohra and tried to look pleased. I didn't want to start off the whole thing by throwing a jealous rage. Part of me wanted to remain superior, the important wife, the one in control of everything. So, I showed nothing of the emotions that were rolling around in my gut.

"So, do you think one night each is a good plan? Alternate nights with Said?" I asked, somehow unable to find any other topic of conversation.

"Um, sure." She nodded. "That's probably the best."

"You can always come and eat with us and stuff, during the day. The girls love having you around," I offered generously. "And will your mother be staying in the apartment downstairs with you?"

"Yes, I think so, and maybe my younger sisters," she added, swallowing a mouthful of coffee.

"Oh, I see." I sipped my coffee also. Today our conversation just felt awkward, whatever we discussed. Things felt out of control, like somehow, we had started a ball rolling and now it was impossible to stop it. Money was needed for the court, money would have to pay for the hotel for the honeymoon, her family was moving in with her downstairs for free… Again, I shut off my thoughts and forced myself to be in the present moment. *Think of the positives*, I told myself. *She will help with the girls, she will be good company when Said is out so much. Said will be committed to taking care of his family more. How could he not take on a better attitude toward his family, now that he had two wives?*

The girls came downstairs, clattering in with a rush of energy. I was glad for the distraction.

"Mama!" They shouted. "Fatima Zohra! Look what Jido gave us!" They pushed in to show their treats to us. Said's father had obviously taken them to the store and bought them chocolate wafers.

"It's almost dinner time," I scolded mildly.

"We can eat them and still be hungry," they insisted. Fatima Zohra and I laughed good-naturedly. I hadn't thought about dinner yet anyway, so maybe it was good they were distracted.

The summer was drawing to a close when a few days later Said announced that he had finally procured the marriage papers. For some reason, now that the moment had arrived, I felt only a numbness about the whole thing. It had taken so many months of planning and work that the sweetness of success was muted. I wasn't so sure anymore that it felt like success anyway.

Life carried on day by day in much the same way. Said's father had met and arranged to marry a younger woman. Zohra was only a few years older than me, but she had the demeanour of a woman much older. She was barren and widowed and as such was not worth much in Moroccan society. She worked at a factory every day for little money, and I think marrying an older man with a pension was the only option for her to have any quality of life. She liked me and Said, and she had taken the chance that life would not be as hard with us as with her own family. None of them really wanted her, she was seen as a liability in a way. I felt sorry for her, it was a hard lot. She had moved in upstairs, quietly and unceremoniously, except that Taher had put new locks on his bedroom door. We had all teased him about this, and he had smiled abashedly. Still, he was married to her now, so why not?

The why not question came into stark view when,

a few days after the marriage papers were finished, Said announced that he and Fatima Zohra would be heading to a nearby hotel for the next three nights.

"You're leaving today?" I caught my breath. I knew this moment was coming, but the reality of the two of them going off to sleep together, to have sex, took my breath away. Would I ever be able to live in the same house as this woman and share my husband with her?

It was too late now to have these doubts. I arranged my face to a neutral expression.

"I'll be back during the days for a bit," he added, "just to see you and the girls."

"Oh, okay…" I trailed off. "Well, um, have a good time." What exactly was I supposed to say? I dropped my hands to my sides and looked down.

"Come here." Said pulled me to his chest, hugging me. I moved stiffly, finding it harder to melt into him than I ever had before. He pulled back, looking me in the eyes. I knew he could feel my resistance, he had always been sensitive to my energy, especially when it had to do with accepting or rejecting him. "I still love you," he said, but it almost came out as a whine.

"Yeah, I know," I answered, trying to sound convinced. When did our marriage become such a dance of placation? I squeezed his hand as I turned away. "Have fun. Honestly, I want you to treat her well," which was the most honest thing I could say. I did want her to be treated well, even if I had never had a honeymoon or a proper wedding. A woman deserved that, she deserved to be celebrated. "I'll see you tomorrow."

I busied myself in the kitchen until I heard them leave. I didn't really want to, but something drew me to go up to the roof to watch the car pull away down the road. As I saw them pull onto the main road, something inside my chest broke, and I sat down sobbing. It was like the tension from the last few years had finally burst, and the dam no longer held back the tidal wave of emotion. I wasn't even aware exactly what I was crying about. The loss of my husband, the loss of my idealistic innocence, the loss of myself. I think a little piece of me died that day, watching the car disappear in the dust.

My mind wandered back to when Said and I had met. Had I really fallen in love with him then? Or had I just convinced myself that I had? He had somehow painted a perfect picture for me, a picture of family life, children, serving Allah together—but was it ever real? Perhaps I had taken on his fantasy without connecting to my own feelings at all. Was that real love?

I slumped down against the wall of the roof terrace, not sure I could muster the willpower to go downstairs and deal with life. I turned as I heard the patter of small feet approaching me.

"Mama? Are you alright?" Omaima looked concerned, in her sweet, six-year-old way.

"Yes, yes, I'm okay. Why aren't you in bed?" I brushed my hand over my eyes and snapped back to reality.

"I didn't know where you were," she said, her voice trembling and her eyes beginning to fill with tears. "Baba and Fatima Zohra went out, and you weren't there!"

I pulled her to me, taking comfort in the warmth of her little body. I still had my girls, my babies, and they needed me. Sighing, I stood up and took her hand. "Come on, habiba, let's go downstairs and get you tucked into bed. It's getting late."

She trotted contentedly beside me down the stairs. It amazed me how easily comforted one could be at that age. She crawled into bed and I sat beside her for a while, stroking her hair. I didn't really want to go yet, I wasn't ready to face the empty bed. It brought up visions I'd rather not see.

"Mama, I love you," Omaima whispered in the dusky light.

"Love you too," I whispered back.

I undressed and climbed into bed, sweet exhaustion robbing me of any thoughts. I slept.

"Hey girls!" I was interrupted in my dinner preparations the next day by Said's jovial greeting. A little too jovial, I thought wryly. Obviously, things were going well on the honeymoon.

"Baba!" The girls ran to give him a hug. Said seemed to be using the kids as a buffer between us; it seemed he was more confident in his welcome from them. Couldn't really blame him. I was feeling a little on the cool side. How were you supposed to feel when your husband had just spent the night with a new wife? I had no precedent for this at all.

Said ventured closer to me. "How are you, baby?"

"I'm alright," I answered. "Are you staying for dinner?"

"Oh, no, I don't think so, Fatima Zohra is waiting for me at the hotel. I just stopped in to see you and the girls."

"Oh, okay, well, we are fine." I busied myself with the dishes. "Don't let us hold you up. You are supposed to be with her for three days." My voice just a little sharper than I meant it to be.

"Yeah, well, I am going." Said sounded disappointed and a little sad, but this was what he wanted. Was I supposed to be cheering him up about his own honeymoon? A bolt of anger rose up in me. I supported him all the time, but this was too much.

"Okay, have fun." I dismissed him nonchalantly, hiding my anger as best I could.

"Alright, well, see you tomorrow."

"Yeah, okay, see you then." I forced a smile onto my face. "Bye."

"You wanted this, you know. I wouldn't have married her if you hadn't told me to," he said a little petulantly.

I turned then, and with a huge effort of will overcame my jealousy enough to smile genuinely. "I guess you're right." At this point it didn't matter how we got here, but I didn't want to lose him completely.

His face softened then, and he looked appeased. "Do you want me to stop in and see you and the girls tomorrow?" he asked in a way that sought reassurance more than offering it.

"Actually, I'm fine. Maybe it's better to concentrate on Fatima Zohra for these couple of days." I wasn't sure I could take another interim visit like this. "She deserves to have a proper honeymoon," I added generously. I knew what it felt like not to have a proper honeymoon, and part of me wanted someone to be happy out of all of this.

"You're such a good Muslim wife and mother!" Said gushed. "How did I get so lucky?"

I blushed and he pulled me into his arms. "I love you, you know."

"Yeah," I answered. He had managed to get his way again.

The next two days passed eventually. In some ways it was a relief. I didn't have to see either Said or Fatima Zohra around. It was just me and the girls. I liked that, it was emotionally relaxing. I didn't realize how much drama we lived with every day until it wasn't there. I got out my sewing machine and began a new project, the girls played together well, it was peaceful.

I could feel my body relaxing without the constant striving to keep Said happy and in a good mood. I also hadn't fully realized how exhausting that was.

Fatima Zohra now lived downstairs as Said's official wife. Her mother and sisters were there permanently as well. So now we all had our own floor. I wasn't sure when we had decided to include her entire family in our arrangements, but Said told me to leave it alone. There were many customs in Morocco I didn't understand and couldn't get my head around, even though I'd been here for three years now. Fatima Zohra replaced Said's mother with trying to teach me how to be a Moroccan wife. She was extremely good at cleaning, and way more efficient than I could ever be. I reluctantly came to respect her for the things she excelled at.

We sorted out a workable truce in the house. Said spent one night with her and the next with me. He wasn't always home for dinner or around much, so making breakfast for him became the most intimate thing we each did as a wife. Neither one of us encroached on that time for each other, although the kids were allowed to go where they wanted, within reason. I usually tried to keep them from going downstairs on her morning until I knew they were up. I don't know if it was me protecting myself or sheltering them from the reality that their dad actually slept with two women.

The one thing I hated right off the bat was the fact that they would come up and shower in the nicer bathroom, which was right outside my bedroom, early in the morning, before prayer time. The only reason a Muslim needed to take a complete shower that early in the morning was if they had had sex or a woman had finished her period. And there was no way that Fatima

Zohra had her period that often! On those mornings, I was awoken to the sound of the water running, and my teeth clenched. *Honestly! I didn't need to know that!*

I had to admit there were certain advantages though. Fatima Zohra came upstairs on the weekends after breakfast, and we usually did the housework together. It was the first time I had really worked together with someone else in any kind of partnership. We both struggled to understand each other's words and meaning. She got the gist of what I was trying to get across in my halting and limited Arabic. When we got onto less definitive topics, like feelings or hopes, it got a little messier.

"Do you find Said sometimes doesn't seem the same as before his mother died?" Fatima Zohra asked me one day.

I looked up at her sharply. What was she referring to? Surely, I would have noticed first if something was wrong. "Like what?" I answered back too quickly.

"Well, like he seems to be not really interested in us, in being here, anymore."

Now that she brought it up, I had noticed he was more distant, but I had just chalked it up to dealing with two wives. But his depressive moods had returned, similar to when we were first married. Was he feeling lost after the initial euphoria of a new experience, a new wife? When things settled into a routine, he seemed to get bored.

"He has talked a few times about going back to the circus work," I said reflectively. "It's probably bothering him that he really doesn't have a proper job, and now he has more pressure to be providing for his family."

"Yes, he promised me a new jellaba for Ramadan," she continued a little petulantly. "I don't have any nice ones."

"You have a couple of nice ones!" I couldn't help snapping back. "What about that cream one you had made just before the wedding?"

"Well that was for the wedding." She looked annoyed. "This would be for Ramadan."

I would never understand the need Moroccan women had for new clothes all the time. It seemed such a waste, or a luxury, all for the sake of appearances. When I needed a new jellaba, I learned how to sew my own and bought cheaper fabric. I didn't care if it was the latest fashion or not. I mean, wasn't that supposed to be an Islamic thing? To not worry about appearances? Wasn't it more important to pray, to be pious, a good wife and mother? I was angry that she would desire and even ask for something for herself, but more than that, I was afraid that Said would capitulate and give her what she wanted. Secretly I would have liked a new outfit also, but this I couldn't admit even to myself.

I let the topic go. There was no point arguing about it, neither of us would likely change our minds. I took down one of the cookbooks I had brought from England and browsed through the pages looking for something that appealed to me. I came across an interesting cake recipe, with ingredients that were readily available in Morocco.

"Look at this!" I said excitedly, showing the picture to Fatima Zohra, our previous clash forgotten for now.

With her limited education and few words of English she couldn't really read the recipe. She knew the letters a little from having studied a bit of French, but she looked up at me to explain the ingredients.

"It is a cake, made with semolina and turmeric." I said the word for yellow in Moroccan, which she understood. "We should try it." I stood up, draining my coffee cup, and headed for the kitchen.

"What about dinner?" she asked. "Do you want me to make a main dish?"

"Yes, that would be great." I smiled. "And I'll do this cake." The camaraderie returned between us. It definitely was nice to have someone to help around the house. "Said should be home for lunch around three, and we can eat together then."

Fatima Zohra nodded and said she would cook downstairs.

"Do you need anything?" I asked, knowing she probably had little in the way of ingredients in her apartment.

"I can go to the market and get a few things," she answered. "If you have 50 dirhams, that should be enough to get a chicken and some vegetables."

I went into my room and got my purse. I passed the money to her.

"If you have enough left to get milk, that would be great."

Somehow, I felt like I needed to have the last word. To not just be the one to hand over money whenever she asked. The work at the school was stressful, and I often felt out of my depth. The one thing that kept me going was the fact that I was now the major breadwinner for the family.

She nodded and took the money. I don't think she liked having to ask me for money any more than I liked having to give it to her. We both felt the same sense of things not being quite right. That there was a missing link. Somehow, Said had managed to extricate himself from the picture altogether. Wasn't it supposed to be him looking after us, his two wives?

"See you later." I kissed her on both cheeks and took our coffee cups to the kitchen. The feeling of something missing stayed with me all morning. Luckily the girls had asked to go and play at the neighbour's across the road; they had a house with a courtyard in the middle. I was not sorry to have them all occupied elsewhere for a couple of hours. Our house was small, and hot in the summertime. Often, when the wind was up from the Sahara, we had to shut the windows to keep the dust from blowing in, making it even more hot and stuffy. Everyone was cranky on those days. The beach was out of the question, the sand would sting as it hit your skin if you tried walking there. Usually the wind lasted only a couple of days before dying down. Afterwards, the

weather would be calm and sunny for a few days.
Those were the beautiful times to go for picnics or walks.

Today the wind was up, and I could feel the sweat
trickling down the small of my back as I filled the sink
with water. I washed the dishes first; the space was so
small, nothing else could be done until I had put
everything away. Then I took out the recipe book and
a mixing bowl and set to work. The ingredients were
simple, and I had everything blended together before
I realized I had not prepared my cake tin. I turned the
small oven on and looked up at the shelf where my tins
were. Where was it? Ugh, not there. Did Fatima Zohra
borrow my cake tin and not return it?

I looked again and not finding it I stormed
downstairs, all hot and bothered, to see if she had it.
The door was locked. Damn, I'd forgotten she was going
to the market first. I could feel the anger and frustration
rise in my throat. All I wanted was for her to leave my
stuff alone. Or at least return things when she was done.
I never locked my door, she could come in whenever
she wanted and borrow anything, but she always locked
hers. How was I supposed to get my stuff back? Why did
she always have to take my things!

I was boiling with rage by now, and I wanted to
hit something. I knew I shouldn't be this upset about
a stupid cake pan, but everything was just below the
surface waiting to be triggered. I was so mad I could
have thrown something. A kind of strangled screech
escaped my lips, as I turned to go back upstairs. Tears

stung my eyes. I grabbed a slipper inside the door and hurled it full force at the wall. The thwack soothed my nerves a little, and I picked up the other one and threw it too. "Damn everything, I hate you! I hate you!" I cried out, not really sure who I was so angry with—Said, Fatima Zohra, myself, God. It all blended together in white fury. I stood inside my apartment throwing slippers at the wall until my arm hurt, and I collapsed on the ground sobbing.

"What's wrong?" I looked up to see Said in the doorway, looking down at me. His expression was a mix of concern and disdain. I cringed.

"I was just upset," I said, wiping my nose and trying to sit up. How had I not heard him coming up the stairs?

"About what?" He almost looked hurt, as if I had hurt him by being upset.

"Nothing," I said, sitting there on the floor. I didn't want to get up and pretend I was fine. Part of me wanted it to all end. "It's nothing important, I guess." I didn't really know how to verbalize my feelings. The rage had left, replaced by a kind of emptiness.

"It can't be nothing," he insisted. "You are throwing things and crying on the floor!" His tone took on an accusatory note.

"I couldn't find my cake tin," I admitted, "and when I went down to ask Fatima Zohra if she had it, the door was locked." I looked down at my hands. I knew it sounded ridiculous, but somehow the feelings it evoked in me were not. I couldn't explain it to him.

I just wanted him to understand. I wanted him to hug me, make me feel loved, take some of the burden of life away.

"Look, you can't just collapse like this over little things," he said, taking on a patient, preaching tone. "Life is what it is, this is your life, you just have to get up and deal with it. We don't get to choose our lives. I know you are a strong woman, get up and do what is yours to do!" He put out his hand and pulled me up.

I took his hand. I wasn't sure I wanted to just keep going. I was done. I didn't want this life anymore, it was too hard. I stood up and kept my gaze down.

"There, that's better." He patted my shoulder. "Stand up and go and finish making your cake. Fatima Zohra will be back soon, and you can get the pan from her." He tapped my bum playfully. I felt dismissed and not in the mood to be teased. I felt he had belittled my feelings, but I had no comeback, as the reason for my tantrum did seem overblown. There were no words for the deep well of anger and resentment and loneliness that created a great chasm in my chest. I turned and walked to the kitchen, not looking at him. I would make the cake, and sit down for lunch with everyone, and look after my kids, and I would try and smile while I did it, but I was not happy, not really.

Chapter
Twelve

ONE BRIGHT SPOT IN MY life at this time was connecting with the other Canadian woman, Aisha. I can't really express the feeling of having a friend who understands. After months of living in the house in Morocco, barely going out, not speaking English except to Said and the kids, it was like a rush of energy came flooding back to me as I settled myself on some floor cushions in her kitchen.

She put down the coffee tray and poured us each a cup. The girls were being amused by her seven children in the other room, and I sighed with relief. I could talk to her in a way I was used to. Aisha understood the difficulties of living in a foreign country, where everything was different. We felt like we'd known each other for years already.

We talked about our husbands. Hers was just looking into getting another wife also. I could talk about the hard things, the jealousy, having to share our things with another woman. Her co-wife would be living upstairs, and there wasn't much furniture up there. It's hard to share when you don't have much yourself.

I told her how I hated hearing Fatima Zohra use the shower just outside my bedroom. I didn't want to know the intimate details of her schedule, especially when it was her day with Said.

We sipped our coffee and just enjoyed being with each other. Our kids were playing happily, and it was nice to just sit and relax for a bit. Aisha never sat for long though, and after her coffee, she jumped up to start cooking. I couldn't imagine having five boys and two girls to cook for; it would be never-ending.

I watched as she deftly set bread in the oven with one hand, the other sprinkling salt into the pot of lentils. She was thin, almost too thin. I found out later she had struggled her whole life with an eating disorder. Her strawberry blonde hair was swept back in a messy bun, and her clothes were certainly not stylish. I could relate to the fact that it was much easier to throw on a pair of leggings and your husband's shirt than to wear anything requiring maintenance.

She was a Canadian-trained nurse, and after that first visit I sometimes bought the vaccine shots for the kids and took them to her to administer, rather than paying another nurse in Tangier. She was interested in health care and wanted to start a centre where women could learn about nutrition and child care. We talked about doing this together, but I was teaching and had no time for anything else, and starting a business as a woman in Morocco was hard.

It seemed we saw less and less of Said these days. Even his dad started to notice that his son wasn't around much. Said didn't seem to want to even be in Morocco anymore. Fatima Zohra and I brought up the subject one evening. Things were quiet, the girls were in bed, and she had come up to sit with me since Said was out late again. I noticed the moon hanging limply in the darkening sky. It seemed as if it too had lost the will to shine brightly.

"Where do you think he is?" she asked.

"I don't know. He said he was going to meet the boys at the café."

"Well, it is my night, and he is never around." She looked frustrated.

"He is not here for my night either," I countered a little defensively.

She shifted uncomfortably. "So why doesn't he like spending time with us? Most men want to spend time with their families."

I didn't have any more answers than she did. All I knew was that when I thought about these kinds of things, my skin crawled and my stomach tightened.

I had thought having two wives would make him better, he would stay home more, be more involved with the family. But so far things just seemed to be getting worse.

"He should be home with his family more," Fatima Zohra continued more forcefully, speaking my thoughts out loud.

Maybe she was right. Maybe he wasn't that great a husband. Perhaps it wasn't all my fault as I had been led to believe. I had never allowed myself to consider that he might be in the wrong. I had always taken responsibility, it had just been easier that way. Now, I didn't want to have to defend his behaviour to her as well as to myself. And what if she had a point? Maybe he should be home with us more. Why wasn't he here? I felt tears pricking the corners of my eyes. He didn't love me, maybe that was it, he didn't really care enough. Did that mean he didn't care about her either? Or the kids? I had no answers to these thoughts, and the doubts were eating away inside me.

"Yeah, I don't know, maybe he is talking to the brothers about work." I was still hopeful that he would stumble on a line of work that would pay him well and allow some ease in our lives here. I knew that was an unlikely reality and a weak excuse on his behalf, but I didn't want to start a fight. I wasn't angry with Fatima Zohra. I wanted to know why he wasn't home too.

"Well, I'm going downstairs." She stood up haughtily. "He better be home soon."

"Good night," I said, not sorry to see her go now.

I suddenly felt exhausted and just wanted to go to bed. It wasn't my night, I didn't want to think about him.

It took me ages to fall asleep, and I was only just there when I heard him come in.

"What are you doing here?" I mumbled sleepily. "It's Fatima Zohra's night."

"Yeah, I know," he replied, "but I was so mad, I came here."

"What's wrong?" I asked, a little irritably. Why did he want to talk to me? Wasn't one of the benefits of having a co-wife that she could take some of the heat?

"The guys I was doing the herbal medicine shop with decided to cut me out."

"Oh." I turned over, knowing I wasn't going to be allowed to sleep through his tirade. "So, what are you going to do?" I knew this wasn't a particularly helpful or comforting question, but I was already working as much as I could.

"I can't stay here and work for nothing," he continued righteously. "This always happens to me. People screw me over, I'm so sick of it."

I sighed. This was his usual go-to complaint whenever life didn't dish up what he wanted.

"Well, you have to do something, you have two wives now." I held my breath as I said this, as I knew he wasn't in the mood to hear it.

"I should have stayed in the circus," he said, continuing on his train of thought.

"Well, I guess you have to decide what to do."

I rolled over again. I could feel my back and shoulders tensing. Once again, I would have to figure out how to make things work. It was a never-ending struggle to make ends meet, and I felt more and more alone in dealing with it all. "Fatima Zohra was waiting for you, so maybe you should go downstairs and talk to her about it." I had my back to him, hoping he would take the hint. I was too tired to deal with his problems right now. If it was me, I'd just find a job, simple.

"Fine, I'll leave you to sleep." His accusing tone made my back spasm, but I kept quiet. "Good night."

"Good night," I answered in as neutral a tone as I could manage.

After he was gone, I rolled over again. I was wide awake. I looked at my phone: one o'clock. Ugh. I would have to get up in a few hours and get the kids and myself ready for school. My mind was working now though. If he wasn't working, we could still manage with my salary. The question was, would he be willing to do that? I thought back over the past few years with him, his many ideas, his many plans, but no follow-through or results. I realized that I had stopped even expecting him to succeed. I just made contingency plans quietly in my head. Like now. I wondered if I could ask to teach the higher grades, make a bit more money, make it work without needing his input.

My plans kept circling round and round. Underneath there was a frustration, an anger that sapped my energy. I closed my mind to all thoughts and willed myself to sleep. I needed that escape.

The next morning, I had a lurking headache. I was tired and irritable and dreaded the long school day ahead. School ran from eight thirty to five. I finished teaching in the nursery at three but stayed on to wait for my kids to finish, meanwhile planning for the next day. Today, I intended to try to talk to the director about teaching some elementary level classes and ask for more money. I was bored of teaching the alphabet, and it seemed we might need money soon.

Sighing, I pulled on the stretchy knit hijab I had taken to wearing now. It was easier to move in and more comfortable to wear for the whole day. I had also started wearing skirts and blouses, with a lab coat over the top, instead of my black burka. The nursery was a messy place, and it was not easy to wear a veil or coat while helping twenty or thirty kids with their snacks and shoes and on the playground. Compromise was the word of the day.

"Come on, girls," I said grabbing my bag. "Let's get in the car, we need to go." Even Hajar was going to school now. She was three years old and could enrol in the youngest nursery class. I herded them all downstairs and out to the car. At least they could all climb in on their own now. I reached in to help with their seat belts. It was a beautiful day, and I tried to smile.

"Assalamu alaikum, Aishah," my co-teacher said as I walked into school. "The director was looking for you."

"Wa alaikum salam, Batoul," I replied in greeting. I liked Batoul, she was one of the few genuinely nice women I had met in Morocco. Many of the people, especially women, seemed to be covering up what they really felt about you, but I felt comfortable with Batoul. At least in so far as work was concerned. I had gotten to know her personally too. She was in her thirties and still not married, which meant she lived at home with her parents and siblings. She wanted to be a wife and maybe even a mother, the ultimate goal of almost all the women here. It was notoriously hard for women her age to find a decent match, as most men wanted younger women. She wasn't particularly pretty in a traditional sense, but I liked her open smile and tender heart.

"Did she say what she wanted?" I asked. It wasn't often that the director bothered herself about the running of the school. She was happy if she was making money, and that was about it.

"She mentioned something about Al Jazeera, a documentary they are doing about foreign women living in Morocco. I think they got your name from one you did before about mixed marriages." A year or so earlier, a few of my women friends had been asked to talk about their experiences being married to someone from a different culture. It had been an interesting discovery for me to hear other women describe the challenges of interracial marriages. "So, they wanted to see if you would be willing to participate. I think she thought it would also be good publicity for the school, if you were filming here," she continued, with a knowing wink.

"Oh, *subhanallah*, praise be to Allah." I raised my eyebrows. "That's interesting. Would you mind taking the children to sing the anthem while I check in with her?"

"No, go ahead," she offered generously. "Go and see what she wants."

I put my bag down in the classroom and hurried back to the main office. The director was on the phone, so I knocked softly and waited. She motioned for me to wait, finished her conversation, then turned and motioned for me to come in.

"Aishah, good morning, how are you?" she gushed, smiling. This was not her usual mode of interacting. *She wants something from me*, I thought.

"Thank you, I am fine," I answered, a little on the defensive.

"So, I have great news! Al Jazeera called and they want to do some filming with you for a documentary about foreign women living and working in Morocco. I told them that we would be most happy to have them come and film at the school." She opened her arms welcomingly. "You are such an asset to our English language program here, and it would be great to promote that."

"Oh, yes, of course." I didn't quite know what to say. The thought crossed my mind to mention my idea of teaching the elementary grades and making more money. It sounded like the perfect time to ask. "I would be most happy to represent the school in the documentary." I smiled warmly. "I was actually going to speak to you today about possibly moving up from the nursery and teaching some of the older grades. I feel I have more to offer than just with the youngest children and would love the opportunity to take on a more challenging role." I stopped short of asking for more money, hoping that would be taken for granted.

"Ah," her smile left her face for a moment, "I suppose we could consider you teaching some of the older children. It is more challenging, and I could only offer you 3,000 dirhams a month," she added quickly.

"Great! Yes, that would be wonderful." I nodded enthusiastically. A thousand dirham increase in my wages was music to my ears right now. The filming couldn't have come at a better time.

"The film crew will be in Tangier next week. I will give them your number also, but we can make sure they begin filming here at the school. I will work you into the older grades as soon as I find another English teacher for the nursery."

"That is great, thank you. I will be ready." I turned to go back to the classroom. The bell had just rung, and the kids would be settling in.

Batoul raised her eyebrows at me as I came back in. I nodded at her and said I'd explain at break time. The children were noisy and rambunctious. It was early in the year, and school was still a new experience for them. I got my chair at the front of the class and called them all to sit down on the carpet in front of me.

"Good morning!" I said cheerfully in English.

"Good morning, Miss Aishah," they all chorused.

"How are you?" I looked at one of the boys in the front.

"I am fine," he answered in a halting voice.

"Good!" I smiled. "How about you?" I pointed to another little girl. "How are you?"

"I am fine," she answered also.

"That's wonderful." I pulled out some flash cards and began asking the different colours. We had been learning blue, red, green, yellow.

"We are going to use some colours to do some painting today!" I said after a few minutes. I indicated to my assistant that we would need the easels set up outside on the patio, as it was a beautiful day. "We will use red, green, blue, and yellow to paint with today." It was a lot of work to have the children paint, but they loved it, and it used up most of the morning. I did not have the head to do much actual teaching today. "Sit still until we get the smocks out, and then you will take turns painting. You can play outside with blocks or on the playground while you wait your turn."

The morning passed quickly with getting the children to take turns painting, and hanging up their pictures to dry. At snack time, we quickly washed out the paint jars and got things cleaned up. The heat was intensifying as the morning passed, and we made sure everyone had a drink. Then it was time to switch classes and do it all over again with the other group. By lunch time we were all tired of running around with paint and keeping an eye on everyone. I took the time after lunch to read them all a story. They liked *Goldilocks and the Three Bears*. It was funny to read them all of the European folk tales when they had so many good stories in their own culture, but the only English books we had were published in the West.

I was always exhausted at the end of a day teaching. Some days were fulfilling and some were horrible, but they were all tiring. I was always grateful to finally get a cup of tea and sit down to reflect and tidy up the classroom while I waited for my older girls to finish school. Usually Batoul and I used the time to plan lessons or prepare materials. I enjoyed working with her, she was someone with whom I could connect. I found it hard to make close friends here in Morocco. Many of the women were stuck in a pattern of disempowerment. The only way they could get what they wanted was to be manipulative and secretive. I hated this and could never bring myself to use the tricks and sly comments that seemed to permeate the culture here. This left me feeling fairly isolated most of the time, and I didn't often seek out the social gatherings that most of the women enjoyed.

Since I had begun teaching, I had the opportunity to interact with more men, and intelligent ones at that. I enjoyed talking about their hopes and dreams and hearing their stories. One teacher told me about his invention of some kind of antenna. I didn't quite follow all the technical aspects, but what struck me was the fact that although he had won recognition for his invention at an international science fair, he was unable to secure funding to patent it in Morocco or to leave the country to work elsewhere. This was only one of many stories of frustration that permeated the whole society here. It didn't seem fair that people in the West had so many opportunities, and here it was so difficult. I felt myself also slipping into the pattern of disempowerment more and more, as every day was the same, and the only thing we did was complain about it.

What would I have to share with the reporters from Al Jazeera? What did they want to hear? What was the truth of a foreign woman living in Morocco? It seemed as though there were many truths. Which one would I share, or more to the point, which one would come across in the documentary?

That evening was my night with Said, and I was excited to share my news about teaching the higher grades, earning more money, being in a documentary. It was a great feeling to be moving again, having some kind of vision and dream that went beyond just getting through the day with four children. I was animated and energetic, more than I had been for a long time.

"So, what do you think?" I prompted him, as he had sat fairly quietly through my exuberant chatting so far.

"That's great, baby, I'm proud of you." His voice was somewhat subdued as he spoke. I looked more closely at him. His eyes had a distant look, almost detached.

"Are you okay? Aren't you happy for me?" I wanted him to celebrate with me. We had made it through so much hardship, and maybe there was a light at the end of the tunnel.

"Of course." He smiled and absently patted my leg. I recoiled as if I'd been hit. What was wrong? I had worked so hard to make our lives work, to keep things going. Why was he acting as if I'd done something wrong?

"I also have something to tell you," he continued, finally looking at me directly. My heart plummeted into my feet. What would he spring on me now, right when I had hope that things were going to get better? "I may go back to England and look for work."

"Why?" I asked, stunned. Hadn't we left England to make a life here in Morocco, a Muslim country? I felt like I was being ripped apart at the seams. "I know it's been hard for you since your mother died, but do you really think you have more chance of finding work in England?"

"I don't know," he admitted sadly. "I could see Philip and maybe work in the circus again."

"Oh!" I was taken aback again. "But you wanted to get out of circus work." I didn't know to call it betrayal, but the knife was twisting in my heart. I had given up almost everything I cared about for him, and he was ready to leave me and just go waltzing back to his past life.

"I know, and I did, but my passion is in the circus, it's all I know." Again, his plaintive look melted my heart. "I am good at it. Maybe it's all I'm good at." He was pleading for affirmation now, and without thinking I responded as I always did.

I took his hand. "You are good at lots of things. You have been a good husband, son, father. You definitely are good in the circus, and if that is where your heart is, then you should go." As I said this, a cold loneliness spread through my body, and tears swam in my eyes.

"Don't cry, baby," he said, brushing the tears away. "I love you so much, you have been so good to me. I know you always understand."

I nodded, not really trusting myself to speak, my mind was such a mix of emotions. My earlier elation at my successes at work and the excitement of being in a documentary had vanished. The wheels were turning frantically in my brain to figure out how to make this work. I knew we couldn't all leave Morocco. We couldn't leave Fatima Zohra so soon after she had joined the family. I reeled with the effort of finding another solution.

"We can make this work, if we have faith in Allah." I had no other answer for now.

I slipped upstairs to the roof for a few minutes, just to gaze at the moon. It had been an elusive companion here, waxing and waning with the days, always marking the time of the month. It felt like an old grandmother, one that made you feel calm but was no more than a sliver of support in a constantly shifting world.

The next few days were a blur. Fatima Zohra was a godsend. She cooked and cleaned and kept everything going in the house so I could manage to work. I was assigned to teach grade two math and English, as well as grade seven science and literature. There were no textbooks or teaching aids. I had no experience in a classroom with thirty or forty kids whose experience of English was minimal and whose idea of discipline was to order me around.

I was only just realizing how different this culture really was, especially for the rich families. Many of the kids grew up in extended family groups where their parents were often travelling or away on business. They were looked after by maids or older relatives, who waited on them hand and foot while simultaneously forbidding them to engage in activities outside of the "proper" Islamic traditions. This system seemed to create entitled but naive kids, whom I found were extremely difficult to teach.

I had assumed that most kids wanted to learn if things were made interesting, but I was quickly finding that these kids didn't want to. They were told what to do, every waking moment, and had no sense of their own self or their own interests. I had no idea what to do. The language barrier made it even harder to bridge the gap between them and me. At first, I tried to make up little skits for them to act out and practice English, but I quickly found that keeping the rest of the class engaged and quiet while a few children were up front was next to impossible. I soon learned to give more worksheets and keep them sitting at their desks most of the time, to maintain some semblance of control in the classroom.

One of the male teachers noticed I was having trouble and offered to come and help keep order when I was giving an exam. I grudgingly admitted this would be helpful. He came into the classroom and gave the grade two class a strong talk.

"Okay, you guys, you must all respect Miss Aishah and be quiet during your test! I will be watching you as well." He walked up and down the aisles, brandishing a ruler ominously. I saw one or two of the kids flinch as he walked by. "You!" He stopped next to Omar, one of the more troublesome boys. "I have my eyes on you." He flicked the ruler at the back of his head, and I saw Omar wince as the end of it made contact.

"Ow!" Omar put his hand up, smiling cockily. I wasn't sure this was what I wanted for my students. Corporal punishment was a little extreme, but the kids had settled down and were quiet as mice. I bit my tongue and handed out the test papers.

"You have thirty minutes to complete as much as you can," I explained. "If you have any questions, raise your hand. Mr. Fouad and I will be watching you. Good luck!" I added, trying to lighten the atmosphere.

"Miss!" Omar nodded his head at me, motioning me to come closer to him. I had to hand it to him for being courageous. Even the smack on the head didn't seem to dampen his spirit. "Miss," he whispered to me as I leaned over his desk, "if I give you 100 dirhams, will you make sure I get an A on my test?" He winked at me conspiratorially.

I stood up, shocked. How did he even think of things like that at his age? I shook my head dazedly. "No, I can't do that. It wouldn't help you learn anything that way."

Omar laughed. "But I don't need to learn anything, I can just pay for stuff."

I shook my head. What in the world did these kids learn at home? I recognized the behaviour as typical of wealthy Moroccan men. They assumed they could get anything if they were charming and had money. I felt deeply troubled at this realization. It was not right that an eight-year-old was trying to bribe his way out of taking a test. I sat down at my desk and let my colleague patrol the class. No one moved while he walked up and down the rows of desks with his ruler.

Was this the only way to get anything done with these kids? I felt tired and overwhelmed. Teaching was difficult and the thought of Said leaving to go back to England made my head ache. If it wasn't for Fatima Zohra, I would have collapsed from the strain and fatigue. I noticed my hands shaking slightly as I made notes for my next lesson. I needed to pull myself together.

Said was leaving that weekend; as usual he had gotten his way. We had just enough money for a ticket from Spain to England, and he had arranged to stay with his friend near London. Neither Fatima Zohra nor I had the energy to try and impose any kind of restraint on him or even make any solid plans. I think we both felt almost relieved. Perhaps he would find a job and be able to send money regularly. He hadn't made much for months, and we all knew it wasn't sustainable.

The morning he left felt strangely like a dream. We got up, he packed his suitcase and said goodbye. He told Fatima Zohra and me to stay at home, no need to come down to the ferry with him.

The girls clung to his legs as he got ready to go. "Baba, don't go! Why do you have to go all the way back to England?" they chorused plaintively. Hajar hid behind Fatima Zohra's skirt, not understanding what all the fuss was about.

And then he was gone. Fatima Zohra and I made coffee and small talk. Family life closed in without him, more easily than seemed possible.

On the Friday after Said's departure, the film crew arrived at the school. They had travelled up from their office in Rabat and were going to spend most of the next two or three days with me and my family. I was a bit nervous but tried not to show it. The school's director escorted them out into the playground to meet me. She was in her element, showing them the school and talking about the great program we offered that combined the Moroccan school system with the

Cambridge English program. It all sounded much more glamorous in her words than I considered it to be in reality. Still, I played along and we sat and chatted for a few minutes. They offered to film at the school that day and then concentrate more on my home and family life tomorrow and the next day. They explained that the documentary would follow four different foreign women's stories of living in Morocco. They seemed especially intrigued that I would support my husband to have a second wife. The more I talked to people, I was learning that even Moroccan women found it hard to accept the idea of sharing a husband.

"So, tomorrow we will film you at home, if that's okay. We would like to interview you and your co-wife. Your husband has returned to England, you said?" I nodded sombrely, the reality hadn't really sunk in yet. "That must be hard for you and the children?" the female reporter prodded gently.

"I guess so, yes," I answered without emotion. "It was necessary for him to go back for work."

"Of course, I understand," she said, smiling, "but how do you and the other wife manage? You must miss him?"

"Yes, of course." I nodded, wondering a little myself. I didn't spend much time contemplating how we managed, I just did what was needed. Kept going. "We help each other, she stays home and I work. She helps me with the girls and around the house. We have become pretty good at fixing things ourselves." I laughed, thinking of the time we had rewired the electrical plug. We had become very resourceful. We had become partners in this twisted relationship triad where one pillar was absent.

The next day being a Saturday, I didn't have to rush and get ready for school. Fatima Zohra came upstairs soon after the kids woke up to help me get ready for the film crew. The house was fairly clean, *alhamdulillah*, thanks to Allah. She began rooting through the girls' clothes to pick out some decent outfits. I didn't have many nice clothes for them besides the navy school uniforms they were required to wear. Over the time we had lived here, many of the nicer dresses had been passed down from sister to sister, until Hajar finally wore them out. Shoes were a constant stress as well. This summer I had resorted to getting them all plastic sandals that could double as both beach shoes and dress shoes.

Fatima Zohra sighed, pulling out some clean T-shirts and shorts. "These will have to do," she said doubtfully. "Come here, girls!" She raised her voice over their playing. Omaima was almost eight years old and was more resistant to being herded up to do things. Safia and Hind were growing up quickly also, their growth spurts making it even more difficult to find clothes that fit them. Hajar still had the round chubbiness of a preschooler. The only issue with her clothes was that they were worn out by the time they got to her.

"Thank you," I mouthed to Fatima Zohra over the girls' heads as they lined up, pushing each other onto the beds as they jostled to get dressed. I went to the kitchen. We were planning to serve tea, a traditional Moroccan custom. Looking around, I realized I didn't have enough glasses for us all, or a nice tray. "I'm just going to see if I can borrow a tea tray and some glasses," I explained, and headed up the stairs to my father-in-law's apartment.

Zohra was up and sitting at the table, preparing herbs for freezing.

"Good morning!" I said.

"Aishah!" She beamed. "Good morning, how are you?"

"I am fine." I blushed slightly, realizing how little I came upstairs these days, now that Safiyya had passed. "You?"

"I am well, praise be to Allah."

"I was wondering if you would mind lending me your tea tray and some glasses." I stumbled a little with the Arabic but managed to convey the gist of my message. "The TV film crew is coming today, and I don't have enough."

"Of course! Take anything you want!" She jumped up to help me find the tea things. She really was a lovely lady. I regretted not spending more time with her.

"Thank you, you are too kind!" I kissed her cheeks. "I'll bring them back this afternoon."

"No rush." She smiled again.

I came back into my apartment to find that Fatima Zohra had successfully dressed the girls and was now working on their hair. I felt a burst of love for this woman, who was now part of our family. She really

had made her place, and I could tell the girls loved her.
A pang of jealousy coloured my feeling just for a
moment as I watched them all around her, laughing and
chattering away in Arabic. I set the tea tray down and
tried to get hold of myself. The film crew would be
here any minute, and the last thing I needed was to cry
in front of them.

I didn't completely understand why doing this
documentary was so important to me, but it somehow
felt like a lifeline. I was not faceless here, people wanted
to see me. Something inside me wanted to be recognized,
to have a voice. I wanted my life to matter.

As if on cue, there was a loud knock downstairs.

"I'll get the door." I almost had to shout over the
excited squeals of the kids. The excitement of something
new always created a frenzy of anticipation.

"Assalamu alaikum," I said, greeting the group of
people who stood at my door with cameras and lights
and a myriad of other black equipment bags. I was a
little taken aback at the scale of this. I'm not sure I was
completely prepared for the reality of filming for the
next two days. "Come in!"

"Wa alaikum assalam. You are ready for us?" It was
a bit of a rhetorical question I thought, given the fact
that they were already unpacked and standing on my
doorstep.

"Of course." I smiled, reaching one hand up
instinctively to check that my scarf was covering my hair.
I had on a long, yellow dress and a white scarf. We were

filming in my house, and I wanted to show that I did not wear dark colours all the time. "Come upstairs and we can set up."

The girls were peeking around the door as we came up the stairs.

"Hello," one of the cameramen said.

The heads popped back inside, and the girls ran to sit next to Fatima Zohra on the sofa. She nodded to the crew as they came in. "Assalamu alaikum."

"This is Fatima Zohra, the second wife." I translated the words directly from English to Arabic, which often gave entirely the wrong meaning to the listener. I hoped I had not offended anyone with my choice of language this time. More times than I could remember I had either hurt or offended Said's parents or extended family by my poor Arabic and lack of contextual understanding of the language. In the end, he had warned me to say no more than good morning, so as not to make a huge issue for him later on. I glanced at Fatima Zohra's face. I had to give her credit, she did not let my inept introduction faze her, at least in public.

She held out her hand in greeting. "Good morning, pleased to meet you. Would you like some tea?"

Of course! The first question to any visitor here in Morocco. I nodded in agreement.

"Well, actually, if you don't mind," the female reporter began, "we were hoping we could film you all having tea as a family. Maybe some shots of you making the mint tea?" She looked at me.

"Oh, um, yeah, I guess so." I could feel my heart rate increase. "My kitchen is very tiny, but we can try that."

They set up and filmed me making the tea, then asked me to serve it to Fatima Zohra and chat with her as we normally would. We made small talk about our day, the kids, the house, the family. It seemed to go well. The film crew did their thing without interrupting us too much. It started to get much easier by the end of half an hour or so, and I was breathing normally again.

"Great! We got some good footage there." The crew looked pleased. "So, we were thinking we could film at the market, if you two went shopping together, and maybe take you up to a café and film near the eucalyptus trees?"

I glanced sideways at Fatima Zohra. We had been shopping together fairly often, but I wasn't sure she was up for being filmed while out and about in Tangier. Surprisingly, she smiled confidently and answered that she would love to go and film at the market. I admired her courageous spirit. She definitely went all out and tried new things. Indeed, not many Moroccan women would consider being a second wife, especially with me being Canadian. I liked her spirit, and I smiled back at her. Again, I felt our kinship, and it warmed my heart.

"That sounds like a great plan," I agreed. "We should just clean up the dishes here, and then we can be ready to go. Should we bring the girls along?"

"I think we can bring them, yes. The crew can help

keep them entertained while we film, and then they are
there if we need them in the shot."

The filming at the market went well. Once they had
the footage they wanted, they asked if we could go out
to the café near the beach. I agreed.

The girls were getting restless and hot.

"Mama, can we get a drink?" Omaima spoke for
all of them, as she often did.

"We are just going to the café now, habiba," I said.
"Can you wait a few minutes until we get there?"

Her expression became pouty, but she nodded,
glancing sideways at the film crew. She knew that fussing
at this point, in front of strangers, would probably not
get her what she wanted.

"We are going to the beach, and I'll get you a
lemonade drink there, okay?"

This assurance settled the matter, and the girls
clambered into the car in anticipation. I pulled out
of the car park and followed the film crew in their car,
driving the ten minutes or so to the beach in tandem.
We drove to where huge eucalyptus trees created an
open forested area. A short walk led to a café overlooking
the Strait of Gibraltar. You could see the Spanish
shoreline, only nine kilometres away. It looked close
enough to swim across, and I could see why many people
tried to get to Europe that way.

The smell of eucalyptus cleared my head as we
seated ourselves at a table on the patio of the café.
The day was a stunning example of Moroccan fall

weather, sunny but not as hot as the summer months. We ordered mint tea for ourselves and lemonade pop for the girls, and the camera crew set up to film us.

By this point both Fatima Zohra and I were beginning to enjoy ourselves, even getting into our roles and becoming bolder with our acting. They filmed us walking up the steps, sitting at the table. We pointed out landmarks to each other as we sat and talked. As the tea was served, Fatima Zohra reached across and fixed my scarf for me with an oddly tender touch. It was a small gesture but done with such caring. It almost felt as though she and I were the married couple, now that Said had left. In a way, I realized then, we were almost happier without him.

The director asked if she could interview me alone. I agreed, and the two of us moved off to another table, followed by the crew. Partway through the interview, I was struck by a sudden look, a shift of her body, almost an impatience. She had been listening to my perfect rhetoric on being a co-wife, mother, and Muslim woman in a foreign country.

Was I happy? she had asked.

Yes, I answered.

Did I miss my home, my family?

Sure, doesn't everyone?

How did it feel that my husband had another wife?

Well there were pros and cons, but mostly things were good.

Did I ever regret becoming a Muslim?

No.

I could hear my voice answering her questions, almost as if I was listening from some distance. I felt strangely disembodied.

She felt the dissonance, I could tell. That piercing look in her eyes as she said, "But are you really happy here?"

I could feel the panic rising like a tide. I held my breath and tried to squeeze it down. The wave of fear was not new, but it was not something I wanted to feel. It threatened to drown my entire existence in its cold, rushing chaos.

"Yes, I am," my voice replied of its own accord, without my brain's input at all.

She looked down at her notes and sighed as if disappointed in me for some reason. I hadn't quite given her what she wanted, even though at that point, I had no idea what that was.

Perhaps she hoped I would rise up and take back my life, that I would confirm her suspicion that Muslim women were controlled and disempowered. Perhaps she wanted a story of the maiden in distress that could be rescued and saved from the throes of a life in servitude to the male dominated, fundamentalist thinking that colours the view of the women in this country. I wasn't sure exactly, and maybe she wasn't sure either. Her shoulders slumped forward slightly, and she wrote a few notes in her book. She didn't speak at all.

Finally, she raised her head and the look was gone.

The rest of the interview was as inspiring as cold porridge. I don't even remember what I said. I only felt the lingering sadness of disappointing her somehow.

The cameraman smiled. "Would you like to come down in the trees here, and we can take a quick shot of you reading Quran?"

"Yes, that would be a great idea," said the director as the crew took down the tripod and picked up the equipment.

I turned to Fatima Zohra. "Could you watch the girls while we do that?"

She nodded, and the girls scampered off with her to look at the camel that was being led around the parking lot for the amusement of the tourists. I picked up my bag and a book of Arabic hadith, sayings of the Prophet Muhammad, and followed the crew down into the trees. The canopy was high and open, and the air cool and fresh under the huge eucalyptus forest. We walked a few hundred metres and stopped when we found a flat stone that was perfect for sitting on.

"You sit here and read out loud. We'll film close up like this so we can hear you." The sound guy moved the mic up near my head. I felt apprehensive, as I didn't have fluent reading skills in Arabic. I flipped quickly through the book and was relieved to find the opening speech that was always recited before the Prophet gave a sermon; I had memorized it for the sisters' circle in Manchester. I opened the book to that page and put my finger on the words.

"Okay, whenever you are ready," the director said.

I looked at the words and took a deep breath, "In the name of Allah, the most merciful, the most kind," I began, and the rest of the speech flowed out almost without thinking. I finished the paragraph and looked up, hoping they would be satisfied with that. "Is that enough?"

"Sure, that was great." The sound guy gave the thumbs-up, and I sighed in relief as I closed the book and deposited it back in my shoulder bag. The crew packed up and we hiked back up the hill and looked down at the beach. The sun was getting low in the horizon, and the director said excitedly, "What about filming you and the girls sitting on the beach, watching the sunset?"

"Okay." I stifled a yawn. The whole day had been tiring and a little surreal. Trying to capture the moments that made my life in Morocco unique was challenging. "I think the girls can last another hour or so. I should go check on them first though."

"Of course." The crew leaned on their car, giving me permission to go chat to Fatima Zohra and the girls on my own.

The girls were still happily playing on the beach, and Fatima Zohra agreed we could probably manage another hour to film the sunset. I turned and gave the crew the thumbs-up. They smiled and waved in return. Picking up the cameras and microphones, they wound their way down near us and began setting up to film again. We sat.

Fatima Zohra and I each had one of the younger girls in our laps. We drew pictures in the sand.

As the sun sank lower in the sky and the colours lit up the waves, I felt the beauty of Morocco sink into my heart. As happens to many young mothers, I rarely seemed to take the time to stop and contemplate how fortunate I was to be alive. It seemed ironic that it took someone filming us for me to take this opportunity, but I was glad nonetheless. I snuggled Hajar in my lap, and the others leaned against us in various positions of repose. It had been a long and exciting day. We would all sleep well tonight.

"Thank you so much. We have finished for today. You have all been amazing." The cameraman lifted Safia up onto his shoulders, and we headed to the parking lot. "We will stop in tomorrow morning to interview you and wrap up, but it will just be in your house."

"Okay, sounds good, thanks to Allah," I answered gratefully.

I chatted to Fatima Zohra on the drive home. "I think it would be fun to have my own TV show." I laughed. "Like Oprah!"

"Sure." She smiled indulgently.

Exciting thoughts and plans flooded my brain. I rarely felt enlivened by ideas anymore, so I relished the feeling, even if my plans were unrealistic.

As we arrived home, my mood was brought back to earth with a clunk. The girls were tired and fussy. It took the combined efforts of both Fatima Zohra and me to quiet them down and get them off to bed. Mission accomplished, we sat and looked at each other. The tiredness crept into my bones, everything began to ache.

Fatima Zohra broke the silence. "So, do you think Said will come back to Morocco?"

"Huh?" I looked at her dazedly. What an odd question. Of course, he would be back. Wouldn't he? I mean, that was the plan. Then again, he had yet to find full-time work, and so far, he had relied on me to give Fatima Zohra her monthly "allowance" out of my own wages. I also paid all the bills and looked after the house. Now that I thought about it, I had expected him to be sending money by now. "I am sure he will be back soon. He did say he was going to work with the circus again." My voice didn't sound overly reassuring, and from the look of her face, Fatima Zohra would agree.

She shifted angrily. "I didn't sign up for this! I didn't get married just to live without my husband all the time and help his family, like a maid."

I understood her anger, but I bristled with the accusation that we were treating her like a maid. We had just spent an amazing day together with the kids. Wasn't I stuck here as much as she was? I thought we shared a special bond, co-wives, partners, housemates, not quite lovers but almost. Anyway, there was no point getting angry. There was no point feeling anything at all really. We were stuck in the same boat, and nothing would change. The truth of this descended on me with a black despair that squeezed all hope from my lungs.

"We will just have to make the best of it," I replied wearily. "What else can we do?"

"Hmph!" She flounced up off the couch. "Well this is not my idea of marriage at all!"

Her footsteps echoed on the steps as she headed down to her apartment, and for some reason I felt like her mood was my fault. Weren't I and the girls enough for her? I knew that wasn't what she meant, but the hurtful words lingered.

The exhaustion of the past few days had seeped into every part of me. Shaking my head dazedly, I headed to bed. I didn't want to think or feel anything. Sleep was a sweet escape.

Chapter
Thirteen

AGAIN, THE DAYS AND WEEKS blurred together. Said had been gone four months now, and life seemed to carry on without him more easily than I would have imagined. Eid-ul-Fitr, the Islamic holiday that descended from the story of Abraham and his son, had come again. God had commanded Abraham to sacrifice his only son, Isaac, to show his obedience and love for his creator. Abraham had spoken to Isaac and explained the dilemma of wanting to please God but not wanting to kill him. Isaac, upon hearing of God's command, told his father he was willing to die and to go ahead and sacrifice him. Abraham laid him on the altar, and just before the blade came down, God replaced Isaac with a sheep. This act of mercy in response to

Abraham's surrender to the will of Allah is what the Muslims remember every year with the ritual sacrifice. In Islam, every family is obligated to sacrifice a sheep on the day of Eid-ul-Adha.

Said had still not sent any money, and Fatima Zohra and I talked about whether we could afford to buy a sheep.

"We have to have a sheep," she insisted. "We have to show that we can afford to buy one."

"But what if we can't?" I was having trouble seeing things the same way. To my way of thinking, if we couldn't afford to buy a sheep, then we didn't buy one, no big deal. But for Moroccans, the status of money was important, and I could see she wouldn't rest until we bought a sheep. I was up against a wall. She had the right, as second wife, to ask for her own sheep. She was already compromising to allow us to get one together. "I'll call Said and talk to him," I offered.

I resented having to be the middleman in these negotiations. I hated having to ask Said for anything. It usually ended up with me feeling needy and selfish. Even if I started off thinking that what I was asking for was perfectly reasonable, he had a way of turning it around and making me feel bad.

"Hey, baby," I began, trying to sound cheerful and nonchalant. "How's things?" I always hoped he would say things were great, never better. And I was always disappointed.

"Well, you know, I'm trying my best," he answered

in an almost whiny voice.

"Oh? I thought you were working now," I prodded, hoping for a shred of good news.

"Well, I am doing some work, but not as much as I'd like yet," he replied grudgingly. "The gym is not that busy. I am still waiting to hear from Philip about the circus."

"Hm, well, keep your chin up." I sounded almost too bright. "So, um, Fatima Zohra wants us to buy a sheep for Eid," I blurted. "Can you send any money?" I rushed through the question, afraid if I didn't get it out, I wouldn't be able to, or he would shut me down before I asked.

"Oh, I don't know," he mumbled. "I don't have anything at the moment."

"Well, Eid is in two weeks. Can you send us something by next week? She really has her heart set on having a sheep. I wouldn't mind either way, but you know, she is Moroccan," I added, trying to explain away my guilty feeling. Why should I feel guilty? Anger also began to creep through my mind. I was busting my gut working here for HIS family. He should be sending money to help, shouldn't he? As doubt crept in, my anger began to leak out, like the air in a balloon that's been pricked. I felt old and tired. I didn't even care anymore. Eid was just another day to get through.

"I'll see what I can do." I heard his voice as if from far away.

"Sure, whatever," I mumbled.

"Don't be like that, baby," he wheedled. "You know I love you. I'm doing my best here."

"Yeah, okay." I was suddenly tired of the whole conversation. "I'll talk to you soon."

"Baby…" his voice trailed off. I knew he wanted me to say I loved him too, to tell him everything would be all right, that I would somehow make everything work. I sighed.

"I have to go." I couldn't do it. Couldn't say "I love you" one more time. "Talk soon," I blurted, then hung up.

Tears stung my eyes as I sat and stared at the phone. I couldn't believe it, I hadn't said "I love you" back. A huge, black hole of a question opened up in front of me. Maybe I didn't love him anymore. My heart raced. The fear was real, but it wasn't because of what I'd not said, it was because I'd realized the deep truth of my feelings. It was too big a realization for the day, for this day. But it was there, and now I knew it was there. I couldn't go on denying it.

I put the phone down on the table and robotically went to check on the girls, the house, anything to keep busy and moving. My heart stopped racing wildly, and I breathed. I didn't know what would happen now, but something had changed in me.

The next morning Said's father came down. It was a Saturday, and I was glad to be on a slower timeline with breakfast and morning chores.

"Good morning!" he said cheerfully, handing out cookies to the girls. I frowned slightly as they ripped open the wrappers and munched on the cookies, leaving their porridge to get cold.

"Good morning, Ba," I answered, using the familiar Arabic name for father. I had slipped into this familiarity more and more since Said left.

"We should go and look at sheep today." He cut straight to the point, as he usually did. "Eid is almost here!"

"Um, yes, we should." I answered uncertainly, wishing for the hundredth time that Said was here to help negotiate these things. "How much money do you think we need to get a decent sheep?"

"A nice sheep for your family would be about 2,000 dirhams," he said proudly. "You need a nice sized sheep."

Two thousand! My breath caught in my throat. "That's a lot." I was stalling. "Could we get something for around 1,500?" I asked hopefully.

His smile faded. "That's not much, you'd only get a small one."

"A small one will do." I spoke hurriedly before he could object any more. "The kids and I don't eat much meat."

"Well, we can try, the market is open today."

"Right, well, um…I guess I can be ready to go in about an hour. Does that sound okay?" I sighed. So much for my quiet Saturday at home. But this would get

Fatima Zohra off my back too. At least, I hoped it would.

I counted out the money I had left and put my final 1,500 dirhams in my bag. I prayed I would have enough to keep everyone happy. I still hadn't heard back from Said, and Eid was coming soon. Heaviness descended on my shoulders. What happened to weekends off and having fun? The days marched onwards with the inevitability of more difficulties to overcome, matching the ominous rain clouds that hung in the sky today. I reached for my oldest jellaba and boots, as I was sure the sheep markets would be muddy and crowded. No point in trying to be anything but practical today.

I wondered if Fatima Zohra would be willing to watch the two younger girls. I wasn't at all sure I could cope with all four of them and a stubborn sheep.

"Good morning!" I called down to her. "Are you awake?"

"Yes, good morning," she replied.

"Ba asked me to go to buy a sheep with him, and I was going to try and get us a small one also," I explained. "Would you watch Hind and Hajar for the morning?"

"Okay." I heard her coming up the stairs. "Did Said send money?"

"No, not yet." My skin prickled uncomfortably. "I'm using all the money I have left to buy a sheep now. Allah willing, he will send money next week."

"Oh." Fatima Zohra looked uncomfortable too. We both felt trapped by our mutual resentment and feelings. It seemed like our husband did not care about either of us. Part of me wanted to comfort and reassure her that everything would work out, or maybe I wanted her to reassure me. I couldn't do anything though. The feeling of worthlessness and loss of hope prevented me.

I turned to the older girls. "Come on, guys, we are going to go out and buy a sheep for Eid."

"Can we pick a cute one?" Omaima asked, excitedly.

"Sure, definitely a cute one for us." I smiled. She had always loved animals. She was big enough this year to help with the sacrifice. It was amazing to me how easily the girls accepted the ritual killing of an animal. They loved helping. This year, Fatima Zohra and I would likely have to do most of the work. It would be good for the girls to be involved.

As we walked through the marketplace, the sounds and smells of the hundreds of sheep assaulted my senses. Every farmer in the area had come to sell the animals they could afford to part with. I looked at the many small groups of sheep, penned in temporary enclosures, waiting to be sold, and wondered if they knew they were being sold as sacrificial animals. Muslims said the sheep knew they were being slain for Allah and felt honoured to be chosen for this role. I had watched the last few years as Said's father had said the name of Allah and drawn a blade across the jugular vein. I had even held the head of the sheep last year as life left its body and the blood spilled out. My mother-in-law had danced in the blood, covering her feet in its sticky redness. "It's good for your health," she had said. Even the girls had joined in the ritualistic dance, wetting their tiny feet and marvelling at the colour.

Taher seemed to know where he was going, so I put my head down and followed. He came to a stop beside a small hut. An old man in a brown wool jellaba was leaning against the frame.

"Good morning," Taher said confidently. "We want to look at your best sheep."

"What's your price?" The man replied, obviously aware of the usual progression of these types of conversations.

"One thousand five hundred dirhams," Taher answered. I heaved a sigh of relief that he had stuck to what I'd told him. I didn't want to be put on the spot for more money than I had.

The man spat on the ground. "That is nothing! I have nothing for under 2,000 dirhams."

"What about that one there?" Taher pointed to a cute, slightly smaller one, over on the side.

"That one?" The man scratched his beard thoughtfully.

"I'll give you 1,500 for that one. It's not even worth that, look at how small he is!" Taher shook his head.

"One thousand seven hundred and you can have him," the shepherd stated.

"One thousand five hundred, that's my final offer." Taher waved his hands to emphasize his point.

"Okay, 1,500." The man held out his hand to shake on it. "Done!"

Taher pulled some short pieces of rope from his pocket and climbed over the fence into the enclosure. He was so confident around animals. I marvelled at the ease with which he hobbled the front feet of the sheep and tied a lead around its curled horns.

"Can I lead him?" Omaima asked eagerly.

Taher handed her the rope, and she almost bounced over the grass as the hobbled sheep shuffled along beside her.

I smiled at her enthusiasm. I knew you couldn't put a price on these kinds of experiences, but somehow there did seem to be a price, a heavy one. I could feel it on my shoulders. Nevertheless, I stopped for a bale of hay on the way home, and we arrived back at the house, triumphantly leading the doomed sheep up the three flights of stairs to the roof.

Taher tied it in one corner and set up a couple of old crates to serve as a shelter in case it rained. We set out some hay and water and left it to get used to its temporary home. We told the girls that the sheep knew it had been chosen as a sacrifice and that it accepted that, even took it as an honour. Deep down I suspected we did that just to make ourselves feel less guilty.

"It's a small sheep," Fatima Zohra commented when I came downstairs.

"Yes, they are expensive this year," I replied, warily defensive. *At least we bought one*, I thought.

"Well, I am going out this afternoon with my mom to get one also," she stated. Something was present in her voice—haughtiness or hurt, I wasn't sure.

"Oh?" I was surprised. Weren't we supposed to do this stuff together? "You are welcome to share this one." I felt the prick of jealousy and anger rising. She'd probably want more money from Said now also, after I went to all the trouble to buy a sheep myself. It was as though she wanted to prove that Said cared more about her than me. "Well, do whatever you want." I tried not to snap back. The day was only half over, yet I felt exhausted. I went past her into the bedroom and changed my dress. She came to the door and stood there, watching.

"Said sent me some money to get one," she added smugly. "I thought you'd want to know."

"Hm," I grunted, facing the other way. I didn't trust myself to answer civilly if I turned around, I might have taken a swing at her. The manipulative bitch. Pulling the sob story to me about needing a sheep, and then going behind my back and doing the same thing to Said. I didn't want to see her right now. I kept my head turned away and headed straight to the bathroom to clean the mud off me. "See you later," I growled.

"Yeah, okay." She left. I waited until her footsteps died away down the stairs then let out a loud growl of frustration. I was mad at her for sure, but most of my rage centred on Said. He had left us in these circumstances, and neither of us felt cared about. What was I doing here anyway? And why would he send her money for a sheep without telling me?

That question sunk deep into my mind and lodged itself there. What was I doing here? Said had been gone for months, and it didn't look like he would come back anytime soon. Was this how I wanted my life to go? What choice did I have? Sighing, I stepped out of the tub. I couldn't even have a real bath, because the electricity was too expensive to heat that much water. I felt beaten down. I didn't even have the mental capacity to consider what else was possible. Every day was a struggle, every dirham was needed.

I wanted to be held, I wanted to feel that everything would be all right, that I wasn't alone. As the tears threatened, I decided to use a calling card and phone Said.

"Hello?" He answered after a couple of rings.

"I just needed to hear your voice…" The tears overflowed, and I sobbed into the phone.

"What's wrong, baby?" He sounded concerned. "Why are you crying?"

"I don't know, it's all just too much…" I blubbered almost incoherently, the stress of the last weeks catching up with me. "I want you to come here, I need you to hold me."

"Aw, you know I love you." His voice did little to soothe me. I made a heroic effort to stop the flow of tears.

"I don't think I can do this on my own." The words tumbled out. I wasn't even sure what I meant exactly. Something had snapped in me. I felt broken. The dream of Hijra, holy pilgrimage to a Muslim country, was no solace anymore. And it wasn't supposed to be just me anyway, was it?

Said tried to keep the exasperation from his voice. "I have a show in half an hour," he said. "You know, you could go back to Canada if you want. I'm not forcing you to do anything."

I was stunned. I could go back to Canada? My mind turned the idea over. A tiny window of hope appeared in the blackness. But how could I go? I had no money, I had spent my last dirhams on the sheep.

I said a distant goodbye and hung up the phone. The girls were playing happily. I went through to the small balcony and looked out, gulping in the fresh air. Was there a way out?

I felt like I was floating through the next few days until Eid. Part of me had left already. All my waking hours I pondered the thought of leaving. Just picking up and going.

The morning of Eid dawned clear and sunny. In a daze, I got the girls ready for prayers. I heard nothing of the talk as we sat in the women's part of the mosque. I went through the motions. Fatima Zohra and I changed into old clothes when we got back and prepared to do the hard work of sacrificing our sheep. We had three to do, as Said's father had bought himself a small sheep as well.

The girls were excited and chattering happily. I smiled. It was nice to see them enjoying the activities. We climbed the stairs to the patio and saw Taher sharpening the knife.

"Good morning, and Happy Eid!" He smiled his toothless smile. He had aged a lot even in the few years we had been here.

"Happy Eid!" We each kissed his forehead.

"Are you ready to bring the first sheep down to the patio?" I asked. He was always careful to bring them down singly so they weren't traumatized by seeing their comrades killed. The patio opened out from their apartment and provided the perfect place to work, being open to the outside but close to the kitchen.

"Yes, I think so." He laid the knife carefully on the window ledge. "Let's get the first one."

Fatima Zohra appeared then also, and we got the things ready. Taher brought down the first sheep. It struggled on the stairs, not wanting to leave its rooftop enclosure.

"Hold the horns, like this," Taher instructed once he had got the sheep on its side. I twisted the head so the throat was exposed. Fatima Zohra helped hold the legs. "Bismillah," Taher said, and slid the knife across the jugular vein. Blood spurted from the wound. I kept hold of the horns, but the feet were free to kick the last of its life out as the blood spilled onto the tiles. A few seconds, and the sheep was still. The girls cheered with delight as they came closer to see. Taher had already wedged a hollow stick into the skin by the hind foot, and Fatima Zohra took the first turn blowing air in under the skin to loosen it. Her face was red with the effort.

Usually it was the man that did the hard work of skinning the sacrificial sheep, but Taher was too old to do much of the work. Fatima Zohra and I held the carcass as it inflated.

"That is good," Taher observed from his seat inside. He came out to help us tie a rope through the hind feet. It then took the combined strength of all three of us to hoist the sheep up and hang it in the doorway.

The blood ran over the tiles, and Fatima Zohra showed the girls how to wash their feet in the red stickiness. It was good for the skin, she told them. To me it seemed an overly dramatic way of celebrating the sacrifice, but I smiled to see them stomping around joyfully. Perhaps there was the possibility of transformation with the death of something else. Maybe the meaning of the sacrifice went a little deeper in my heart this year, as I thought about how my life had already changed so much. Would a sacrifice be required in order to move forward with my life, for myself and my girls? I watched as they continued to stomp happily in the blood, the redness staining their little feet. Was I ready to let go of everything I'd built here?

I wiped the sweat from my forehead, not caring that I was smearing blood on my face. I took a smaller knife and began the tedious work of detaching the skin from the meat. This was meant to be done quickly, while it was still fairly easy to separate. I made a few nicks in the fleece, it was definitely harder than it looked. Taher criticized my efforts but only half-heartedly. We still had two sheep to go, and there was no room for perfection.

After what seemed like hours but was really only about half an hour, the fleece was hanging from only a few sinews on the legs. I cut through the last cords and pulled down the skin, which flopped onto the tiles. It was surprisingly heavy. I managed to load it into a washtub before flopping down myself. One down!

Zohra, Taher's wife, handed me a glass of water, and I nodded gratefully. She had been busy in the kitchen preparing to cook the first meat over the barbecue. It really took a lot of people to get through this process. I thought about how in Canada we would just buy meat at the store. No matter how much you understood intellectually where meat comes from, the hands-on experience was totally different.

Somehow, we managed to get through sacrificing and skinning three sheep, and by then, the smell of meat cooking over the coals was making my mouth water. I washed my hands in a tub of water and wiped them on my mendeel as I ducked into the darker living room upstairs. Zohra was crouched over the small barbecue, and Taher was sitting on the couch. He really was getting too old for this type of work, I could see the strain on his face. I felt a twinge of guilt. Said should have been here to help his father with this yearly ritual. I wondered vaguely what he was doing in England. It seemed like forever since we'd seen him. I remembered his words: "You could go back to Canada, you know." I felt trapped here, and yet I cared about these people, they were family now. I was supporting them. I wondered what they would do if I left.

"Here, have some meat." Zohra handed me a skewer fresh off the grill.

"Thank you! This looks amazing." I smiled. "I worked up an appetite."

I grabbed a warm loaf of bread and opened it to put my meat inside. It smelled delicious.

"Mm," I nodded appreciatively. "It's so good. Thank you!"

Zohra helped get everyone a sandwich, and the girls sat down hungrily to enjoy the Eid feast, the first of many over the next few days. There were special meals to be prepared with each of the body parts of the sheep. The head was charred and used to top heaping plates of couscous, the brains were fried up with eggs for breakfast. Taher held up the balls of his sheep for me to see.

"These are for you, my daughter." He laughed and winked.

I laughed too. I was game to try them, but they didn't look that appetizing dangling from his hand.

As I finished my sandwich and mint tea, I could feel my eyes drooping. I hadn't realized how tired I was until I sat down and had some food.

"I think I am going to go down and have a quick nap, if we are done here for now." I yawned.

"Yes, yes, go and rest. The sheep have to hang for now anyway." Zohra shooed me out and began wiping off the table.

"Thank you for the food. It was lovely." I got up stiffly. "Come on, girls. Let's go downstairs for a bit."

I put the kettle on to heat some water and took it to the bathroom. I stripped off my dirty clothes and stepped into the tub. The warm water felt so amazing, I could have stayed there all day. I wished I could have a proper bath. I dripped the last bit of water down my chest and stepped out to dry myself. The stiffness was settling into my body already from this morning's work. I prayed the girls would behave for half an hour and let me lie down.

I looked in the mirror, and my eyes glazed over. I couldn't even see the person I was looking at. Where were the contours of her face? The edges seemed all blurry and indistinct.

I closed my eyes and opened them again, willing myself to see. A woman's face stared back, brown eyes, soft cheeks, a slightly pudgy nose, wavy hair. I looked into her eyes, and as I stared I felt inexplicably sad. The more I looked, the more the depth of her sadness came over me.

I turned away, not wanting to feel with her, for her. It was too much to bear. But something pulled my gaze back. I glanced at her sideways, wanting her to smile, to say everything was okay.

"Nothing to see here," I said, prompting her to leave me alone. She stared back with the liquid brown of her eyes and saw into my soul. I shivered.

This is stupid. The Voice was back with a vengeance.

I mean, eye-gazing with yourself? How is this going to help anything? You're still alone.

"Be quiet," I told The Voice, surprised at my own boldness. "I don't need you anymore," I said clearly and more loudly than I was planning. "You can go. I am going to take back my life." Now that I had come this far, I wasn't backing down.

The Voice deflated like an old balloon. *You need me*, he wheedled, a little of the sneer coming back into his words.

"No, Voice, I don't. I know I can do this now. I can live on my own. I want to see her."

A shiver went through me as I said these words, and I turned to fully face my reflection. I reached out my hand toward her, and she reached back. I could see a tear threatening at the corner of her eye. She wanted me as much as I wanted her.

"I love you," I whispered, with more feeling than I'd felt in a long time. I could feel her warmth begin to seep into me, inhabiting my body with her essence. "You're back." I could see the tears running down her face now, and they matched my own.

I gazed at her wonderingly for a few more minutes. Her face was clear and full of gentle empathy. I could feel my body respond to her loving gaze, and I realized that for right now, I didn't feel lonely at all.

Thankfully, the children had put on the cartoon channel. I left the bedroom door open and lay down on the bed. I could see them out of the corner of my

eye for a couple of minutes before drifting off to sleep.
I awoke with a start when Hajar crawled into bed next
to me. Pulling at my shirt, she made it clear what she
wanted. Sighing, I rolled over and allowed her to pull
my breast to her mouth. She was almost four years old
now but still found comfort in suckling, and I had
decided the benefits outweighed the downsides of
continuing to breastfeed. I was too exhausted to
negotiate or find an alternative for her. It was easy.
She settled into a rhythm and her eyes fluttered closed.
It had been a long and exciting morning.

I stayed still, allowing her to fall asleep, then got
up without disturbing her. The others had fallen asleep
on the couch watching cartoons. Smiling, I turned off
the TV and left them to nap for a bit. I made some tea
and sat down in a corner, taking in the view of my
apartment. Now that the work of Eid was over, my
thoughts returned to the idea of moving back to Canada.
Could I stay here? For what? Said had no plans to return
to Morocco on a permanent basis anytime soon. I was
not sure my life plan had ever included supporting his
extended family here in Tangier on my own. Fatima
Zohra didn't really want me or the girls, she wanted
a husband and family, and it was becoming clearer that
I couldn't give that to her. I didn't have it myself.

—————

"Hello?"

"Oh, hey, Dad." I tried to sound nonchalant. I had

hoped to speak to Mom first. I didn't quite know what I wanted to say. Now that I was on the phone, I struggled to find the words to sum up my feelings. "How are you and Mom?" I wanted to cry, I missed them, I missed home. Life just felt so hard here.

"We are good," he answered, never having been a great conversationalist.

There was a pause, and I wondered where to start. "We just sacrificed the sheep here, for Eid. Said didn't make it home," I started, the words tumbling out. "I've been getting really stressed at school lately. I had to sit down at the break the other day because I was shaking so much." My lip quivered and the tears that had been just below the surface started rolling down my cheeks. "I don't know if I can take it here anymore," I blurted out between sobs.

"Don't cry," Dad said gently, which just made me cry harder. "You can just come home if you want." I wasn't sure if he had thought of this scenario before or not. They had always seemed supportive of my choices in life, but his answer had been so confident and quick. Maybe they had known all along I wasn't really happy?

"I can't," I answered. "I haven't got any money, I have all my stuff here, I don't know…I don't know if I can just leave."

"If you need to come home, then just come. I can book tickets for you and the kids. Leave everything there. Nothing material is so important that it's worth this much stress." His voice was understanding and loving. When he said it, it actually sounded possible. Was it possible? Could I just walk away? The tight cords around my chest relaxed a little as I realized I could. His voice soothed me in a way I hadn't felt in a long time.

"Okay," I said softly. "Okay, I think I should come home," I said more confidently. "I can't take it here anymore, without Said."

"Okay, I'll look for tickets." My dad's businesslike manner felt reassuring.

"I'll hand in my notice this week. There is a school holiday coming up in two weeks. I can say I'm leaving then. Thank you, Dad, I love you." Tears choked my throat as I said these last words. I couldn't remember ever feeling so close to my dad before. It felt good, warm, comforting, supportive, this feeling of being held by a man.

I hung up the phone, feeling so many things all at once I was bursting. I was leaving! I was leaving… My mind shut down, it was like an overload. The girls stirring on the sofa brought me back to reality.

"Mama," Hind's curly head peeked around the pillow. "I'm hungry."

"Hm, maybe we should see if Auntie is downstairs. We could see if they want to have tea together." The girls were much more comfortable visiting downstairs than I was; they considered everyone in the house fair game. I had interacted a little with Fatima Zohra's mother since the marriage, enough to know she would understand my wanting to leave. She herself had raised four daughters on her own in Morocco after her husband had left, and I knew it had not been easy.

"Yeah!" Omaima sat up sleepily then too.

"Okay," I said laughing, "let me go and see what they are up to downstairs."

Fatima Zohra's mother, Khadija, was lying on the sofa. The room was dark, as the only windows were in the bedrooms and the light didn't reach into the living room.

"Assalamu alaikum, Auntie." I went in quietly, trying to judge if she was asleep or just resting. She beckoned me in and I went over to sit near her. "The girls wanted to come down and have tea together if you are up for that." I hesitated, worried yet again that my Arabic was not good enough to encompass the nuances of politeness that these negotiations required. I tried to read her response to tell if she actually wanted to or was just going along with my request.

"Oh, the dear girls." She smiled and pushed herself to an upright position. "Bring them down, of course!"

"I'll get some bread from the store," I offered. "It should be open again now. Do we need anything else?"

"No, I'll make the tea, and we have chocolate spread and cookies," she said. I smiled in return and stood to go get the girls and the bread. They loved the family time that these holidays provided. Tomorrow would be the time to visit relatives in the village. I hadn't been out there since Said had left for England. It was a long drive, and I felt

awkward going on my own. Taher had lost interest in
visiting the village since Safiyya had passed away.

"Okay, guys, we are having tea downstairs,"
I called to the girls, "and before we go down, I have
some news. We are going to go to Canada for awhile."
I decided the less information the better at this point,
hoping they would just be excited about the trip and
not ask too many questions.

"Yay!" The squeals blended with the excited
shuffling of four girls putting on their flip-flops for
the trip downstairs. "We love Canada! That's where
Granny and Grandpa live!"

"Yes, that's where Granny and Grandpa live,"
I said as I threw on my scarf and coat and grabbed
my purse.

I followed the girls as they scurried downstairs.
"I'm just going to the store," I called out, then left
through the main door. I could hear the tea preparations
going on inside as I pulled the heavy metal door closed
behind me. The bright sun dazed me for a second.
I squinted and dropped my gaze, walking quickly to
the small shop next door.

"Two loaves of bread, please," I said quickly in
Arabic. I counted out the change and added a hasty,
"*Eid Mubarak!*" as I put the money down on the counter.

"Mommy, there is chocolate spread!" Omaima
exclaimed as I re-entered the house. "Come quickly
with the bread." It was like they hadn't eaten in weeks.

I smiled at her exuberance. "Here, habiba,"

I handed her the loaves, "take these to Auntie."

I slipped out of my coat and tied the ends of my scarf behind my neck so they wouldn't get in the way. I entered the dimness of the downstairs apartment.

"Put the light on, Aishah," Khadija said as she swept past me with the teapot steaming.

"Auntie, I have some news," I plunged in, as everyone took their places with me around the table. Fatima Zohra began pouring the tea. "I have decided to go back to Canada with the children."

There was an uncomfortable silence as everyone waited for me to continue. "Said can't come back here for a while, and I can't support everyone here with just my wages from the school." My voice wavered a little, and I looked straight at Fatima Zohra's mother. "I can't stay, I will end up like you…" My voice trailed off.

She nodded, the look in her eyes telling me she understood. No more words were needed. She had struggled to raise four girls on her own in a place where women were not supposed to be alone. I knew that in order to survive she had done things she would never speak about. Fatima Zohra didn't look up. I could see her lips clamped tightly together. Guilt rose up in my throat, but I choked it down. I had to leave, it was the only way.

Khadija passed me a glass of tea and whispered, "Go, dear, it is better."

I nodded silently, sneaking a glance at Fatima Zohra and trying to make eye contact. I hoped everyone else would leave the topic alone now. I wanted to enjoy this last Eid in Morocco. I couldn't imagine ever coming back, not really. I had never asked to be Fatima Zohra's life partner—I had wanted our husband to be there with us. The reality was clear now though. My time in the land of Islam was done.

I noticed the picture of the mosque hanging on the wall, the crescent moon perched precariously on the top. I had never seen it look so sharp and thin before. I shuddered. What would the next step in my journey bring? Would I ever be back in the land of the crescent moon?

I knew in my heart that I was leaving for good— the land, my religion, my Moroccan family, and maybe my husband.

I did not have anything else to say, and not long after, I rose to go upstairs. Entering my apartment, I tore the scarf off my head, took a deep breath, and ran my fingers through my hair. I felt lighter than I had in years. I could breathe.

Epilogue

DEAR READER, you may be wondering what happened next. Did I leave for Canada as planned? Did I stay with Said or end the marriage? What happened to Fatima Zohra? Did I stay a practicing Muslim? And most importantly, did I finally find and experience love? Some of these questions can be answered easily, but many of the answers crept their way into my new life, bursting out months or even years later. My transformation took time, my freedom was hard won, and my love story is still being formed. There are some things I'd like to share with you though, some wisdom I gleaned from my years of covering myself and finally emerging from the cocoon of my illusions.

I did leave Morocco a couple of weeks after this last Eid celebration. Me, four girls, and ten suitcases flew halfway across the world to return to my homeland, Nova Scotia. It was February and the snow was piled two feet high as we got off the plane in Halifax. We loaded the suitcases and the girls into two cars; my parents had thoughtfully brought both. We settled in for the hour-long drive to the house I had grown up in. Cresting the hill and looking out over the Minas Basin to the cliffs of Blomidon, my heart felt strangely peaceful. I needed to come back to myself, and there was nowhere in the world that could help me do that better than this land I called home. I sighed and settled back in the seat, enjoying the feeling of being taken along for the ride and knowing it would end well.

I am not going to say it was an easy transition. I struggled with old emotional baggage around my family. I searched for the next direction in my work life, and I still did not have a clear answer to the question of my relationship with Said. He was still working in the UK. As I was complaining one morning to my mom about how I felt stuck because I had to look after four girls on my own, she shocked me by replying, "You could just put them in foster care and go, no one is forcing you to do this, you have a choice."

I was taken aback by this even as the truth of it settled like a stone in my stomach. I could just walk away, but would I be able to live with myself? I had begun to see a bioenergetic therapist for counselling, and just having a place to be seen and heard was beginning to release my repressed emotions. I loved my girls. In a way, they were the meaning in my life right now. I was beginning to understand that my dream to empower women had to begin at home with myself and with my girls.

"You have four beautiful girls. Did it ever occur to you that you are already doing your life's work by

raising them to be embodied and powerful women?"
a friend asked me. I listened with ears that were finally
ready to hear. I could do this. I could still create a life
I wanted, and loving my daughters was a crucial part
of my own journey.

With renewed interest in learning, I returned to school
to study massage therapy. My degree in physiology from
years ago finally made sense in the context of my life,
and I thrived in the learning environment, graduating
with top marks and a new passion. One cannot work
with the body without being transformed, and by the
end of the two-year course I had enough confidence
to move out on my own with my kids.

In a last-ditch effort to commit to my love
relationship, I sponsored Said to come to Canada as
a permanent resident. Almost as soon as he came, I knew
it was a mistake. Instead of working with me teaching
acrobatics at the local circus school, he preferred to work
with a girl who had the time to devote to training and
to doting on him full-time. I barely saw him at home,
and I only knew he was in Canada because of the bills
he racked up on my credit card. Added to this stress was
the fact that I was no longer so interested in practicing
Islam. I had written this fact in my diary and absent-
mindedly left it open on the kitchen table one morning.
I came down to find Said crying. He said in a raspy
voice, "You don't want to be a Muslim anymore?" and
pointed at my book.

I sighed and realized I was relieved, in a way, that

he had found out. "No, I don't think I do."

In the most dramatic way I had ever seen, he collapsed on the floor crying. I stood and looked at him, not knowing what to do, and for the first time felt like I didn't have to do anything. I knew I had moved on from caring what he thought. I was finally free.

A week later, I asked him to move out and cancelled his credit card on my account. He left for Montreal in the car my parents had bought for him. It took time to fully disengage from the emotional entanglement that I had mistaken for love in this relationship with Said. He would try and pull me back into his games, but I knew I no longer needed him to survive. I was also painfully aware that he had drained me in so many ways. I now had people in my life who pointed out to me my own follies in relationships. My ability to create a fantasy that didn't in fact exist was so good, I had fooled myself.

The grief was ongoing. Would I ever experience a loving partner? Was it even possible?

Around the time Said left, I was broken-hearted again, this time by my eldest daughter, Omaima, wanting to return to Morocco. She would not let the topic go, and finally with trepidation, I let her go back to live with Fatima Zohra. Fatima Zohra and Said had recently had a baby boy. It felt like a gut punch to know she had succeeded in this one thing that I couldn't do; I'd only had girls. Now, even my own child wanted to be with her. I couldn't stop the thoughts from eating away at me, like the waning moon that slowly ebbs into darkness.

Finding solace in my massage work and my own inner growth with counselling, I held my breath in the darkness and slowly adjusted to the idea of being with myself and with God, the Beloved, in a new way. Looking for love from others had not worked when I had not found integration within myself. The divine feminine face of God called to me, and I made a pilgrimage to Mexico City to the Virgin of Guadalupe. With guidance I found myself in love with this new version of Spirit that was both Father and Mother. I was no longer a child waiting to be taken care of but a fully-fledged woman, in love with myself in a new way.

My erotic energies began to flow again, and I embraced them with curiosity.

Am I attractive? I wondered. *Would someone be drawn to me sexually?* It had been so long since I had let this part of myself be seen, I felt like a newborn in the world of adult relationships. I searched for and found a program in intimacy coaching and somatic sex education and embarked on a profoundly connecting adventure of erotic awakening. I met myself in this place of pleasure and a few lovers also, who helped me rewrite the script of what men and love could look like in my life.

Finally, at one of my week-long training sessions to complete the somatic sex education program, I met my new partner. It started as an attraction, but we both realized we were interested in making something more lasting. Declan is Irish, and I loved that he could actually pronounce my name properly because of his similar

Celtic roots. The only obstacle in our way was the 6,000 kilometres between us. He lived in Vancouver and I was still living in Nova Scotia. It wasn't long before he took a huge leap and flew across the country to see me. I had never before been pursued with such dedication, and I kind of liked it.

I liked it enough to pursue a long-distance relationship for a year before finally inviting him to move in with me. Now, two years later, we are building a life together as well as a beautiful healing sanctuary in the Annapolis Valley. I have realized that partnership and committed love is very different from the flashy attraction I mistakenly believed was true love before. Someone you can count on, come home to, and plan a life with is a miraculous gift.

My girls are grown now and almost flown the nest. I have not lost everything in the process of life as I once feared. I am perched on the precipice of a new chapter. Wisdom has been hard won, and love has become an embodied reality. Gratitude flows from my heart to all of the people who played a part in my story—even the villains have a place in the plot. Thank you.

Author
AILSA KEPPIE

AILSA IS A LIFELONG STUDENT of self-awareness and spiritual connection. She finds expression of her personal view on life and relationships through writing, coaching, and working with the body. Expanding the feeling of aliveness both in herself and the people she comes into contact with is something she finds enriching and fulfilling.

In her younger days, Ailsa desperately sought fulfilment and inner peace. She studied music, science, dance, and the performing arts in an attempt to find her place and a way to contribute to the world. During this time of expansion and exploration, there was an underlying fear. Fear that she was not enough, fear of not being perfect, and a fear of being seen.

At the age of twenty-five, these fears consumed her and she retreated into Islamic fundamentalism and a polygamous marriage. She started wearing a burka in an effort to regain some sense of herself. Over the years, as she nursed her mother-in-law and raised four daughters, the containment of her chosen life became too constricting and she began to wonder if this path was truly the one for her. Finally, the overwhelming desire to once again be seen in the wider world prevailed, and she left her life in Morocco to return home to Canada.

She continued to raise her daughters on her own and spent a decade learning and practicing the healing arts, which has finally led to a readiness to share her story, from a place of self-knowing. Through the process of diving deeply into the religion of Islam and living that way of life for many years, she has learned to embody the diversity of another culture as well as the "way of peace" that is Islam. Ailsa continues her work these days with somatic coaching, teaching, and writing. She focusses on healing relationships—with ourselves, others, and the planet.

Learn more about Ailsa on her websites:
www.pleasureforhealth.com
www.ourceltichearth.com

Follow her on Social Media:
@pleasureforhealth
@pleasureforhealthyrelationships

Acknowledgements and gratitude

I'D LIKE TO THANK my parents, Maggie and Duncan Keppie, for giving me opportunity for life. My ex-husband Said, for allowing me to learn so much about myself in relationship. My co-wife Fatima-Zohra for being a second mom to my daughters and an indispensable part of my life in Morocco. My daughters for giving me reasons to keep going when the going was tough. For all my therapists and teachers who supported my journey and to my devoted partner Declan, for knowing we were meant to be life partners.